Computers and Education

António José Mendes • Isabel Pereira • Rogério Costa

Editors

Computers and Education

Towards Educational Change and Innovation

 Springer

António José Mendes
University of Coimbra, Portugal

Isabel Pereira
Polytechnic Institute of Leiria, Portugal

Rogério Costa
Polytechnic Institute of Leiria, Portugal

British Library Cataloguing in Publication Data
A catalogue record for this book is available from the British Library

ISBN: 978-1-84996-680-1   e-ISBN: 978-1-84628-929-3

Printed on acid-free paper

9 8 7 6 5 4 3 2 1

springer.com

Table of Contents

Editors' Introduction

This book contains a collection of the best papers presented at the VII International Symposium on Computers and Education (SIIE 05), which took place in Leiria, Portugal on November 16th–18th, 2005. This symposium was organized by the School of Education of the Polytechnic Institute of Leiria.

SIIE has been organized in Portugal in odd years and in Spain in even years. It represents a collaborative effort between the communities that in both countries investigate the educative utilization of ICT – Information and Communication Technologies. In more recent editions the symposium had also a strong participation of researchers coming from Latin-American countries, especially from Brazil.

It has been a tradition of SIIE to invite each year internationally recognized speakers. This year the keynote speakers were António Dias de Figueredo (University of Coimbra), Pierre Dillenbourg (École Polytechnique Fédérale de Lausane) and Rosa Maria Carro (Universidad Autónoma de Madrid).

The Symposium included the following main topics:

- Design, development and evaluation of innovative educational environments
- Web based courses, tools and resources
- ICT in special education
- Collaborative learning
- Distance learning supported by Information and Communication Technologies
- E-Learning in Higher Education
- Innovative experiments using ICT in educational context
- Teacher training on the utilization of ICT in education
- Methodologies for ICT use in educational context
- Social aspects of the utilization of ICT in education
- Educational applications of ubiquous computing

The papers included in this book are revised and translated versions of those included in the symposium proceedings.

The paper selection was based on the opinion and classification attributed to the submitted papers by the Program Committee (PC) during the symposium paper selection. At that stage each paper was revised by at least two PC members, which included recognized researchers from several countries. From the 175 submitted papers, the PC accepted 72 to presentation in the symposium, which means that the acceptance rate was around 41%. The authors of the 26 best classified papers were invited and accepted to produce revised and translated versions of their papers. The 27th paper included in the book is the basis text for the invited talk Prof. Rosa Maria Carro gave during the symposium.

The Editors would like to thank all persons that collaborated in the symposium organization. In special we would like to thank the authors and PC members for all their work. We would also like to thank the School of Education of the Polytechnic Institute of Leiria for organizing the symposium.

António José Mendes
Isabel Pereira
Rogério Costa

List of Contributors

Mercedes Gómez Albarrán
Universidad Complutense de Madrid, C/ Profesor Jose Garcia Santesmases
s/n 28040, Madrid, Spain
albarran@sip.ucm.es

Luis Anido-Rifón
Departamento de Enxeñería Telemática, Universidade de Vigo, Spain

Raúl Arriola
Facultad de Informática, Universidad Complutense de Madrid

Ana Maria Ponzio de Azevedo
Fundação Faculdade Federal de Ciências Médicas de Porto Alegre
and Postgraduate Program of Computer Science applyed to Education,
Universidade Federal do Rio Grande do Sul (PGIE–UFRGS),
Rua Sarmento Leite, 245, Sala 309, CEP 90050-170, Porto Alegre, RS,
Brazil
anzevedo@fffcmpa.edu.br

Luís Barbeiro
School of Education, Polytechnic Institute of Leiria, Portugal
barbeiro@esel.ipleiria.pt

Crescencio Bravo
Computer Engineering School, Department of Information Technologies
and Systems, University of Castilla – La Mancha
Crescencio.Bravo@uclm.es

Manuel Caeiro-Rodríguez
Departamento de Enxeñería Telemática, Universidade de Vigo, Spain
Manuel.Caeiro@det.uvigo.es

Rosa M. Carro
Department of Computer Science and Engineering, Tomas y Valiente,
11 Universidad Autonoma de Madrid, Campus de Cantoblanco,
28049 Madrid, Spain
Rosa.Carro@uam.es

Ana A. Carvalho
University of Minho, Portugal
aac@iep.uminho.pt

Sónia C. Cruz
University of Minho, Portugal

Paulo Dias
Universidade do Minho, 4700 Braga, Portugal

Guillermo Jiménez Díaz
Universidad Complutense de Madrid,
C/ Profesor Jose Garcia Santesmases s/n 28040, Madrid, Spain
gjimenez@fdi.ucm.es

Fernando Díez
Department of Computer Science, Universidad Autónoma de Madrid,
Spain
fernando.diez@uam.es

Lizandra Estabel
Computer Center in Special Education (NIEE),
Federal University of Rio Grande do Sul (UFRGS),
Porto Alegre – Rio Grande do Sul – Brazil
estabel@cpovo.net

Baltasar Fernández-Manjón
Universidad Complutense de Madrid
balta@fdi.ucm.es

Rafael Gil
Department of Computer Science,
Universidad Autónoma de Madrid, Spain

Maria João Gomes
Universidade do Minho, Portugal
mjgomes@iep.uminho.pt

Marco A. Gómez-Martín
Universidad Complutense de Madrid,
C/ Profesor Jose Garcia Santesmases s/n 28040, Madrid, Spain
marcoa@fdi.ucm.es

Pedro A. González-Calero
Universidad Complutense de Madrid,
C/ Profesor Jose Garcia Santesmases s/n 28040, Madrid, Spain
pedro@sip.ucm.es

Pedro Henriques
Universidade do Minho, 4700 Braga, Portugal

Isidoro Hernán-Losada
Departamento de Lenguajes y Sistemas Informáticos,
Universidad Rey Juan Carlos, Móstoles, Madrid
isidoro.hernan@urjc.es

Susana de la Iglesia
Facultad de Informática, Universidad Complutense de Madrid

Carlos A. Lázaro-Carrascosa
Departamento de Lenguajes y Sistemas Informáticos,
Universidad Rey Juan Carlos, Móstoles, Madrid
carlos.lazaro@urjc.es

Gustavo Brandalise Lazzarotto
Fundação Faculdade Federal de Ciências Médicas de Porto Alegre
and Postgraduate Program of Computer Science applyed to Education,
Universidade Federal do Rio Grande do Sul (PGIE–UFRGS),
Rua Sarmento Leite, 245, Sala 309, CEP 90050-170,
Porto Alegre, RS, Brazil

Sandra Lopes
Universidade do Minho, 4700 Braga, Portugal
sandralopes@di.uminho.pt

Maria José Loureiro
Department Didáctica e Tecnologia Educativa; Universidade de Aveiro
zeloureiro@dte.ua.pt

Sofia Malheiro
Universidade Aberta
sofiamalheiro@gmail.com

Célio Gonçalo Marques
Instituto Politécnico de Tomar Quinta do Contador,
Estrada da Serra, 2300-313 Tomar, Portugal
celiomarques@ipt.pt

Ivan Martinez-Ortiz
Centro de Estudios Superiores Felipe II
imartinez@cesfelipesegundo.com

Emilia Miranda
Escola E.B. 2/3 Dr. Carlos Pinto Ferreira,
Centro de Competência Nónio da Universidade do Minho
emiranda@mail.telepac.pt

Luísa Miranda
Polytechnic Institute of Bragança
lmiranda@ipb.pt

Carlos Morais
Polytechnic Institute of Bragança

Carla Morais
Faculty of Sciences of the University of Oporto
carlamorais@imediato.pt

António Moreira
Department Didáctica e Tecnologia Educativa;
Universidade de Aveiro
moreira@dte.ua.pt

Paulo Moreira
Escola E.B. 2/3 Dr. Carlos Pinto Ferreira,
Centro de Competência Nónio da Universidade do Minho
paulo.moreira@nonio.uminho.pt

Pablo Moreno-Ger
Universidad Complutense de Madrid
pablom@fdi.ucm.es

Lina Morgado
Universidade Aberta, Portugal
lmorgado@univ-ab.pt

Eliane Moro
Computer Center in Special Education (NIEE),
Federal University of Rio Grande do Sul (UFRGS),
Porto Alegre – Rio Grande do Sul – Brazil

Adelina Moura
Escola Profissional de Braga
adelinam@netcabo.pt

Martín Llamas Nistal
Departamento de Enxeñería Telemática,
Universidade de Vigo, Spain

João Noivo
Universidade do Minho DSI, Campus de Azurém,
4800-058 Guimarães, Portugal

Manuel Ortega
Universidad de Castilla-La Mancha, Spain
Manuel.Ortega@uclm.es

João Paiva
Faculty of Sciences of the University of Oporto
jcpaiva@fc.up.pt

Raquel Pedrosa
Edulearn
raquel.pedrosa@eduweb.pt

Alda Pereira
Universidade Aberta, Portugal
amp@univ-ab.pt

Luísa Pereira
Department Didáctica e Tecnologia Educativa;
Universidade de Aveiro
lpereira@dte.ua.pt

Paula Peres
Instituto Politécnico de Contabilidade e Administração do Porto,
Universidade do Minho
p_peres@iscap.ipp.pt

Angie Phillip
Universidad de Castilla-La Mancha, Spain

Pedro Pimenta
Instituto Politécnico de Contabilidade e Administração do Porto,
Universidade do Minho
pimenta@dsi.uminho.pt

Anabela Pinho
Department Didáctica e Tecnologia Educativa;
Universidade de Aveiro
apinho@dte.ua.pt

Javier Piquer
Facultad de Informática,
Universidad Complutense de Madrid

António Quintas-Mendes
Universidade Aberta, Portugal
quintas@univ-ab.pt

Filipe Rocha
University of Minho, Portugal

Luísa M. Romero-Moreno
Department of Languages and Informatics Systems,
University of Seville, Avd. Reina Mercedes s/n, 41012 Seville, Spain
mariaro@lsi.us.es

Asunción Sánchez
Universidad de Castilla-La Mancha,
Spain

Pedro Sánchez
Universidad de Castilla-La Mancha,
Spain

Pilar Sancho
Universidad Complutense de Madrid
pilar@sip.ucm.es

Lucila Santarosa
Computer Center in Special Education (NIEE),
Federal University of Rio Grande do Sul (UFRGS),
Porto Alegre – Rio Grande do Sul – Brazil
lucila.santarosa@ufrgs.br

Danielle Santos
Paulista State University – Technology and Sciences College,
Rua Roberto Simonsen, 305, CEP 19060-900, Presid. Prudente,
SP, Brasil
dani_asn@yahoo.com.br

Antonio Sarasa
Facultad de Informática,
Universidad Complutense de Madrid
asarasa@sip.ucm.es

Elisa Schlunzen
Paulista State University – Technology and Sciences College,
Rua Roberto Simonsen, 305, CEP 19060-900, Presid. Prudente,
SP, Brasil

Maria Isabel Timm
Fundação Faculdade Federal de Ciências Médicas de Porto Alegre
and Postgraduate Program of Computer Science applyed to Education,
Universidade Federal do Rio Grande do Sul (PGIE–UFRGS),
Rua Sarmento Leite, 245, Sala 309, CEP 90050-170,
Porto Alegre, RS, Brazil

José A. Troyano
Department of Languages and Informatics Systems,
University of Seville, Avd. Reina Mercedes s/n,
41012 Seville, Spain

Joana Valente
Edulearn

J. Ángel Velázquez-Iturbide
Departamento de Lenguajes y Sistemas Informáticos,
Universidad Rey Juan Carlos, Móstoles, Madrid
angel.velazquez@urjc.es

Mário Veríssimo
NRC-APPC Rua Garcia de Orta, Vale das Flores,
3030-188 Coimbra, Portugal

Milton Antônio Zaro
Fundação Faculdade Federal de Ciências Médicas de Porto Alegre
and Postgraduate Program of Computer Science applyed to Education,
Universidade Federal do Rio Grande do Sul (PGIE–UFRGS),
Rua Sarmento Leite, 245, Sala 309, CEP 90050-170,
Porto Alegre, RS, Brazil

Applications of Adaptive Hypermedia in Education

Rosa M. Carro

Department of Computer Science and Engineering, Tomas y Valiente, 11
Universidad Autonoma de Madrid, Campus de Cantoblanco
28049 Madrid, Spain
Rosa.Carro@uam.es

1 Introduction

Adaptive hypermedia (AH) has been used for web-based teaching and learning from its origins until nowadays [14]. In this paper I will go through some of its applications in the area of education, starting from the earliest ones, which dealt with guiding each student individually when surfing electronic books, to the most recent ones, related to mobile and ubiquitous systems. During this journey through AH educational applications, the way of applying AH in each of them will be commented, as well as the way in which we have done it in our group, in the Department of Computer Science of the Universidad Autonoma de Madrid.

2 Applications of AH for Education

In general, an AH system is a system based on hypertext and hypermedia that stores some personal features about the user in a user model and applies this model in order to adapt several visible aspects of the system to the user [13]. In this section, different applications of adaptive hypermedia for education will be described.

2.1 Individual Guidance

The earliest applications of AH in education found in the literature date from the beginnings of the 90s [30, 44]. In 1996, Brusilovsky defined the first classification of AH methods and techniques [13], which has been widely used as the basis of AH since then. One of the first applications of AH in the e-learning area, which is still widely used nowadays, involves the use of AH methods and techniques for guiding each student individually when interacting with e-courses. Old e-courses mainly consisted of electronic books with chapters and sections to visit, and links leading to them [15, 45]. New e-courses tend to be more oriented to support the achievement of activities, according to the constructivism theory [12]. Chapters and sections are replaced by activities to be performed, and the navigational guidance offered attempts to propose the most suitable activities to be tackled by each student at each learning step. The main decisions to be taken when developing these types of applications deal with [17]:

- The student features to be considered with adaptation purposes.
- The type of adaptation to be provided (navigational, content, both of them).
- The activities that will be performed by the students, as well as the different possible relationships between them, which can vary depending on the type of the student which the e-course is intended for.
- The different multimedia contents to be offered to each type of student to facilitate his/her learning when accomplishing each activity.
- The relationships between activities and contents.
- The specification/implementation of pedagogical strategies to be used to support the individual guidance through the activities defined.
- The AH methods to be used during the learning process, as well as the techniques for their implementation.

Some examples of AH educational systems are: ELM-ART [15], AHA [29] and WHURLE [54]. Concerning our work, we have developed TANGOW [19], which supports the specification and delivery of adaptive e-courses. These courses are based on the separation of abstract tasks (activities to be tackled, such as *solving a problem related to digital circuits*), content fragments (variants of pieces of contents related to these tasks, i.e., the statement of the specific problem related to digital circuits to be solved by a certain type of students) and adaptation rules (which support the specification of the different relationships between tasks and the adaptative guidance desired during their execution). More details can be found at [20].

In order to provide individual educational guidance to the users it is necessary to store information about each of them in the *User Model*, which is stored and maintained by the system [46]. In order to construct user models, different methods can be used, such as those based on stereotypes [44], overlays [27], machine learning [64] or Bayesian networks [50] among others. In our case, we use a combination of stereotypes and overlays, storing also each action performed by the students. This combination proved to be sufficient and simple enough to satisfy our needs.

One of the user features that can be modelled is the learning style, defined as *"characteristic strengths and preferences in the ways people take in and process information"* [33]. Different learning style models have been developed by experts in psychology, such as the ones by Myers-Briggs [10], Kolb [47], Dunn and Dunn [32], Herrmann [40] or Felder-Silverman [34]. The way of adapting educational resources to the student's learning styles has risen a lot of debate. Some researchers bet on providing the guidance according to the students' learning style, in order to help them to learn in the way they prefer [39, 41], while others favours doing it the other way round, in order to help them to acquire not so developed skills. Some experiments comparing both approaches have been done [59].

In our case, we use Felder-Silverman's model to adapt, according to the student's learning style: i) the strictness/flexibility of the navigational guidance, ii) the type of activities to be proposed, iii) the order in which activities are suggested, according to their type (theory, examples, exercises), and iv) the multimedia contents to be used for page generation. Adaptation is done favouring the student's learning style [58].

2.2 Adaptation in Collaborative Applications

Individual learning can be pretty effective, but it is well known that the involvement of students in collaborative activities contributes to knowledge acquisition [31]. Moreover, a proper accomplishment of collaborative activities can facilitate the development of student's personal and social skills which might not be so strengthen when learning individually, such as making ideas explicit, communicating with others, reasoning, arguing, negotiating, etc. Furthermore, it reduces the potential isolation of students learning through the Web, and supports the communication among them to exchange ideas, doubts, knowledge and so on [7, 55].

Collaborative activities have been used with educational purposes in traditional classrooms since the 70s [63]. In the 80s, a new area of research emerged: Computer-Supported Collaborative Learning (CSCL) [60]. Since then, numerous researchers and developers have made use of the results of psychological studies to bring those into collaborative applications. Some of the theories used in CSCL are [48]: the Sociocultural Theory [63], the Constructivism Theory [12] and the Situated Cognition Theory [11]. They all assume that individuals are active agents that are seeking and constructing their knowledge within a meaningful context.

In some systems, adaptation techniques have been used to adapt several aspects of the collaboration. This is the case of EPSILON [61], WebDL [37], COALE [36], SMART-Learning [8] and the collaborative version of TANGOW [21]. In this last one, adaptation supports the runtime decision about some issues such as: i) the (in)convenience of proposing collaborative activities to certain types of students, ii) the best time (point of the course) to propose collaborative activities to specific students, depending on their profile or their previous actions, iii) the more appropriate set of collaboration tools to support the activity accomplishment for each type of student, or iv) the specific problem statement to be presented to a group of students. More details about the formalism that supports the specification of the adaptation capabilities of the courses are given in [22].

A relevant aspect for collaborative work is the group formation. There are some studies regarding how group formation influences its performance in traditional classrooms [43]. In these studies it is stated that homogeneous groups tend to be better at achieving specific aims. However, when heterogeneous groups are analysed, they outperform homogeneous groups in a broader range of tasks. Therefore, the way in which students are grouped may affect the results of the learning experience.

This motivated us, firstly, to find out the influence of learning styles on the outcome of collaborative work developed by self-selected groups, if any; and secondly, to elaborate on the way this knowledge can be used for grouping students automatically in adaptive e-learning systems. In our system, there exist three possibilities of group formation: i) the students can group themselves, ii) the teachers can form the groups, or iii) the system groups the students automatically according to grouping rules. These rules can be either specified by each course responsible or selected from those provided within the system by default. The default rules indicate that the students will be grouped according to their features, as well as to their performance at the time at which any group must be formed. We have developed a mechanism to process these rules and, therefore, to support grouping on-the-fly [38].

During the last months we have been studying the impact of learning styles and group homogeneity/heterogeneity on the results obtained by students in collaborative tasks. We carried out a case study with 166 students of Computer Science, and we found out that some dimensions of the learning style model (namely active-reflective and sensing-intuitive) seem to affect the quality of the resulting work [5]. We are preparing similar experiments for different subjects in order to get information about this type of correlations in other disciplines. Variations might occur from one course to another, which might make difficult to compare the results obtained. However, the aim is to evaluate whether it is feasible to find a reasonably good set of grouping rules for each course to be used for grouping users automatically.

2.3 Adaptive Assessment and Games

Another relevant element to be provided in adaptive courses is (self-) assessment. To this respect, there are a lot of works dealing with the inclusion of tests, exercises, problems and practical individual/collaborative tasks in them. Regarding the assessment of free-text answers, NLP techniques can be used, as in Atenea [2]. Atenea is a Computer-Assisted Assessment tool developed in our group for scoring short student answers automatically. It uses statistically based evaluation procedures to process the students' replies in order to correct them and to give them a score along with the corresponding feedback. Atenea and TANGOW have been integrated, as explained in [3]. Adaptation techniques can be used in order to present the most appropriate assessment elements to each student. In this direction, SIETTE [26] supports dynamic generation of tests. The questions are dynamically selected, from those defined by the teachers, in order to fit the student's level of knowledge.

Games constitute another useful and enjoyable resource to support self-assessment and also to motivate students and to promote learning. Educational games have been used with this purpose for a while. Adaptation is normally used in educational games to vary the difficulty of the games according to the students' progress. However, there are many other possibilities. For example, in ECOTOONS [18], the educational goals, the activities to be performed by the users, the organization and sequencing of activities, the games to be played, and the game stories, are selected or dynamically generated taking into account the user's features and behaviours.

2.4 Authoring, Visualization and Content Generation

The richer an adaptive application is, the more complex its development turns out to be. The specification of the adaptation strategies intended for an e-course is a pretty hard task. This is why many systems incorporate them hard-coded. However, other systems support their configuration and specification. In these cases, there is a clear need of authoring tools to facilitate this task. Until the time being, each system has its own niche and deals with adaptation in a particular way. Therefore, existing authoring tools are directly related to the corresponding AH system.

However, there is still a need of facilitating the authoring task, since authoring tools usually require previous knowledge about AH, adaptive courses and the behaviour of the corresponding system. AH can be used for helping course developers to overcome that. In [28], semi-automatic generation of platform-independent AH is proposed. It reduces the workload, although it still requires experience in the creation of adaptive courses. In our group, the authors of [56] present an adaptive tutorial for secondary-school teachers with no knowledge on AH. In the tutorial, teachers are provided with course templates, automatically selected according to their needs, and are taught how to instantiate them to reach their goals.

The authoring process can also be improved by the use of visualization tools that support the representation of adaptive courses. Adaptive courses are not easy to visualize, since the final course (both structure and contents) can be different for each student depending on their features and also on their previous actions. With the aim of facilitating their visualization, some tools have been developed. Some of them are based on hyperbolic geometry [23]. Others are based on graph direct manipulation, as [35], developed in our group, that uses multiple focus plus context techniques to avoid display clutter and information overload; navigation through the graph is animated in order to avoid loss of orientation; and multiple views of the same data can be generated, each with independent settings for filtering, clustering and zooming.

Regarding the generation of multimedia contents, there exist different possibilities, such as the elaboration of contents from the scratch, the reuse and modification of existing contents, or the use of natural language processing (NLP) techniques to create different content versions. Normally, contents are labelled with metadata to facilitate the adaptation. Metadata is either associated to separate multimedia files or set at certain key points inside them (i.e., in videos). In some cases, ontologies are used to organise the contents [42]. TANGOW makes use of annotated multimedia content fragments that can be related to any task. The most suitable fragment variants, among those available, are selected for each student to compose the corresponding web page on the fly. Even collaboration tools are provided separately, so that the most appropriate ones can be put together during the generation of collaboration workspaces [22]. Besides, NLP techniques have been used in Welkin [4], a multilingual system that analyses source texts, stores information about them in a database, and uses this information to generate on-the-fly adaptive contents according to some of the user's features.

2.5 Mobile Learning

The earliest adaptive web-based educational applications were commonly accessed from personal or even shared computers. However, the quick development of mobile and wireless devices and technologies have facilitated the access to the Internet from a wider range of locations with more flexibility. This has made possible mobile-learning (M-learning), defined as *"e-learning through mobile and handheld devices using wireless transmission"* [49]. In this type of learning environments, the students' location, as well as their available devices and time, can vary from one time to other. Therefore, they should be considered in order to propose the most suitable activities to be performed at each time, as well as the most appropriate contents to be shown. Some existing M-learning systems are [52, 53]. In our case, we have used adaptation techniques to support the generation of mobile learning environments in which the students can perform a variety of activities. Given a specific user accessing the system in a particular context, the system suggests him/her the most suitable learning activities to be accomplished in that specific situation, and compose the web pages accordingly [51]. Not just the users' context, but also their personal features (including learning style), preferences and actions are considered, to provide a more complete adaptation. For example, the same activity can be appropriate for a user in a certain context while being inadequate for other user in the same context, because of his/her particular learning style [51]. In this environment, it is important to decide whether a user should be interrupted at a certain moment in order to be informed about the availability/recommendation of new activities. In our case, we have used adaptation techniques to support the configuration of alerting services [6].

2.6 Evaluation

The evaluation of the benefits and appropriateness of adaptive hypermedia for education is not an easy task [65]. In [38] the author proposes a set of methods and techniques for evaluating AH. When performing empirical experiments it is usual to compare the results obtained by students using an adaptive version of a course versus those obtained by students accessing to its non-adaptive version [16]. Even if the results obtained by the former are better, it does not guarantee that this course is completely adequate. Therefore, it is important to evaluate whether the adaptation strategies are proper, and to try to detect aspects that could be improvable.

With the aim of detecting possible fails or improvement possibilities in TANGOW-based courses, as well as of trying to propose suggestions about the actions to be performed to improve them, we have developed the "continuous empirical evaluation approach" [57]. It assists the course designers in the evaluation and maintenance of courses, by analysing the course description along with the user data (including actions performed when interacting with the course and surveys). Apart from the huge complexity involved in trying to obtain the right conclusions given a set of usage data, there are other limitations for the evaluation process: the number of data needed in order to obtain conclusions for each type of student [25], and the difficulty of testing the evaluation tool itself. In [9], a simulation-based technique is proposed as a way of testing evaluation tools based on TANGOW-log analysis. The authors also present Simulog, a tool that implements the simulation technique itself.

3 Conclusions

There are numerous applications of AH for education. Some examples have been shown in this paper, although there exist many others, such as, for example, adaptive simulations [1]. Currently, each AH educational system has its own representation models, adaptive strategies, mechanisms, and so on. The reuse of resources has been addressed. In this direction, some work has been done regarding one-to-one protocols [24], standards such as LOM or IMS, and web-services [62] to give support to the semantic web approach. Yet the reuse of resources is not enough. Reusing other elements such as the user model and the adaptation model would be much richer. In recent international conferences and workshops the discussion about the need of reusing these elements has arised. Not only their reuse, but also their composition, would allow everyone to benefit from their integration, giving rise to new and more complete AH systems, adapted to the corresponding specific needs. Some efforts have been done in this direction, and this is one of our current main aims. There is still a lot of work to do to be able to reuse different existing adaptive information systems to compose new ones.

References

1. Alfonseca M, de Lara J (2000) Integration of Simulation and Multimedia in Automatically Generated Internet Courses. Computers and Education in the 21st Century. Kluwer Academic Publishers, 47–54

2. Alfonseca E, Pérez D (2004) Automatic Assessment of Open-ended Questions with a BLEU-inspired Algorithm and Shallow NLP. Advances in Natural Language Processing. LNCS 3230: 25–35

3. Alfonseca E, Carro RM, Freire M, Ortigosa A, Pérez D, Rodríguez P (2004) Educational Adaptive Hypermedia meets Computer Assisted Assessment. Procs. of the 2nd Int. Workshop on Authoring of Adaptive and Adaptable Educational Hypermedia, at AH 2004, Eindhoven, pp. 4–12

4. Alfonseca E, Rodríguez P, Pérez D (2004) Welkin: Automatic Generation of Hypermedia Sites with NLP Techniques. LNCS 3140: 617–618

5. Alfonseca E, Carro RM, Martín E, Ortigosa A (2006) The Impact of Learning Styles on Student Grouping for Collaborative Learning: A Case Study. User Modeling and User-adapted Interaction. Special issue on User Modeling to Support Groups, Communities and Collaboration 16(3–4): 377–401

6. Andueza N, Carro RM (2006) Supporting Configurable Alerting Services in Mobile Learning Environments. In: Procs. of the 8th International Symposium on Computers in Education, Leon, Spain, vol 1, pp. 326–333

7. Barros B, Verdejo MF (1998) Designing Workspaces to support collaborative learning. Tasks and Methods in Applied Artificial Intelligence. LNAI 1416: 668–677

8. Benkiran MA, Ajhoun RM (2002) An Adaptive and Cooperative Telelearning System. SMART-Learning. International Journal on E learning 1(2): 66–72

9. Bravo J, Ortigosa A (2006) Validating the Evaluation of Adaptive Systems by User Profile Simulation. Lecture Notes in Learning and Teaching, 479–483

10. Briggs KC, Myers IB (1997) Myers-Briggs Type Indicator. Consulting Psychologist Press, Inc. Palo Alto, CA

11. Brown JS, Collins A, Duguid P (1989) Situated Cognition and the Culture of Learning. Educational Researcher 18(1): 32–42

12. Bruner J (1966) Toward a Theory of Instruction. Harvard University Press, Cambridge

13. Brusilovsky P (1996) Methods and Techniques of Adaptive Hypermedia. User Modelling and User-adapted Interaction 6:87-129 (Reprinted in: Adaptive Hypertext and Hypermedia, Kluwer Academic Publishers, 1–43 1998)

14. Brusilovsky P (2000) Adaptive Hypermedia: From Intelligent Tutoring Systems to Web-based Education. Intelligent Tutoring Systems. LNCS 1839: 1–7

15. Brusilovsky P, Schwarz E, Weber G (1996) ELM-ART: An intelligent tutoring system on World Wide Web. In: Frasson C, Gauthier G, Lesgold A (eds) Procs of the 3rd Int Conf on Intelligent Tutoring Systems, pp. 261–269

16. Calvi L (2000) Formative Evaluation of Adaptive CALLware: A Case Study. Adaptive Hypermedia and Adaptive Web-Based Systems. LNCS 1892: 276–279

17. Carro RM (2002) Adaptive Hypermedia in Education: New Considerations and Trends. Procs. of the 6th World Multiconference on Systemics, Cybernetics and Informatics, vol 2, pp. 452–458

18. Carro RM, Breda AM, Castillo G, Bajuelos AL (2002) A Methodology for Developing Adaptive Educational-game Environments. Adaptive Hypermedia and Adaptive Web-based Systems. LNCS 2347: 90–99
19. Carro RM, Pulido E, Rodríguez P (1999) Dynamic generation of adaptive Internet-based courses. Journal of Network and Computer Applications 22: 249–257
20. Carro RM, Pulido E, Rodríguez P (2002) Developing and Accessing Adaptive Internet-based Courses. Virtual Environments for Teaching and Learning. World Sci. Publishing Company 111–149
21. Carro RM, Ortigosa A, Martín E, Schlichter J (2003) Dynamic Generation of Adaptive Web-based Collaborative Courses. Groupware: Design, Implementation and Use. LNCS 2806 191–198
22. Carro RM, Ortigosa A, Schlichter J (2003) A Rule-based Formalism for Describing Collaborative Adaptive Courses. Knowledge-based Intelligent Information and Engineering Systems. LNAI 2774: 252–259
23. Cassidy K, Walsh J, Coghlan B, Dagger D (2006) Using Hyperbolic Geometry for Visualisation of Concept Spaces for Adaptive eLearning. Lecture Notes in Learning and Teaching, 421–426
24. Celik I, Stewart C, Ashman H (2006) Interoperability as an Aid to Authoring: Accessing User Models in Multiple AEH Systems. Lecture Notes in Learning and Teaching, 408–413
25. Chin D (2001) Empirical Evaluation of User Models and User-adapted Systems. User Modeling and User-adapted Interaction 11(1–2): 181–194
26. Conejo R, Guzmán E, Millán E, Trella M, Pérez-De-La-Cruz JL, Ríos A (2004) SIETTE: A Web-Based Tool for Adaptive Testing. International Journal of Artificial Intelligence in Education 4(1): 29–61
27. Conlan O, Dagger D, Wade V (2002) Towards a Standards-based Approach to e-Learning Personalization using Reusable Learning Objects. In: Procs. of the World Conference on E-Learning in Corporate, Government, Healthcare and Higher Education, pp. 210–217
28. Cristea A, Stewart C (2005) Automatic Authoring of Adaptive Educational Hypermedia. Web-based Intelligent e-Learning Systems: Technologies and Applications, pp. 24–55
29. De Bra P, Calvi L (1998) AHA! An open Adaptive Hypermedia Architecture. The New Review of Hypermedia and Multimedia 4: 115–139
30. de La Passardiere B, Dufresne A (1992) Adaptive navigational tools for educational hypermedia. In: Tomek I (ed): Procs. of the 4th International Conference on Computers and Learning, Berlin, pp. 555–567
31. Dillenbourg P (1999) Collaborative learning: cognitive an computational approaches. Elsevier, Oxford, UK
32. Dunn R, Dunn K (1978) Teaching Students Through Their Individual Learning Styles: A Practical Approach. Reston Publishing, Virginia
33. Felder RM (1996) Matters of Style. ASEE Prism 6, 4:18–23
34. Felder RM, Silverman LK (1988) Learning Styles and Teaching Styles in Engineering Education. Engineering Education 78(7): 674–681

35. Freire M, Rodríguez P (2004) A Graph-based Interface to Complex Hypermedia Structure Visualization. In: Procs. of Conf. on Advanced Visual Interfaces. ACM Press, pp. 163–166
36. Furugori N, Sato H, Ogata H, Ochi Y (2002) COALE: Collaborative and Adaptive Learning Environment. CSCL 2002. Boulder, USA, pp. 493–494
37. Gaudioso E, Boticario JG (2002) Supporting personalization in virtual communities in distance education. Virtual Environments for Teaching and Learning. World Scientific Publishing Company, pp. 327–362
38. Gena C (2005) Methods and Techniques for the Evaluation of User-adaptive Systems. The Knowledge Engineering Review 20(1): 1–37
39. Gilbert JE, Han CY (1999) Adapting instruction in search of a significant difference. Journal of Network and Computer Applications 22: 149–160
40. Herrmann N (1990) The Creative Brain. Lake Lure, NC: Brain Books
41. Hong H, Kinshuk D (2004) Adaptation to Student Learning Styles in Web Based Educational Systems. In: Procs. of World Conference on Educational Multimedia, Hypermedia and Telecommunications. Lugano, Switzerland, pp. 491–496
42. Iksal S, Garlatti S (2004) Adaptive Web Information Systems: Architecture and Methodology for Reusing Content. In: Procs. of EAW'04: Engineering the Adaptive Web. Eindhoven, The Netherlands, pp. 36–45
43. Johnson DW, Johnson FP (1975) Learning Together: Group Theory and Group Skills. Pearson Education.
44. Kay J (2000) Stereotypes, Student Models and Scrutability. Intelligent Tutoring Systems. LNCS 1839: 19–30
45. Kay J, Kummerfeld RJ (1994) An individualised course for the C programming language. In: Procs. of 2nd International WWW Conference, Chicago, IL. URL: http://www.cs.usyd.edu.au/~bob/kay-kummerfeld.html
46. Kobsa A (2001) Generic User Modeling Systems. User Modeling and User-Adapted Interaction 11: 49–63
47. Kolb D (1984) Experiential Learning: Experience as the Source of Learning and Development. Prentice Hall, New Jersey
48. Koschmann T (1996) Paradigms Shift and Instructional Technology. CSCL: Theory and practice of an emerging paradigm. Lawrence Erlbaum Associates, New Jersey, USA, pp. 1–23
49. Ktoridou D, Eteokleous N (2005) Adaptive m-learning: Technological and Pedagogical Aspects to be Considered in Cyprus Tertiary Education. Recent Research Developments in Learning Technologies. Formatex, Badajoz, Spain, pp. 676–683
50. Li X, Ji Q (2005) Active Affective State Detection and Assistance with Dynamic Bayesian Networks. IEEE Transactions on Systems, Man, and Cybernetics: Special Issue on Ambient Intelligence 35(1): 93–105
51. Martín E, Carro RM, Rodríguez P (2006) A Mechanism to Support Context-Based Adaptation in M-Learning. EC-TEL 2006, LNCS 4227: 302–315
52. Maths4Life project: http://www.mboard.org.uk
53. MOBIlearn project: http://www.mobilearn.org/

54. Moore A, Brailsford TJ, Stewart CD (2001) Personally tailored teaching in WHURLE using conditional transclusion. Procs. of the 12th ACM conference on Hypertext and Hypermedia, Århus, Denmark, pp. 163–164
55. Muehlenbrock M, Hoppe U (1999) Computer supported interaction analysis of group problem solving. In: Procs. of the Computer Support for Collaborative Learning Conference, Stanford Univ., Palo Alto, pp. 398–405
56. Muñoz F, Ortigosa A (2006) An Adaptive Course on Template-based Adaptive Hypermedia Design. Lecture Notes in Learning and Teaching, 345–354
57. Ortigosa A, Carro RM (2003) The Continuous Empirical Evaluation Approach: Evaluating Adaptive Web-based Courses. User Modeling 2003. LNCS 2702: 163–167
58. Paredes P, Rodríguez P (2002) Considering Learning Styles in Adaptive Web-based Education. In: Procs. of the 6th World Multiconference on Systemics, Cybernetics and Informatics, vol 2, pp. 481–485
59. Pillay H, Willss L (1996) Computer assisted instruction and individual cognitive style preferences in learning: Does it matter? Australian Educational Computing 11(2): 28–33
60. Slavin RE (1980) Cooperative Learning. Review of Educational Research 50(2): 315–342
61. Soller A (2001) Supporting Social Interaction in an Intelligent Collaborative Learning System. Int. J. of Artificial Intelligence in Education 12(1): 40–62
62. Stynes P, Conlan O (2006) Architectural framework for the composition and delivery of adaptive educational support services. Lecture Notes in Learning and Teaching, 156–163
63. Vygotsky LS (1978) Mind in society: The development of higher psychological processes. Harvard University Press, Cambridge MA
64. Webb G, Pazzani MJ, Billsus D (2001) Machine Learning for User Modeling. User Modeling and User-Adapted Interaction 11(1–2): 19–29
65. Weibelzahl S, Weber G (2002) Advantages, Opportunities, and Limits of Empirical Evaluations: Evaluating Adaptive Systems. Künstliche Intelligenz, 3/02 17–20

Protocols of Coordination and Structured Communication in Synchronous CSCL Environments

Crescencio Bravo

Computer Engineering School, Department of Information Technologies and Systems, University of Castilla – La Mancha
Crescencio.Bravo@uclm.es

1 Motivation

Software Engineering studies the principles and methodologies for the development and maintenance of software systems. The Collaborative Systems (CS) are a kind of software system that are particularly complex to develop, especially when they support distributed synchronous collaboration. For example, it is difficult to carry out an exhaustive test because of the multiple interactions of different types that occur between the users. In this situation, the use of tested components facilitates development and provides quality. On the other hand, the software patterns facilitate the collection and application of experience. A pattern is a valid *solution* to a common *problem* in a specific context. Components and patterns follow the reuse principle and allow the improvement of software development.

The CSCL (Computer-Supported Collaborative Learning) and CSCW (Computer-Supported Cooperative Work) are the two scientific areas that make up the CS. In [4] Collis identifies the main contributions of the investigations in CSCL and CSCW. For instance, some essential characteristics of CSCL that differentiate it from CSCW are the influence of the teacher, the importance of structuring the group activities and of establishing shared aims, and the utilization of theoretic frames and computer support based on constructivist and cognitive learning theories.

Some of the teaching-learning methods that are usually used in CSCL are Problem-Based Learning, Project-Based Learning and Learning by Design. Taking these methods as a frame of reference, a CSCL environment allows the users to carry out an activity such as solving a problem, developing a project or designing an artefact. In the collaborative learning underlying these activities, two kinds of interactions take place: negotiation and argumentation [5]. Communication, coordination and decision-making are tasks which are necessary for implementing the negotiation and argumentation processes.

The contribution of this article consists of the proposal of a set of collaboration protocols for coordination and decision-making processes and for structured communication. These protocols make up a collection of design patterns to be used in the development of synchronous CSCL environments. Examples of these processes in different systems will be shown, in order to exemplify the use of such protocols. These examples represent proposals of user interfaces, and therefore constitute patterns for human-computer interaction (HCI).

Different authors have proposed pattern systems for HCI [6], although these patterns do not approach collaborative interaction. Although patterns for Groupware do exist, they do not consider CSCL aspects. In [8] the authors formalize collaborative learning patterns by means of IMS Learning Design. Nevertheless, the general patterns these authors propose do not approach specific coordination processes and they do not deal with user interface aspects. Therefore, there are no specific collections of design and interaction patterns for CSCL environments.

Support structured methods in CSCL are presented in the next section. In Section 3, different protocols for structuring coordination processes are shown, including decision-making and communication, and some implications regarding the user interface are discussed. Finally, the article concludes with an analysis of the protocols proposed and outlines the future lines of work.

2   Structuring the Support for Collaborative Learning

In Collaborative Learning, two support methods are distinguished [9]:

- Global methods that structure the collaboration at general level.
- Structured or guided methods of collaborative learning that provide protocols to structure the learners' dialogue and actions.

In [4] Collis also highlights the importance of structuring learning activities. The Learning Protocols (or Collaboration Protocols) are an integrated learning support that describes how to carry out and apply constraints, rules and methods of structuring of the processes in a CSCL environment [11]. The collaboration protocols, understood as guided methods of collaborative learning, are based on the theories of the psychological scripts. In cognitive and social psychology, the general knowledge regarding a routine sequence of related events is commonly known as a script. According to this approach, the collaboration protocols are a set of useful scripts for collaborative learning, expressed as executable methods with roles, events and explicit actions.

The collaboration protocols can be represented by means of State Diagrams. Each state represents the execution of a task in a shared workspace. In each workspace the users carry out actions such as communicating or manipulating artefacts. The transition to other workspaces is triggered by means of the users' actions or when a specific situation is reached, such as the occurrence of a time-out or when the artefact reaches a certain condition.

3 Coordination, Decision-making and Communication Protocols

In order to describe collaboration protocols, several formalisms can be used: the extended Activity Diagrams of AMENITIES [7], State Diagrams, etc. A Conversational Graph [1] allows the contribution types issued by the users and the relationships between these contributions to be shown. The graph nodes represent the contributions and the arcs, which are directed according to which contributions reply to a given contribution, thus determining the order of emission. In a conversation there are initial, final and intermediate contributions. In addition, contributions issued by the users or automatically issued by the system can be distinguished. The former are represented with a rectangle, and the latter with a rectangle with rounded corners (see Fig. 1). However, conversational graphs only show the contribution types and their relationships, so that more detailed techniques, such as State Diagrams, are required to express the working of the protocol.

Protocols for coordination, decision-making and communication are presented in subsequent subsections. The final subsection discusses user interfaces to be used to support these protocols.

3.1 Processes Based on Proposals and Agreements

In this type of processes, a leading student makes a proposal of a value for a variable, of the execution of an action, etc. The remaining students in the group have to reply to this proposal with an agreement, disagreement or abstention. This procedure is described by the conversational graph in Fig. 1.

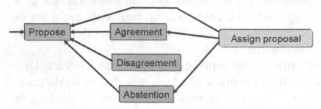

Fig. 1. Conversational graph of a process based on proposals and agreements

This scheme represents a process for a single proposal. However, it is common for users to carry out many proposals in parallel during a task. In this case, in order to reply to a proposal this has to be identified previously. A more detailed conversational graph would allow, for instance, a proposal to be replied to with another proposal, that is, a counterproposal. However, these more complex structures are more typical of asynchronous collaboration processes, in which the users have more time to think and to select the most appropriate conversational act at any moment.

3.2   Request and Release of Resources

In this scheme, the users request resources, and take control of them if they are available. However a resource can only be owned by one user, and cannot pass to another user until it has been released by the user who had control over it. Frequently, the assignment of resources is made by order of request. A typical situation in which this process is applied is when there is a floor control which is not managed by the system and that must be negotiated among the users. The conversational graph of this protocol (Fig. 2) contains two user contributions (request and release) and one system contribution (assign).

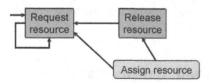

Fig. 2. Conversational graph of a process to request and release a resource

3.3 Democratic Processes

A democratic process avoids replying to contributions. In this protocol the system has to calculate the value to be assigned to a variable as the users make proposals. The system should have a configurable method which defines how to obtain the variable value from the values proposed and depending on the variable type. In the DomoSim-TPC environment [3], the Parameter Definition tool (see Fig. 4) uses a democratic process. This tool manipulates two kinds of variables: numeric and alphanumeric. Numeric variables are calculated as the arithmetic mean of all the values proposed, whereas for alphanumeric ones the most voted value is taken.

3.4 Decision-making Processes

The three coordination processes presented above are characterized by generating a system action as a result of adopting a specific proposal or negotiating the control of a resource. On the contrary, a structured decision-making process is a more guided process that is implemented as a voting process. In a voting process, a user makes a voting definition, then this user and his/her partners vote (the users can issue an abstention vote), and finally the system counts the voting results and shows them to the group. In so doing the users are responsible for using the results to carry out some action, and therefore a system action is not generated automatically.

A voting process consists of formulating a question for the users. There are three types of voting procedures that correspond to three types of questions: those which have a yes-no vote as an answer, those which have a numeric value as an answer, and those which have a value from a list of possible values as an answer.

3.5 Structured Communication

Many synchronous CSCL environments incorporate communication functionalities in the supported tasks. Communication is another means for negotiation and argumentation. In this situation, a structured communication interface can be an excellent complement, presenting three potential advantages:

- It provides the explicit representation of certain communication acts (for instance, the act *why...?*) that encourage learners' participation.
- It can reduce the writing load and facilitate coordination, allowing the learners to focus more on the task and on the reflexive interaction.
- It avoids problems of understanding the natural language.

The language underlying structured communication takes the form shown in the conversational graph in Fig. 3. There are initial messages (*i*, *k*) and messages that reply to others (*j*, *l*, *m*). There are also messages that can have more than one reply (*i*), and communication cycles are possible (*i*, *l*, *m*, *i*, ...).

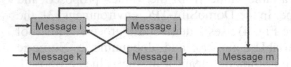

Fig. 3. Conversational graph of a generic structured communication

3.6 User Interfaces for Coordination, Decision-making and Structured Communication

In this section, some example user interfaces to support the protocols presented in the previous subsections are shown. Fig. 4 (a) shows the Parameter Definition tool of DomoSim-TPC [3], which allows the learners to give values to different variables by means of proposals, agreements and disagreements. There is a row for each parameter. The user interface supports multiple proposals, from several users and for several parameters simultaneously. The panel in Fig. 4 (c) allows the students to decide when to compile. This supports one proposal from each user. The arrangement of this user interface is different to the previous one: all the contributions are inserted in a list. Thus, the contribution to which a reply is to be made has to be selected from a list.

In Fig. 4 (b), the Parameter Definition tool of DomoSim-TPC is shown again, but in this case the tool is configured to support a democratic process, so that agreement and disagreement contributions are not needed. Fig. 4 (d) shows the user interface to manage the floor control in Co-Lab [10]. There are buttons to request and release control as well as to cancel a request. The decision-making process is implemented in the Voting Tool of DomoSim-TPC [3]. Fig. 4 (e) is an example of definition of a *list-of-values* voting type. The COLLEGE system [2] incorporates a structured chat (Fig. 4 (f)) implementing the structured communication protocol. The tool controls the correct use of the messages according to the communication structure. For example, the messages *I think so* or *I don't think so* can only reply to a message *I think that...*

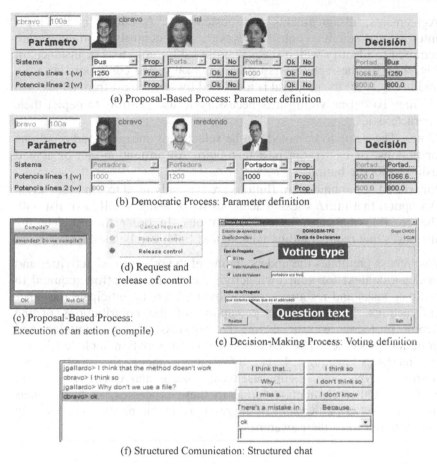

(a) Proposal-Based Process: Parameter definition

(b) Democratic Process: Parameter definition

(d) Request and
release of control

(c) Proposal-Based Process:
Execution of an action (compile)

(e) Decision-Making Process: Voting definition

(f) Structured Comunication: Structured chat

Fig. 4. User interface examples for some collaboration protocols

The example user interfaces in Fig. 4 constitute a collection of interaction patterns, since they involve a solution for the problem of designing a user interface for a coordination, decision-making or communication process. However, several solutions to designing a user interface for such processes exist. The following are some ideas which are put forward for analyzing which user interface elements (controls) are more suitable to support a specific collaboration protocol and how to issue their corresponding contributions.

- Proposals: Usually, buttons are used to make proposals. The data set that characterizes a proposal (variables and values) must be defined using other user interface controls, such as check boxes, lists or text fields.

- Agreements, disagreements and abstentions: A button is the most intuitive and suitable control. However, other controls or strategies are required to identify which specific proposal to reply to. For instance, in Fig. 4 (a, b), the reply refers to the proposal of the corresponding row, and in Fig. 4 (c) the proposal is identified by selecting it from a list.
- Voting: To define voting it is necessary to use controls to depict their characteristics.
- Votes: The value to be voted can be selected by means of radio buttons or buttons, or be written in a text field. An abstention can be issued using a specific button.
- Structured communication: Buttons are typically used to send messages. An option that utilizes less space consists of using a pulldown list with the possible messages instead of buttons. In order to complete the messages that require additional text, text fields can be used.

Awareness facilitates the understanding of the other users' activities and provides a context for your own activity, reducing the effort required to coordinate tasks and resources, and allowing users to anticipate the other users' actions. Therefore, the perception of the contributions of the different protocols is crucial for the progress of argumentation and negotiation processes. The main awareness information included in the user interfaces in Fig. 4 is: information about the contributions (occurrence, type, data, issuing user, etc.), beeps and visual signals (see Fig. 4 (c)). Other elements external to these processes, such as panels showing the list of participants in the sessions, including their photos, help the users to reinforce their awareness.

4 Conclusions and Future Work

In this article a collection of collaboration protocols that allow the modelling of coordination, decision-making and communication processes in CSCL environments has been presented. In addition, examples of user interfaces to enable the necessary human-computer-human interaction to support these processes have been shown. These protocols are, in fact, patterns, since they represent a problem (to coordinate a task or collaborative action) and an effective solution (a coordination model) in a given context. More specifically, patterns for processes based on proposals and agreements, processes for request and release of resources, democratic processes, decision-making processes, and structured communication processes have been proposed. From the example user interfaces, guidelines from which patterns for HCI derive can be extracted. Each protocol and its user interface can be implemented by means of software components, so that by making a component-based development, CSCL environments could be constructed by composing building blocks (components).

The protocols proposed develop the principle of structuring. This structuring facilitates the storage of the students' tasks and actions, and of their interactions on the user interface, which allows the later analysis and study of the work carried out, which is a characteristic issue in CSCL.

With respect to the limitations of the protocols presented, they do not provide mechanisms to avoid both the lack of participation and the conflicts of intentions. From the point of view of software development, the need exists for methods for the modelling of collaboration processes, so that direct engineering is facilitated. To reach this objective, it is necessary to use formal description techniques to represent the protocols and the patterns without ambiguity, in order to facilitate their computational processing and to represent and apply previous experiences. In this respect, it will be necessary to link the elements of the user interface with the types of contributions and the working of the protocol. This is our current line of work.

Acknowledgments

This work is supported by the Consejería de Educación y Ciencia, Junta de Comunidades de Castilla-La Mancha (Spain), in the PCI-05-006 project.

References

1. Barros B (1999) Aprendizaje Colaborativo en Enseñanza a Distancia: Entorno Genérico para Configurar, Realizar y Analizar Actividades en Grupo. Ph.D. thesis, Departamento de Inteligencia Artificial, Universidad Politécnica de Madrid
2. Bravo C, Redondo MA, Mendes AJ, Ortega M (2006a) Group Learning of Programming by means of Real Time Distributed Collaboration Techniques. In: Lorés J, Navarro R (eds) HCI related papers of Interacción 2004. Springer (The Netherlands), pp 289–302
3. Bravo C, Redondo MA, Ortega M, Verdejo MF (2006b) Collaborative Environments for the Learning of Design: A Model and a Case Study in Domotics. Computers and Education 46 (2): 152–173
4. Collis B (1993) Cooperative Learning and CSCW: Research Perspectives for Internetworked Educational Environments. In: IFIP Working Group 3.3. Working Conference, Lessons from Learning, Theme B. Archamps, Francia
5. Dillenbourg P, Baker M, Blaye A, O'Malley C (1996) The Evolution of Research on Collaborative Learning. In: Espada E, Reiman P (eds) Learning

in Humans and Machine: Towards an Interdisciplinary Learning Science. Elsevier, Oxford, pp 189–211

6. Fincher S (2000) Patterns for HCI. Pattern gallery. http://www.cs.kent.ac.uk/people/staff/saf/patterns/gallery.html

7. Garrido JL, Gea M, Rodríguez ML (2005) Requirements Engineering in Cooperative Systems. In: Requirements Engineering for Socio-Technical Systems. IDEA GROUP INC, USA, pp 226–244

8. Hernández D, Asensio JI, Dimitriadis Y (2004) IMS Learning Design Support for the Formalization of Collaborative Learning Patterns. In: Proceedings of 4th International Conference on Advanced Learning Technologies. Joensuu, Finland, pp 350–354

9. Mancini BM, Hall RH, Hall MA, Stewart B (1998) The Individual in the Dyad: a Qualitative Analysis of Scripted Cooperative Learning. Journal of Classroom Interaction 33 (1): 14–22

10. van Joolingen WR, de Jong T, Lazonder AW, Savelsbergh E, Manlove S (2005) Co-Lab: Research and Development of an On-line Learning Environment for Collaborative Scientific Discovery Learning. Computers in Human Behavior 21: 671–688

11. Wessner M, Hans-Rüdiger P, Miao Y (1999) Using Learning Protocols to Structure Computer-Supported Cooperative Learning. In: Proceedings of the ED-MEDIA'99, World Conference on Educational Multimedia, Hypermedia & Telecommunications. Seattle, Washington, pp 471–476

Components of an EML Proposal for Collaborative Learning Modelling

Manuel Caeiro-Rodríguez, Martín Llamas Nistal, Luis Anido-Rifón

Departamento de Enxeñería Telemática, Universidade de Vigo, Spain
Manuel.Caeiro@det.uvigo.es

1 Introduction

Up to 2003, most e-learning standards related with learning contents have followed a well-established educational model: a learner receiving or accessing information and resources under the control of a computational system [9]. This is the most common model in the majority of existing e-learning systems. Furthermore, it is suitable for the needs of the great part of schools, companies and users. Nevertheless, there exist many pedagogical approaches that cannot be supported on this particular model. As an example, pedagogical approaches based on collaborative learning ideas are not supported.

To overcome this limitation, the *Open University of the Netherlands* (OUNL) developed several years ago a proposal named as *Educational Modeling Language* (EML) [6]. A main purpose of this EML was to support the computational modelling of educational units (e.g. a course, a lab practice, a seminar) in accordance with different pedagogical approaches. Among them, the support of pedagogical approaches based on collaborative learning was one of the main goals. In 2003, the efforts of the OUNL produced the publication of the IMS *Learning Design* (LD) specification [7], currently EML *de facto* standard. This standard does not impose the pedagogical approach of educational units. Nevertheless, IMS LD has not achieved a definitive solution to support the computational modelling of collaborative learning educational units. Some authors have described extensions to LD supporting collaborative issues [4, 10]. Anyway, they consider a narrow view of the problem and comprehensible solution remains to be developed.

This chapter introduces the main components of an original EML proposal to support collaborative learning pedagogical approaches. The main idea underlying this proposal is the separation of concerns: instead of attaining the computational modelling of educational units as a whole it considers its decomposition in several separated and independent concerns, named as perspectives. The obtained EML proposal, *Perspective-oriented Educational Modeling Language* (PoEML), has been developed to enable the evaluation of this separation of concerns approach. The chapter contains a description of PoEML main components in relation with collaborative learning requirements.

The rest of the chapter is organized as follows. Next section briefly introduces some of the main requirements needed to support collaborative learning approaches. In Section 3, the main components of the PoEML proposal are introduced, distinguishing among perspectives, entities and behaviours. The paper finishes with some conclusions.

2 Collaborative Learning

Broadly speaking, collaborative learning involves a situation in which two or more people learn or attempt to learn something together [1]. Despite of this definition, there is not agreement on a common interpretation of what collaborative learning means. Depending on the application collaborative learning may involve two or several participants, interactions may be produced freely or in a constrained way, synchronous or asynchronously, the collaboration may involve communication among participants or the performance of an activity in conjunction, etc.

Computer-Supported Collaborative Learning (CSCL) is concerned with the development of computer-based systems to support collaborative learning. Similarly to collaborative learning, CSCL involves a great variability and heterogeneity of approaches and solutions. The literature in this field [3, 8] can be approached by considering the following three main functionality areas:

- *Communication*. Communication encompasses the process of transfer and exchange of information that takes place between participants. Typical communication tools are: e-mail, desktop conferencing systems, chat, etc. In education, the provision of communication functionalities usually involves mechanisms to control the management of communication functionalities (*conference model*) and the participation of users (*conversation model*).

- *Co-operation.* Sometimes the collaboration among a group of people is centred on the access and change of a shared set of data. In these situations, the goal of the collaboration is the construction of this shared data. Examples of systems that provide these functionalities are shared editors, virtual whiteboards, shared repositories, etc. These functionalities usually involves some control mechanisms: access rights, floor control, version control, etc.
- *Coordination.* Coordination is considered as the process of managing dependencies. There are different ways in which coordination can be supported. Two extreme approaches are distinguished: (i) normative models that try to structure collaboration by restricting the tasks to be performed; and (ii) collaborative systems that take flexibility to the extreme, leaving the coordination to the users and simple mediating in the interaction (i.e. supporting communication and co-operation). In practice, none of the extreme approaches can be discarded and several intermediate solutions can be considered [5] (e.g. awareness, contraints).

3 PoEML Components for Collaborative Learning

PoEML (*Perspective-oriented Educational Modeling Language*) has been proposed as a new EML to perform contributions that enable the development of these languages. It is based on the following premise: "*to attain the computational modeling of educational units not as a whole, but by decomposing the modeling problem in several as independent as possible separated parts (namely: perspectives)*". The different parts are related among them in accordance with a task scheme to obtain a comprehensible solution. In this way, we hope to obtain an expressive and flexible modelling solution. The perspective approach may enable the modelling of more educational situations incrementally (e.g. collaborative learning), while maintaining the modelling of common situations in a simple way. In addition, the modelling in separate (and as independent as possible) perspectives enables to change the modelling in one perspective without affecting to the others. The purpose of this work is to evaluate this modelling approach to contribute to the EML standardization process.

The PoEML proposal has identified twelve perspectives to support the computational modelling of collaborative learning educational units. These perspectives do not only enable the modelling of collaborative learning, but also other pedagogical approaches such as individual instruction or adaptive learning. Anyway, the description of the complete set of perspectives and PoEML modelling components will be too large. Therefore, perspectives are briefly introduced next and then the main components of the

PoEML proposal are described. The PoEML components are arranged in two sections: *PoEML entities* represent abstract or concrete things involved in an educational unit, and *PoEML behaviours*, used to model the coordination of the previous entities.

3.1   PoEML Perspectives

PoEML perspectives are divided into a core set and an optional set. The perspectives included in the core are:

- *Functional. What has to be done in the UoL.* This one is concerned with the goals that have to be attained in the course. These goals are intended to drive the work of participants. But, this perspective does not deal with the participants that have to perform them, neither about the environments where they should be performed. It simple involves the decomposition of goals into their possible sub-goals in accordance with a hierarchical aggregation; the featuring of the goals (e.g. mandatory, optional, and prohibited); the input and output parameters; etc.
- *Social. Who is to perform each goal in the UoL.* It considers the featuring of roles (e.g. learners, academic staff, profile); the assignment of participants to roles; the aggregations of participants (e.g. groups, teams); etc.
- *Informational. What data and artefacts are available to perform each goal in the UoL.* It involves data-types (e.g. Boolean, file, array); the assignment of values (e.g. copy, transfer); etc. These data may be associated with environments, roles, goals, etc.
- *Structural. How the goals of the UoL are intended to be performed.* This perspective supports the arrangement of other perspectives elements in appropriate aggregations to indicate *who* is intended to perform *what*, using *what data and artefacts,* etc. Basically, this perspective considers a *task structure* relating *goals*, *participants*, *environments* and the rest of the elements. This *task structure* is organized hierarchically in correspondence with the hierarchy of goals.

The rest of the perspectives are optional as they are not always required. The *structural perspective* relates all of them. These perspectives are the following:

- *Operational. Which operations are required to perform each goal in the UoL.* It comprises the applications and services that can be used (e.g. simulators, editors, and communication and collaboration services). We are only interested in the capacity to model the functionality of such applications and services. To support their management and control we propose other perspectives: *authorization*, *awareness* and *interaction*.

- *Organizational. The organizational structure required to perform the UoL.* This information may be used to constrain other perspectives. For example, the assignment of a participant to a certain role may depend on his/her organizational position.

- *Process. The order in which goals are intended to be performed.* It indicates whether a set of goals have to be performed in sequence or parallel, to set synchronization points, etc.

- *Temporal. The time at what goals are intended to be performed.* Without temporal constraints, a goal is always initiated when its preceding goal finishes.

- *Authorization. The access rights users have to perform operations.* This perspective enables to determine the available actions for each participant and group (e.g. public/private artefacts). In collaborative scenarios it is usual that different participants have different authorizations.

- *Awareness. The runtime information that has to be provided to participants about what other participants have done or are doing.* For example, in educational experiences it is very important that teachers know about the progress of their learners. Anyway, it is worth to notice that as important as providing this information to a teacher it is to provide not too much info in order to facilitate the teacher work and not to overload him/her.

- *Interaction. How the interaction in applications and services is managed.* We have considered the following forms of management and control: (i) *session control*, to manage the initiation and termination of systems; (ii) *membership control*, to manage the resources involved in a system; (iii) *floor control*, to manage the way in which participants are intended to collaborate; (iv) *conversation control*, to manage the communications between the participants.

- *Causal.* It indicates *why to perform a UoL*: the learning objectives, the learner pre-requisites, etc. This perspective has already been thoroughly analysed and discussed in the context of *Learning Objects* (LOs) promoting the first e-learning standard: *The IEEE Learning Object Meta-data* [9]. In any case, this perspective is not specifically about coordination.

3.2 PoEML Entities

PoEML Entities enable the modelling of the basic elements that made up an educational unit. They are used to feature the properties and the relationships of these elements. Then, *PoEML Behaviours* enable to specify how *Entities* are coordinated in order to support their interoperation.

3.2.1 EducationalScenario

An *EducationalScenario* (ES) represents a unit of education at any level of granularity or specificity. The *ES* entity is the aggregation point where all other elements are anchored. Particularly, an *ES* is intended to: (i) achieve a certain *Goal* or set of *Goals*; (ii) that have to be attained by a particular *Participant* in a *Role*; in a specific *Environment* composed by (iii) a set of *Artefacts*; and (iv) *Tools* that represent *applications* and *services*; (v) in the context of a certain *OrganizationalStructure*; (vi) considering a certain *Order* in the way in which *ESs* are intended to be attempted; and (vii) *TemporalSpecifications* on their performance (init a finish time); and involving a set of rules that control and manage (viii) the *AuthorizationSpecifications* of the involved participants to invoke operations; (ix) the *Awareness* they receive during execution; and (x) the *Interaction* produced on *applications* and *services*. In addition, *ESs* can be related among them using reflexive aggregation relationships. Therefore, it is possible to model a large *ES* composed by several *sub-ESs*. In addition, ESs may involve.

3.2.2 Goals

Each *ES* needs to indicate at least a *Goal*. It is not a learning goal (e.g. to know about birds), but a performance goal that directs the efforts of a person in the development of an activity. The PoeML modelling of goals enables the establishment of reflexive aggregation and specialization relationships among goals (belonging to the same or different *ESs*). In this way, it is possible to maintain different *ES* and *Goal* organizations. Anyway, *ESs* and *Goals* use to maintain related arrangements. *Goals* are characterized through the following artefacts

- *Pre-conditions*. Constraints that must be satisfied to enable the *Goal*.
- *Post-conditions*. Constraints that must be satisfied to complete the *Goal*.
- *OutputArtefacts*. They are the produced results. It may be the state of consecution of the *Goal* (e.g. failed).
- *InputArtefacts*. They are the resources required to perform the *Goal*.

3.2.3 Roles

A *Role* is an active entity responsible for performing an activity. It can represent a single person or a group. In the case of groups it is possible to define the group structure. *Roles* of the same *ES* can be related using reflexive aggregation and specialization relationships. In addition *Roles* can be related with properties to indicate the features that must be maintained for the *Role*. In case of a learner these features may involve: profile, portfolio, etc. In the case of a teacher capabilities, curriculum, etc.

3.2.4 Environments

Environments represent the places where *Roles* can perform their work towards the achievement of *Goals*. An *Environment* is made up by *Artefacts*, *Tools* and by other *Environments* through a reflexive aggregation relationship. Conceptually, an *Environment* constitutes a delimited space of elements where other PoEML specifications can be applied in a uniform way (e.g. to authorize access to all the artefacts of an environment).

3.2.5 Data and Artefacts

Data in PoEML is included in *Artefacts*, which act as resources to maintain information. It is possible to model different types of artefacts: Boolean, integer, real, string, date, time, binary file, text file, etc. Reflexive aggregation and specialization relationships between artefacts are also supported. *Artefacts* are mainly intended to be included in *Environments* enabling their use in the ES. In addition, *Artefacts* may be associated with *Goals* (input and output artefacts), with *Roles* (features), with *Tools* (operations and events) and with certain *PoEML behaviours*.

3.2.6 Tools: Applications and Services

PoEML Tools are included to support the modelling of external functionalities. In general, EMLs do not try to support all the functionality involved in e-learning systems. On the contrary, they were proposed as integrative specifications that take advantage of existing systems. PoEML enables this integration by the description of functional and non-functional features of applications and services. This featuring is considered syntactically or semantically, by the reference of external vocabularies, taxonomies and ontologies. In addition, it is enabled the modelling of operations, events and permissions. This entity is used to support the modelling of communication and co-operation functionalities required in collaborative learning.

3.3 PoEML Behaviours

Behaviours enable to specify how *PoEML Entities* are coordinated in order to support their interoperation. The coordination requirements are supported by the first five *behaviours*, which enable the specification of different coordination issues. The last three behaviours are very important to support the models to control and manage communication and co-operation functionalities.

3.3.1 Process (Sequencing)

Process is about the order in which *ESs* (tasks) can/should be performed. PoEML includes a reduced set of constructs (sequence, parallel, branch and boucle) because *PoEML Process* behaviour is only concerned about ordering. Other proposals (e.g. workflow languages and systems) also use the process behaviour to decide the activities that need to be performed (e.g. optional and mandatory activities), namely: coercion.

3.3.2 Temporal Dependencies

Temporal dependencies are included to indicate when ESs must/can be initiated and finished, and when operations need to be invoked. Without temporal specifications ESs are always initiated in accordance with the *process behavior*. By separating process and temporal behaviours it is possible to model them almost independently. Possible dependencies are solved by establishing a priority.

3.3.3 Goal Dependencies

Goal dependencies enable to specify the behaviours of a *Goal*. The coercion degree is used to indicate if a goal is mandatory or optional. This degree can be determined in accordance with different kinds of constraints (e.g. conditions, events, decisions). The *multiplicity* factor is included to enable the specification of the number of times a *Goal* needs to be achieved. The *performance* feature enables to establish cancellation mechanisms.

3.3.4 Participant Assignment

Participants (learners and teachers) need to be assigned to the *Roles* that are modelled in each *ES*. In a similar way, participants are also arranged into groups. These assignments may be performed in accordance with different mechanisms: selection, election, conditions, association, etc. In addition, a participant may be assigned to different *Roles* in different *ESs*.

3.3.5 Data Flow

This behaviour refers to the transfer of information between *Artefacts*. Data is transferred from one ES to the next in accordance with the *process*. This is known as synchronous data flow. There is another kind of data flow known as asynchronous in which data is transferred or copied in accordance with a an event or condition satisfaction.

3.3.6 Interaction

Interaction is about the invocation of operations in external tools in order to facilitate their management and control for the educational unit. These interactions are produced in accordance with events or conditions satisfied during the runtime. It is possible to model complex interactions involving the combination of several simple operations.

3.3.7 Awareness

PoEML supports the specification of *awareness* specifications indicating which events need to be captured in what elements and how they need to be processed in order to detect certain situations. The operations proposed in PoEML have been taken from the composite event literature: aggregation, filtering, correlation, etc. Eventually, these event processing structures can be used to notify certain participants, feed event management tools or to specify other behaviours (e.g. interaction).

3.3.8 Authorization

Authorization is supported by enabling the assignment of permissions to *Roles*. The permissions used are referred to *Artefacts* and *Tools*. In addition, it is required to indicate the object of authorization.

4 Conclusions

This paper introduces the main components of the PoEML proposal to support the computational modelling of educational units, particularly in accordance with collaborative learning approaches. The modelling of these approaches is very complex involving the managing of many different issues [2]. The approach presented in this proposal involves the separation of concerns. In this way, it is possible to consider the modelling of educational units in an systematic and incremental way, enabling the modelling of complex scenarios while solving the common problems in a simple way.

Acknowledgments

We want to thank *"Ministerio de Educación y Ciencia"* for its support to this work under grant *"MetaLearn: methodologies, architectures and languages for E-learning adaptive services"* (TIN2004-08367-C02-01).

References

1. Dillenbourg P (1999) What do you mean by collaborative learning? In Dillenbourg P (eds) Collaborative-learning: cognitive and computational approaches. Oxford: Elsevier, ch. 1, pp. 1–19
2. Dillenbourg P (2002) Over-scirpting CSCL: the risks of blending collaborative learning and instructional Design, In Kirschner PPA (eds) Three worlds of CSCL. Can we support CSCL. Open Universiteit Nederland, pp. 61-91
3. Ellis E, Wainer J (1999) Groupware and computer supported cooperative work. In Weiss G (ed) Multiagent systems: a modern approach to distributed artificial intelligence. MIT Press, pp. 425–457
4. Hernández-Leo D, Asensio-Pérez JI, Dimitriadis YA (2004) IMS Learning Design support for the formalization of collaborative learning patterns. In Proccedings of the ICALT
5. Jørgensen HD (2004) Interactive process models. Ph. D. Thesis, Norwegian University of Science and Technology
6. Koper R (2001) Modeling units of study from a pedagogical perspective – The pedagogical metamodel behind EML. Open University of the Netherlands
7. Koper R, Olivier B, Anderson T (Eds.) (2003) IMS learning design information model. IMS Global Learning Consortium
8. Raposo B, Pimentel MG, Gerosa MA, Fuks H, Lucena CJP (2004) Prescribing e-learning activities using workflow technologies. In Proceedings of the CSAC'04, pp. 71–80
9. Rawlings A, van Rosmalen P, Koper R, Rodríguez-Artacho M, Lefrere P (2002) Survery of Educational Modelling Languages (EMLs). Version 1, CEN/ISSS Workshop on Learning Technologies
10. Turani A, Calvo R (2006) Sharing synchronous collaborative learning structures using IMS learning design. In Proceedings. of the 4th International Conference on Information Technology Based Higher Education and Training

Analysis of Engaged Online Collaborative Discourse: A Methodological Approach

Sofia Malheiro, Lina Morgado, António Quintas-Mendes

Universidade Aberta
sofiamalheiro@gmail.com, lmorgado@univ-ab.pt, quintas@univ-ab.pt

1 Introduction

Messages in computer-mediated conferencing are widely acknowledged as a new, hybrid form of communication. They contain some of the strengths and weaknesses of speech and of writing, but it is not quite clear how good they are to make the most of those strengths and minimize the weaknesses in online learning environments.

In fact, to deepen the analysis of student participation in discussion forums integrated in online distance training courses is of the utmost importance in order to produce strong evidence about the learning taking place and the construction of knowledge that might occur.

As Fahy reminds us [3], researchers should be able to describe online interactions in a less impressionistic way and measure them more efficiently. We can thus consider some studies in which transcriptions of the computer-mediated conferences were examined in a more precise manner.

Henri [5] centered his analysis on the learning processes perceived in the messages. His model grants particular emphasis to content analysis.

Gunawardena [4] took Henri's model further and shifted the emphasis to the nature of the dialogue taking place, highlighting the importance of the analysis of interaction itself.

Lally [6], taking into account Henri's content analysis and Gunawardena's interaction analysis concluded that the networked collaborative learning environments "provide means to evaluate and confirm the nature of the existing complex relations between teaching and learning which are not accessible in conventional classrooms".

In her research, Xin [13] tried to create an interpretative framework which allowed for measuring the quality of engaged collaborative discourse (ECD) in computer conferencing. To that end, she used three sub-scales that measure, respectively, the Communication Processes, the Intellectual Engagement and the Use of Moderating Functions in ECD. These three sub-scales will then be combined into a single scale that aims at measuring the Overall Quality of Engaged Collaborative Discourse.

This is the conceptual frame in which we conducted an empirical study, having as object an Online Trainers Training Course offered by Universidade Aberta. This work systematizes the main methodological constraints we faced when we used Xin's scales to analyse the level of engaged collaborative discourse in a discussion forum, part of the module "Models of Online Training: Collaborative Learning", with the objective of determining the nature of the interactions that took place.

2 Collaborative Learning and Cooperative Learning

Piaget, although criticized for not having favoured the social element in cognitive development, did consider the importance of interactions and social interactions in explaining learning and development. For him [11] "it is precisely the constant interchange of thoughts with others that allows us to decentre and assure the possibility of coordinating internally as relations that emanate from different points of view". In his book *Sociological Studies* [11], Piaget tries to find a sociological explanation, as opposed to a psychological explanation of cognitive growth. The basic concept of the subject's action upon the object remains, with the difference that the "I" has now become "We" and that the actions give way to interactions or "conducts that modify one another, forms of cooperation, that is, operations performed in common or in reciprocal correspondence" (p. 22).

Continuing Piaget's work, Perret-Clermont [10] concentrated on the influence of interactions on cognitive development, using the results of the studies conducted by Doise & Mugny [2] which showed that, under certain circumstances, pair work was better than individual work. It follows from these considerations that learning takes place inside each individual, but can be prompted by social exchanges, i.e. social interactions and culture play, in this perspective, a prominent role in the individual's cognitive development. This is the basic principle of Cooperative/Collaborative Learning, which in this case follows the socioconstructivist approach.

Vygotsky [12], on the other hand, postulated that the higher psychological processes appear firstly in social relations in the form of interpersonal processes, then becoming intrapersonal or individual.

The justification for the social origin in the higher psychological processes lies, according to Vygotsky, in the mediation performed by tools. These tools can be physical (tools that control the environment) or psychological (signs, language in particular), and the relation of the human being with them is active and transformative.

The move from the interpersonal (social) to the intrapersonal (individual) process happens through interiorization, which is "the internal reconstruction of an external operation" [12: 74]. Both oral and written language are made of symbols used in human communication which, when interiorized, create new forms of thinking. The interiorization of socially rooted and historically developed activities constitutes the basic feature of human psychology [12: 76].

Learning is thus a social process that takes place through the possibilities created by the subject's mediations in a given social and historical context, since, as Ratner [12: 160] points out, "the individual does not face things with a solitary conscience. He is a member of a social community and depends on other people for material, behavioral and psychological help". We therefore reassert Vygotsky's conviction that social interaction is the origin of and the driving force behind learning and intellectual development [12].

Pierre Lévy [8] also incorporates the sociocultural approach to learning when he proposes the virtual learning communities, the collective construction of shared knowledge and the networked collaborative/ cooperative learning. To learn with others, reformulating knowledge through the critical perspective of others, is important to strengthen reasoning and communication skills. The fundamental assumption of the collaborative/cooperative models is that the acquisition and development of knowledge, skills or attitudes is not an inherently individual process but rather results from group interaction.

In the context of his Cognitive Ecology theory, Pierre Lévy [7] states:

> intelligence or cognition are the result of complex networks where a great number of human, biological and technical actors interact. It is not 'I' who am intelligent but 'I' with the human group of which I am a member, with my language, with a whole heritage of intellectual methods and technologies (p.135)

There is, however, some controversy about the use of the terms "cooperative learning" and "collaborative learning". The debate of "collaboration" versus "cooperation" is a complex one. It is possible to state, on a first approach, that both paradigms are based on a constructivist epistemology, with a special relevance to the learner's active role.

In the distinction put forward by Panitz [9], the term "collaboration" corresponds to a "a philosophy of interaction and personal lifestyle where individuals are responsible for their actions, including learning and respect the abilities and contributions of their peers".

The term "cooperation" is viewed, by the same author, as a "structure of interaction designed to facilitate the accomplishment of a specific end product or goal through people working together in groups". Cooperative learning is thus defined by a set of processes that help individuals interact to achieve a common goal.

Dillenbourg [1] also views collaboration as different from cooperation. This author distinguishes the concepts along three main characteristics: a) degree of symmetry in the interaction, b) shared goals and c) division of labour. For him, situations can be characterized as more or less collaborative or more or less cooperative according to these three criteria.

To move from the theoretical elaboration on collaboration and cooperation to the empirical analysis of interactions, seeking to understand the ways in which dialogue and cooperation take place online is our strong motivation in this phase of searching for valid tools and methodological procedures to analyse interaction in computer mediated communication.

3 Analysis of Engaged Collaborative Discourse

For Xin [13], to create an interpretative framework that permits the measuring of individual learning and engaged collaborative discourse in online discussions implies the establishing of a process that is synergetic and, simultaneously, allies design and development at the theoretical and instrumental level, allowing for the articulation of some of the variables. Thus, Xin proposes three subscales that after being combined will produce a single scale that measures the overall quality of engaged collaborative discourse (ECD).

First Subscale – Measurement of the Communication Processes

"Sustained group communication is reflected in its members' contributions to the discourse and their interaction with others" [13: 155].

In this perspective, the concept of *participation* is related to contribution and interaction. To measure the "quantity" of communication three rating questions are used, which aim at describing the level of individual participation on a given discussion topic and in a given period of time. They are:

- **Login activities** – Number of times an individual makes a request to download waiting messages from the server in a given time period; number of messages read by an individual at a given point in time.
- **Quantity of contribution** – Number of messages posted by an individual in a given discussion topic and the total number of words in those messages.
- **Quantity of interaction** – Number of references made by an individual to previous contributions in a given time period in a given discussion topic.

The results from these three rating questions allow a classification of the individual according to six levels of communication: Peripheral; Minimal Participation; Basic; Regular; Frequent; Active.

This subscale thus tries to answer the questions of "How much" and "How often" an individual contributes and interacts. However, it does not answer the question regarding the "Quality of participation" of the individuals.

Second Subscale – Measurement of Intellectual Engagement

To establish a rubric for measuring the quality of intellectual engagement Xin [13] uses three rating questions that try to describe the level of Intellectual Engagement of an individual in a given discussion topic during a given time period. They are:

- **Coherent with the teacher's agenda for the discussion** – The most basic requirement for participation in ECD is to be able to follow the teacher's agenda and post relevant and understandable contributions.
- **New ideas and points of view** – Contributing with new ideas and new points of view are important indicators of intellectual involvement and understanding, and can happen at any time in the discussion.
- **Relation with other contributions** – Elaborating on and relating to one or several previous contributions happens in the negotiation, construction and integration zones.

The answers to these three rating questions allow the classification of the individual according to five levels of intellectual engagement: Poor, Minimal, Fair, Competent, Excellent.

This subscale is not independent from the Communication Subscale. Both point to levels of intellectual contribution and interaction. The first is more focused on the quantitative aspects, the second on the qualitative ones.

Third Subscale – Measuring the Use of Moderating Functions

This third subscale measures the use of Moderation Functions by the individual – student or teacher/tutor – in a discussion topic, in a given period of time.

Moderation functions describe the tasks to be performed so as to facilitate and support the communication processes (1st subscale) and the intellectual engagement processes (2nd subscale).

To establish the scale for measuring moderating functions three rating questions are used:

- **Opening comment** – Almost exclusively the teacher/tutor's responsibility; it means to open a discussion announcing the topic(s), contents, goals, etc.
- **Setting discussion norms and agenda** – Generally these aspects are the teacher's responsibility, and have to do with organization, calendarization, delegation and assessment.
- **Referring materials** – Indication of referring materials, bibliography, etc. that support learning.

The answers to these three rating questions allow to classify the individual – student or teacher/tutor – according to a scale of use of moderating functions that comprises five levels: Basic, Effective, Active, Strong and Expert, for the student; and Minimal, Basic, Effective, Strong and Expert, for the teacher/tutor.

Unidimensional Scale – Measuring the Quality of Engaged Collaborative Discourse

The three subscales previously presented set up the basis to build a Unidimensional Scale that allows the measuring of the Quality of Engaged Collaborative Discourse, using a set of interpretative anchors for the interactions that occurred. But according to Xin [13], to use all the possible combinations they offer, ordering them from low to high, would result in an overly complex and confusing overall scale of no practical use. On the one hand, the communication, intellectual engagement, and use of moderating functions are closely related, so inevitably there are some overlaps among the levels of the three subscales. On the other hand, the combinations work at a theoretical level but might not translate into real life settings in one-to-one terms. Therefore, the author proposes a scale to measure the Quality of ECD comprising six levels: Peripheral, Minimal, Basic, Normal, Competent and Excellent. This scale is considered to be unidimensional and hypothetical, but provides an interpretative framework that allows the drawing of a progression map of the individual's performance in a given online course adopting a collaborative learning approach.

4 Results: The Application of the Subscales to a Discussion Forum

This work systematizes the main methodological constraints we faced when we used Xin's scales to analyse the level of engaged collaborative discourse in a discussion forum, part of the "Online Trainers Training Course" offered by Universidade Aberta, with the objective of determining the nature of the interactions that took place. We used Xin's "Scale of Engaged Collaborative Discourse" [13] to analyse the discussion forum of a one-week module containing 52 messages. Results for the Subscale 1 are shown in Table 1.

Table 1. Measuring the communication processes

Trainee's Code	Login activity		Contribution level				Interactivity level			
	Yes	No	N	O	R	A	N	O	R	A
Subject 1	----	----				10				7
Subject 2	----	----				8			6	
Subject 3	----	----			5			3		
Subject 4	----	----		2				1		
Subject 5	----	----		2						
Subject 6	----	----		2						
Subject 7	----	----				7			5	
Subject 8	----	----			6				6	
Subject 9	----	----			5				4	
Subject 10	----	----		1				1	0	
Subject 11	----	----		1				1	0	
Subject 12	----	----		2				1	0	
Subject 13	----	----		3				1	0	
TOTAL	----	----	0	13	16	25	0	8	21	7

Legend: N (None); **O** (Occasionally); **R** (Regularly); **A** (Actively)

Our intention to apply this scale met its first drawback when we realized that the functions that would allow us to quantify the login and download activity of the individuals in the discussion forum were not implemented in the system used to deliver the course. This obviously prevented us from assessing the quantity of login activity.

We have considered as *Quantity of Contribution* the number of messages posted by a given individual in that discussion forum, dividing the total amount of 52 interventions by the participants. This process revealed systematically the participants that contributed the most to the discussion and those that did not even take part in it.

We have taken as *Quantity of Interaction* the number of messages related to one or more previous contributions, in a merely quantitative perspective, which equals to saying that we counted the branches in the discussion tree ignoring the contents of the contributions.

The attempt to apply this first subscale met yet another important drawback. Although some of the contributions were inserted as replies to other messages, they didn't reveal any indicator of relation with one or more previous messages after content analysis had been performed. This makes it obvious that often a quantitative analysis without articulation with a qualitative approach distorts the validity of the data obtained.

The 2nd subscale – "Measuring Intellectual Engagement" – has a qualitative nature, which implied an analysis of the meaning of the transcriptions (see Table 2).

Table 2. Measuring intellectual engagement

Trainee's code	Coherent w/ teacher's agenda		New ideas and new points of view	Interactivity level				
	Yes	No	N/I	Y/L	YS	N/I	Y/1	Y/M
Subject 1	5	5	6	4		4	6	
Subject 2	4	4	3	5		4	3	1
Subject 3	3	1	4			1	1	2
Subject 4	1	1	2			1	1	
Subject 5	1		1			1		
Subject 6	2		2			2		
Subject 7	4	2	5	1		3	2	1
Subject 8		6	6			3	3	
Subject 9	2	2	3	1		1	3	
Subject 10		1	1					1
Subject 11	1		1					1
Subject 12	1		1			1		
Subject 13	1	1	2			1	1	
TOTAL	25	23	37	11	0	22	20	6

Legend: N/I (None or Insignificant); **Y/L** (Yes but with little supporting arguments); **Y/S** (Yes with strong supporting arguments); **Y/1** (Yes with relating to one previous contribution); **Y/M** (Yes with relating to multiple previous contributions)

In fact, the discussion forum analysed was focused on a lively discussion among the trainees about a text provided by the trainer. This aroused the need to elaborate also a content analysis grid for the text being discussed, since it was the only way in which we could classify the participants contributions according to Xin's proposition concerning new ideas and/or new points of view.

Finally, when we tried to apply the 3rd scale, "Measuring Moderating Functions in ECD" (see Table 3), and since the discussion was not subdivided to allow for small group work, the results obtained indicate that the trainer was the only participant to assume moderation functions. In a more cooperative-oriented task, an intragroup analysis would certainly result interesting.

Table 3. Measuring moderation functions

Trainee's code	Opening comment?		Setting norms?		Setting agenda?		Referring materials	
	Yes	No	Yes	No	Yes	No	WO/E	W/E
Subject 1	2		6		4		2	3
Subject 2			2					1
Subject 3			1					
Subject 4								
Subject 5								
Subject 6								
Subject 7								
Subject 8			1					
Subject 9								
Subject 10			1		1			
Subject 11								
Subject 12								
Subject 13								
TOTAL	2	0	11	0	5	0	2	4

Legend: WO/E (Without Explanation); **W/E** (With Explanation)

When we combined the three subscales in search for a result that measured the quality of engaged collaborative discourse, we actually obtained an individual indicator of each participant's performance, although conditioned by the aforementioned methodological constraints. Notwithstanding, the application of Xin's three subscales didn't allow us to analyse the engaged collaborative discourse among the participants as a collaborative learning group.

5 Final Considerations

The study presented here is still an ongoing one. The subject of computer mediated collaborative learning and the level of engaged collaborative discourse on the part of the participants are highly relevant for our research. Our use of Xin's subscales was not intended to describe rigorously the quality of engagement and produce results accordingly; our aim was to test this methodology, mapping its fragilities when applied to the analysis of asynchronous interactions in a discussion forum.

The classification proposed by Xin for the results obtained in the different subscales and at various levels of performance strikes us as being somewhat subjective. Since the results are organized in a qualitatively ascending order, without clearly specifying the criteria for the positioning in one or the other subsequent level, it is hard for another researcher to apply these procedures in a different context.

There is still a long way to go in the analysis of computer mediated communication if satisfactory levels of reliability, validity and replicability are to be attained in the analysis performed by different researchers. Only valid measurements can support assertions on the nature of asynchronous dialogue and its potential to generate insightful and sound arguments and discussions, in other words, on their true pedagogic potential. Valid measurements certainly presuppose relevant categories of analysis. In that sense, we feel that Xin's model, although it may require necessary contextualizations and improvements, might serve as an excellent point of departure to establish solid methodological foundations for the analysis of online educational interactions.

References

1. Dillenbourg P, Baker M, Blaye A, O'Malley C (1995) The evolution of research on collaborative learning. In: Reiman P, Spada H (eds) Learning in humans and machines: towards an interdisciplinary learning science. Elsevier, Oxford, pp 189–211
2. Doise W, Mugny G (1984) The social development of the intellect. Oxford: Pergamon Press
3. Fahy PJ (2001) Addressing some common problems in transcript analysis. International Review of Research in Open and Distance Learning, 1:1–5
4. Gunawardena CN (1991) Collaborative learning and group dynamics in computermediated communication networks. Unpublished manuscript, University Park, Pennsylvania: The Pennsylvania State University
5. Henri F (1992) Computer conferencing and content analysis. In: Kaye A (ed) Collaborative learning through computer conferencing. Heidelberg: The Najaden Papers NATO ASI Series Springer-Verlag, pp 117–136
6. Lally V, Laat MFD (2002) Cracking the code: learning to collaborate and collaborating to learn in a networked environment. In: Proceedings of the CSCL 2002 Conference, Boulder, Colorado, USA
7. Levy P (1990) Les technologies de l'intelligence. Paris: La Découverte
8. Lévy P (1999) Cyberculture. Paris : Odile Jacob
9. Panitz T (w/d) Collaborative versus cooperative learning – a comparison of the two concepts which will help us understand the underlying nature of

interactive   learning.   Available   in: http://home.capecod.net/~tpanitz/
tedsarticles/coopdefinition.htm
10. Perret-Clermont AN (1980) Social interaction and cognitive development in
children. London: Academic Press
11. Piaget, J (1995) Explanation in sociology. In: Piaget J (ed), Sociological
studies London: Routledge, pp 30–96. (Original work published in 1950)
12. Vygotsky LS (1978) Mind in society: The development of higher
psychological processes. Cambridge, MA: Harvard University Press
13. Xin C (2002) Validity centered design for the domain of engaged
collaborative discourse in computer conferencing. Ph.D. thesis, Brigham
Young University

Adding Constraints to a Virtual Course Using a Formal Approach to the Interactions in Collaborative Learning

Luisa M. Romero-Moreno, José A. Troyano

Department of Languages and Informatics Systems, University of Seville,
Avd. Reina Mercedes s/n. 41012 Seville Spain
mariaro@lsi.us.es

1 Introduction

Computer Supported Collaborative Learning (CSCL) is a research area whose central aspects are the concepts of interaction and participation in an educational way. Artificial Intelligence (AI) methods give interesting solutions to the construction of CSCL systems [8, 9]. However, in order to establish the learning model it is necessary to formalize the concept of interaction, hence the organization and structure of the process must be defined. The use of collaborative learning favours a distribution of knowledge in communities which improves working within a group.

There have been a great deal of empirical research and theoretical issues in collaborative learning that have offered different approaches on how to learn in a group. At the moment, the most important goal is to analyse the group as a unit. The system can be treated as some independent cognitive units which exchange messages or as a single cognitive system which has own laws.

The initial problem was to analyse whether and under what constraints collaborative learning was more efficient than individual learning. Recently the question has shifted in both theoretical and empirical terms, and researchers are trying to understand the role of interactions which appear in collaborative web-based educational systems. This change requires new tools and methods for the analysis and modelling of interactions.

However, collaborative learning is not only a frame which has positive effects on the students. Collaboration is a complex social structure in which two or more people interact with each other and where some interactions occur with interesting effects. It is necessary to stop using general concepts and start fixing categories of interactions.

In the educational community, some people use collaboration and cooperation interchangeably. Cooperation is a division of the labour among participants, as an activity where each person is responsible for a portion of the problem, whereas collaboration is a mutual engagement of participants in a coordinated effort to solve the problem together.

Defining collaboration as the non-distribution of labour does not avoid the problem. Some division of tasks may occur in collaboration: for example, the student who has more to explain about the problem takes the tutor role, while the others become observers, monitoring the situation. The observers can contribute by criticizing and giving different points of view. Cooperation and collaboration do not differ in terms of whether or not the task is distributed. In cooperation the problem is divided into independent sub-problems; in collaboration, cognitive processes may be divided into intertwined layers. In cooperation, coordination is only required when assembling partial results, while collaboration is "a coordinated synchronous activity that is the result of a continued attempt to construct and maintain a shared conception of a problem" [1, 2].

In this work is described a formal description of the interactions which are produced among the students on a virtual course. This course should be integrated into a collaborative web-based educational system. In order to specify where and under what constraints collaborative learning is more effective, the system must be characterized by a set of parameters, which include those referring to interactions. We define the variables that permit the interactions to be studied in a formal and systematic way. A virtual course is thereby designed and the integrated constraints required are given.

2   The Group as a Unit

We adopt a constructivist point of view [5], which suggests that the individual cognitive development is the result of a conjunction of causality: a given level of individual development allows participation in certain social interactions which in turn produce new individual states which make more social interaction possible, and so forth.

The constructivist approach borrows its structural framework together with the main concepts from Piaget's theory, which were used to account for development: conflict and the coordination of perspective (centralizations).

The original theory emphasized individual aspects in cognitive development and inspired a group of psychologists (Genevean Schools, 1970's) who developed a systematic investigation into how social interaction affects individual cognitive development.

From this perspective [3], the most important question becomes under which conditions cognitive conflict might be induced. One answer may be a pair of students who are at different stages of cognitive development. It is stressed that subsequent individual progress cannot be explained by one student simply modelling the other, more advanced students are important too. Learners at the same level of cognitive development, but who enter the situation with different perspectives, can also benefit from conflict interactions. AI web-based educational systems show that the performance of a network of problem-solving agents is better when there is some inconsistency in the knowledge of each agent. These findings concern the heterogeneity of a multi-agent system. The logical concept of conflict can be modelled in terms of knowledge or beliefs and integrated into maintenance systems or dialogue models.

The concept of a group as a single system is similar to the computational concept agent, and hence the idea of agent can be used to express a functional unit, a cell or a representation of the world. The size of a distributed system is the designer's choice. It is a parameter which the designer employs to understand phenomena that are invisible on another scale. This model supports a system whose different layers of agents with various scales within may be compared to communication among agents at level n and at level $n+k$.

In terms of empirical research, it is very important to establish whether and under what laws collaborative learning is more efficient than individual learning. Researchers have controlled independent variables (size of the group, communication media, group heterogeneity and intellectual or developmental level, and so on). However, the variables can be influenced in a way that makes causal links between conditions and effects of the collaboration, very difficult to structure. On the other way, when the collaboration is supported via AI in collaborative web-based educational systems, the design of the system causes an impact on the collaborative process. The intervention has methodological consequences: the researcher may have control over some aspect of collaboration (establishing rules, distribution of activities, determining the division of collaborative work). The effects of the AI upon collaborative-based educational systems have pedagogical aspects [6, 7]: support of the type of interactions that are expected to promote learning. The following are the main goals and their variables for the study of the interactions in an AI collaborative web-based educational system:

- **The goal is efficacy in collaboration:** in this case the independent variable is collaborative work versus individual work. The choice of the dependent parameters varies according to what the investigators mean by more efficient. The most important measures are the improvement of monitoring and regulation techniques.

- **The goal is to analyse under which conditions the collaboration must be produced:** in this analysis, we establish that numerous independent variables should be studied. These are the composition of the group, the feature of the task and context of collaboration. The first variable, composition of the group, covers several other independent variables such the as the number of members, their gender and the differences between participants. Group heterogeneity is the most interesting variable. Usually students present diffcrent levels of knowledge or domain expertise. We have considered objective and subjective expertise differences. These differences provide necessary conditions for the socio-cognitive conflict, for the constructivist approach. It is very important to determine the optimal degree of differences. If it is too small, it may fail to trigger interactions. If the difference is too large, there may be interaction at all. However, heterogeneity is also a function of the size of the group.

- **The goal is to study individual prerequisites:** collaboration does not benefit an individual if he is below a certain knowledge level. We consider here the absolute level of the individual, not his level relative to the group. From Piaget's point of view, a rich interaction gives an individual knowledge.

- **The goal is to study task features:** tasks that have been commonly used in collaborative learning include skill acquisition, joint planning, and categorization and memory tasks. Tasks should also promote differences in perspectives or solutions.

The independent variables shown so far do not have simple effects on learning, but interact with each other in a complex way, for example, the interaction between the composition of the group and the task features. If the group is heterogenic, the most interesting task may be meta-cognitive or meta-mnemonic roles, and for a homogeny group, the tasks may be understanding and skills.

3   Formal Approach to the Interactions

The most important aspect to analyse is to establish under what conditions an AI in collaborative web-based educational system is more efficient than individual learning. To this end, the analysis determines what interactions are produced and what effects are caused.

Our contribution to formalize the interactions is to consider the following items:

- **Studying the relationship between categories of interaction and the independent variables:** general level of ability and the specific level of expertise. In groups where the highly qualified student is the domain expert and the low - ability student the "novice", the interaction is characterized by tutoring. In a group where the high-ability student is the "novice", the interaction involves collaboration.

- **Assessing how elaborated is provided help by one learner to the other.** This level of elaboration goes from giving the right answer to providing a thorough explanation and discussion. It concerns the conditions in which each category of interactions is more likely to occur. Learning from receiving explanations is submitted to several conditions which may not be observed by the explainer, e.g. the fact that the information must be delivered when the student needs it. These effects, called self-explanation, have a computational model. The main concept is that the instantiation of general knowledge with particular instances creates more specific knowledge, a situation that appears in machine learning under the label "explanation-based learning" [4]. An explanation is not a simple message delivered by one student to another, but the result of joint attempts to understand each other. Furthermore, AI collaborative web-based educational systems should consider the use of the digital library, technical papers, web pages, and so on.

- **Studying the relationship between categories of interaction and learning outcomes:** Explanations are more frequent when the group is moderately heterogeneous (high-ability and medium-ability students) and when the group is homogeneous, composed of medium-ability students. Some other group compositions are detrimental to the quality of explanations: homogeneous highly qualified students (because nobody can collaborate) and heterogeneous groups with high, medium and low-ability (because medium-ability members are almost excluded from interactions).

At the moment, the AI collaborative web-based educational systems allow exciting possibilities such as synchronous shared workspaces and educational hypermedia. This does not mean that older technologies should be superseded. Asynchronous text provides a time of reflection on messages and information interchange.

4 Design of a Virtual Course

In the development of our course, we consider it can be applied to a collaborative web-based educational system that is integrated in distance learning supported by information technologies or e-Learning in higher education in general. However, when the experiments, which following this formalization, are implemented, more specific designs can be presented.

We consider that this type of virtual course is independent from the Internet platform for e-Learning currently in use (WebCT, LUVIT, and so on). All of these have similar functions (chats, forums, mails, electronic blackboards, automatic generating groups, publications of contents, electronic calendars). However it is very important to specify the didactic materials, which should be fully accessible: accessible for everybody and materials dedicated to specific subgroups. Materials can be supportive to a traditional lecture and interactive tutorials. They should include exercises, tests, case of studies, library and additional documents. The digital format may permit labelling, in accordance with the educational standards.

To this end, we present a model of a virtual course establishing some constraints which point out the formal approach to the interactions.

- **Constraints under conditions of collaboration**
  - C_{11} Fixing the monitoring conditions
  - C_{12} Accepting a constructivist approach
- **Constraints under the features of tasks**
  - C_{21} Establishing procedural tasks
  - C_{22} Establishing acquisition – knowledge tasks
- **Constraints under individual prerequisites**
  - C_{31} Establishing that the initial level of the group can permit collaboration
  - C_{32} Defining asymmetric collaboration (with student-tutor)
  - C_{33} Supervising the expertise of the student-tutor who expresses the result of the tasks
  - C_{34} Supervising the effects of the assistance (in order to monitor them)
- **Constraints under collaboration conditions**
  - C_{41} Establishing the size of the group as 15 students
  - C_{42} Defining the individual differences which permit the collaboration
  - C_{43} Defining the learning tasks according to the didactic tools

These constraints represent the initial conditions of the course which integrates an AI in collaborative web-based educational systems. They integrate formal interactions, and hence the methodology should include these constraints in different courses and to extract the conclusions.

Some C_{ij} may be altered in order to maintain another constant, and thereby contracting the result of others.

5 Conclusions and Future Work

In this paper we have presented a formal approach to the concept of interactions, which are produced in the context of an AI collaborative web-based educational system. The two most important aspects in this work are: the specification of the relevant variables that are present in an interaction of a collaborative group of students and the application to a virtual course by the formal constraints.

In order to represent this conceptualization we will need to use a knowledge-based representation, ontology in fact, that will be specified using the owl language.

We conclude that collaboration should no longer be used in a general way and only formal categories of interactions should be referenced. The methods and techniques from the Semantic Web must be both incorporated into the analysis of the interactions and added to the design of the collaborative web-based educational systems.

Acknowledgments

This work has been partially supported by the Spanish Science and Education Ministry (TIN 2004-07246-C03-03).

References

1. Dillenbourg P, Self JA (1992) A computational approach to socially distributed cognition. European Journal of Psychology of Education. Vol VII, No 4: 352–373
2. Dillenbourg P, Baker M, Blave A, O'Malley C (1996) The evolution of research on collaborative learning. In Learning in Human and Machine: Towards an interdisciplinary learning science. E. Spada & P. Reiman (Eds) Oxford Elsevier: 189–211
3. Hsiao JW (1998) CSCL Theories. Technical Report Department of Computer Science University of Texas
4. Koschmann T (1996) CSCL: Theory and practice of an emerging paradigm. Lawrence Erlbaun Associates, Inc, New Jersey

5. Romero LM, Troyano JA (2005) Incorporación de las teorías de aprendizaje y conocimiento en colaboración a un modelo de curso virtual. I jornadas sobre el uso de las TICs en la UNED
6. Romero-Moreno LM, Troyano JA (2005) Aportaciones de una formalización de las interacciones producidas en un entorno que integra aprendizaje colaborativo al diseño de un curso virtual. Actas VII Simposio Internacional de Informática Educativa: 245–249
7. Romero-Moreno LM, Troyano JA (2006) Aplicaciones de los Estándares Educativos a los Sistemas Virtuales de Formación Colaborativos: Especificaciones para la Herramienta LAMS. Actas IV Congreso Iberoamericano de Telemática
8. Verdejo MF, Barros B, Rodríguez-Artachom M, Sopron Hungary MA (2001) Proposal to support the design of experimental learning activities. Proceedings ECSCL'2001, Maastrich McLuhan Institute: 633–640
9. Verdejo MF, Barros B, Mayorga JI, Read T (2003) Designing a semantic portal for collaborative learning communities. Current Topics in Artificial Intelligence, CAEPIA-TTIA 2003. Springer

An Experiment in Collaborative Writing

Paula Peres, Pedro Pimenta

Instituto Politécnico de Contabilidade e Administração do Porto,
Universidade do Minho
p_peres@iscap.ipp.pt, pimenta@dsi.uminho.pt

1 Context

In this article an experiment of collaborative work is described; it was held in an Internet environment of a Computer science discipline in the Accounting and Administration course of ISCAP, where 26 first-year students participated. This subject was lectured between September and December 2004 in a traditional class room, complemented with a distance developed collaborative work. Student's easy access to the Internet was an essential condition for the success of this project's implementation. The Institute has some rooms equipped with computers connected to the Internet, available for free access by the students. Nevertheless, an inquiry was carried out at the beginning of the semester to check the kind of technologies access the students had: 93% of the students had a computer at home and 73% of these had their computer connected to the Internet (see Table 1):

Table 1. Results of the inquiry on the use of the internet

Question	Answer
Have computer at home	93%
Have access to the Internet	73%
Type of Internet connection	65% CableNet
	25% ADSL 20% Modem
Frequency of internet use	85%
Frequency of e-mail use	72%
Have a home page on the Internet	13%

2 Planning

2.1 Learning Objectives

The main objective was that the students should understand the essential factors to be analysed when they want to buy a new monitor, printer or personal computer, including a laptop. It was intended to create a collaborative report which includes the main characteristics of each hardware group, the available market solutions and the choices that they would make. Parallel to this work, we also wanted to evaluate the potentialities of the forums as a collaborative writing and as a tool for the communities of practice. Each student is seen as a member of a community of practice in a dynamic learning process. At the end of all the activities a report would be created by the community in accordance with the structure shown in Table 2.

Table 2. Report to be produced by the community

Options of the Hardware	
Personal Computers	Main characteristics
	Market Solutions
	Our choices
Monitor and Printer	Main characteristics
	Market Solutions
	Our choices
Laptop	Main characteristics
	Market Solutions
	Our choices

2.2 Work Groups

According to the Jonhson brothers [3], an ideal type of group does not exist. The productivity is not determined by its members but by the way they work together. Sometimes it is an advantage to create homogeneous groups to reach specific goals. In the majority of the situations the constitution of heterogeneous groups is better, in order to share ideas between students of different contexts, abilities, experiences and interests. Thus, they can know different perspectives and methods of problem resolution and become involved in more complex thoughts. For this experiment and in a random mode, the groups shown in Table 3 were formed.

Table 3. Workgroups

Group	Number of Students
Group C18D1: 26 Students	Group A: 8 Students
	Group B: 9 Students
	Group C: 9 Students

2.3 Technological Context

All the groups worked in the *yahoogroups* environment. It was chosen the Brazilian version due to the inexperience of most of the students in using discussion groups and in order to avoid the linguistic barrier. In the available tools, the space of messages, database and files were used.

2.4 Schedule

The works were carried out in the first semester of the 2004/2005 school year.

3 Activities

Activity 1:

Each student, looked at a hardware catalogue, identified their option for an eventual purchase of a new personal computer, with monitor and printer, and also a laptop.

Activity 2:

Groups creation and assignment of the subjects to each group according to the following structure:

- GA: Personal Computers
- GB: Monitors and Printers
- GC: Laptop

Creation of the *yahoogroups* space for each group, as shown in Fig. 1:

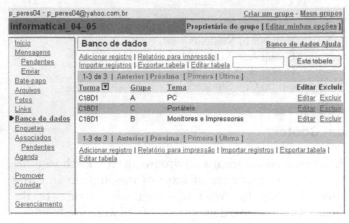

Fig. 1. Area of work of each group

Activity 3:

Each group searched their subject on the Internet.

Activity 4:

Each group wrote a text which included the main characteristics that were important when they need to buy the hardware. At the end of this activity, each group inserted their text, in their *yahoogroups* space.

Activity 5:

The teacher presented the continuity rules (see Table 4): Each group would have to continue the work started by another group, criticizing constructively and supported by the research that they would have done about the Market solutions:

Table 4. Rules of continuity

Activities Groups	Main characteristics	"Critical" + Market solutions
GA	Personal Computers	Monitors and Printers
GB	Monitors and Printers	Laptop
GC	Laptop	Personal Computers

For example, group A that made a summary of the main characteristics of the personal computers, would have, at this stage, to read the work developed by group B, about monitors and printers, search on the internet the market solutions and criticize the work constructively. Example of the one criticism done:

"...your work does not show the availability of boards like soundboard, On-board hardware, modem, etc.
Also it does not show USB input and, memory cards."
Group C

Activity 6:

Each group discussed, accepted or rejected the criticism done, while a final version about the hardware characteristics was being created. They inserted the updated text in *yahoogroups* space.

The Students expressed their eventual doubts about the criticism done in the discussion forum, in *yahoogroups,* that support the project. The formal record can be seen in Fig. 2.

	Assunto	Nome/E-mail	ID Yahoo!	Data
79	Trabalhos de grupo	p_peres04	p_peres04	Qua 11/10/2004
80	Trabalho de grupo C da turma C1901 sobre PCs	charlene_d354	charlene_d354	Qua 11/10/2004
81	Elementos do GrupoC da Turma C18D	lilianapinto_18	lilianapinto_18	Qua 11/10/2004
82	Aluno da turma C19D1	ricardo_silvestre373	ricardo_silvestre373	Qua 11/17/2004
84	escolha portáteis/aula	isabel_2980668	isabel_2980668	Qui 11/25/2004
85	Trabalho de informatica	mortagancakes2004	mortagancakes2004	Ter 11/30/2004
86	Duvida	sara2030570	sara2030570	Ter 11/30/2004
88	Problema	sara2030570	sara2030570	Ter 11/30/2004
89	Problema	sara2030570	sara2030570	Ter 11/30/2004
90	Re: Duvida	p_peres04	p_peres04	Seg 12/6/2004
91	Re: Problema	p_peres04	p_peres04	Seg 12/6/2004
92	Escolha de Portátil	anafonsaca_30	anafonsaca_30	Ter 12/7/2004
94	Escolha do melhor portátil	claudia_253	claudia_253	Qui 12/9/2004
96	Trabalho Final	saradiogo_18	saradiogo_18	Qui 12/9/2004
97	Trabalho final	ana_2030269	ana_2030259	Qui 12/9/2004
99	Não consegui colocar o trabalho de Grupo no yahoo groups	vitor_c2000	vitor_c2000	Qui 12/9/2004
100	Re: Trabalho final	p_peres04	p_peres04	Seg 12/13/2004
101	Re: Não consegui colocar o trabalho de Grupo no yahoo groups	p_peres04	p_peres04	Seg 12/13/2004
103	Apresentação do Trabalho!	carina_leite2004	carina_leite2004	Qua 12/15/2004

Selecionar todos - Limpar todos

[Apagar]

79-103 de 106 | Anterior | Próxima [Primeira | Última]   Msg # [ir]   Data | Assunto

Fig. 2. Discussion forum of support to the project

Activity 7:

The teacher presented the continuity rules (see Table 5): Each group would have to continue the work started by another group, criticizing constructively and choosing one of the solutions presented.

Table 5. Rules of continuity

Activities Groups	Market Solutions	Criticism on one work + Choices
GA	Monitors and Printers	Laptop
GB	Laptop	Personal Computers
GC	Personal Computers	Monitors and Printers

For example, group A, that presented the available market solutions for the monitors and printers would have, at this stage, to read the work developed by group B, about laptops, criticize constructively the choices shown and select their choice for an eventual purchase of this hardware component.

Activity 8:

Each group discussed, accepted or rejected the criticism done, while a final version about the hardware characteristics was being created. They inserted the updated text in *yahoogroups* space.

At the end of these stages a report was obtained, inserted in the *yahoogroups*, constructed collaboratively, which could help them when they needed to buy new hardware equipment. An example can be seen in Fig. 3:

Arquivos			Arquivos Ajuda
Adicionar arquivo | Criar arquivo de texto | Adicionar pasta			
Arquivos > C18D1		1823 Kb usados de 20480 Kb total	
Nome e descrição	**Tamanho Enviado por**	**Data Editar Excluir Cortar**	
Relatório.doc Trabalho Final (Relatório)	58 k ligiadelca	08/12/2004 Editar Excluir Cortar	
informatica.xls Trabalho Final em Excel	296 k ligiadelca	08/12/2004 Editar Excluir Cortar	
Arquivos > C18D1		1823 Kb usados de 20480 Kb total	
Adicionar arquivo | Criar arquivo de texto | Adicionar pasta			

Fig. 3. Stored final report in *yahoogroups*

Activity 9:

Final examination that includes a question about the subject discussed. The students should choose a personal computer to be used by an accountant. Between two options they would have to select the one that, in their opinion, would be more efficient in order to answer their professional needs and, at the same time, justify their selection.

4   Evaluation/Characterization of the Learning Process

The biggest barrier faced by the students was unfamiliarity while using the collaborative tools, which were easily overcome through continuous use. After the first experience in the group activity, supported by the technologies, the students started to demonstrate a greater competence in the use of the information tools and developed their activities faster. The students needed time for experimentation and recognition of the work environment and its functionalities; in this sense the teacher's help was sometimes necessary.

The students showed difficulties creating a text in their own words. This difficulty of synthesis, understanding and developing ideas was a characteristic present in all the process.

In the first activity, where the students had indicated the hardware equipment that they would choose if they had to buy a new equipment, they presented some gaps supporting their options. In general, they supported their choices in the cost associated, defending that the quality of the equipment is proportional to its price.

In the last activity, in which a new choice of an equipment was requested, this time to be used for supporting accounting activities, their choices were more consistent. Other characteristics, beyond the cost, were referred. For example:

"the price of computer A is higher than computer B because it has a better graphical board but for accountants this is not so important..."

"computer A has more memory and accountants use some programs with more costumer information..."

5 Conclusions and Recommendations

The collaborative text creation showed an important support in the dynamics of the learning community of practice, in which the individuals are capable of accepting the other individual's ideas and creativity in a collective evolution.

The communication in a collaborative environment, especially in a discussion forum, allowed the participants to reflect on their colleagues' contributions and to prepare their interventions in a more qualitative way. It was verified, as the Jonhson brothers state, that when people present their conclusions and justifications to others they prepare their knowledge more carefully. In this context Karanyan and Crowe affirm that the time that the students have to think about their answers, in an on-line discussion, promotes the quality and the relationship of their ideas [4]. At same time it supports different learning styles, as Zafeirious [5] underlines, "has intervening that they are capable to immediately participate in the group while others need more time to construct their interventions".

The discussion forums use was the creation base of the virtual community of practice, to help the information exchange, knowledge and experiences. Forums allowed the creation of an institutional memory preventing the forgetting of "what" and "how" they learned with the chosen strategy inherent (learning history). The register of the explicit and tacit knowledge could be applied to the new learning situations.

With the hypertext writing containing texts, photos and videos of computer assembly, a plural production was obtained of the knowledge in a collective and interactive form providing the exploration of the cognitive and communicational potential of cyberwriting.

Some students presented different options when questioned individually or when they presented their group options. When they reviewed their texts, they accepted many of the suggested proposals by other groups; this confirms the premises defended by the Johnson brothers when they affirm that people are uncertain of their points of view and try to form a new solution, qualitatively better through the understanding of the perspectives and the reasoning of other people.

A positive aspect of the collaborative writing work is the necessity of understanding the main ideas so as to be able to criticize. In this work were to be seen some of the premises pointed out by Freitas & Freitas [2], about practice of collaborative learning such as: an improvement of the interpersonal relationships, of the abilities to criticize thought, a greater capacity to accept the other's perspectives and the acquisition of the necessary abilities to work in groups.

The school must take into account the educational process form to incorporate the technology consciously to prevent that these are imposed disorderedly and without a pedagogical source. It is necessary to reflect on the use of the Internet, and especially of collaborative environments, the direction to optimize the learning beyond the classroom. It is also imposed to investigate new forms to explore this collaborative world and to determine how the students learn on-line.

This experiment proved that direct contact with the teacher and the interactions in the classroom is essential. The students need an experimentation and recognition time of the tools and its functionalities. In this sense the intervention of the teacher was sometimes requested. As is related by Smaltino & Muffolletto (quoted by [6]) "it is the teacher who marks the difference in the learning environment. The decisions that the teacher takes concerning the selection and integration of the TIC influence the learning". In last instance it could be necessary a new generation of teachers, educated in environments sensitive to these needs [7].

This type of activity is well accepted by the students and it does not demand a teacher with a good knowledge of the Internet. In this experiment some students had difficulties in access to the environment. It is important to guarantee the minimum technological conditions necessary to prevent that. This type of difficulty can promote loss of interest and absenteeism.

In the collaborative context it is necessary to enhance the fact that all the contributions are registered and identified with the author's name and the insertion date, available for further consultation and/or reuse. This fact contributes to the explicitation of the tacit knowledge generated by the community which resulted from the experiment.

The Internet thus facilitated the construction of the knowledge in a collaborative mode, in a learning community of practice. In this way "barriers are broken, allowing to the group of participants to see and to discuss the material in study" [5], whichever methodology for the use of collaborative environments is concerned, enhances the importance of a good planning and an orientation focused and organized it in concrete and well limited activity in time. Otherwise, the probability of dispersal of the intended objectives grows. As Beaudin states it is necessary to provide guidelines to help the students to prepare their answers on-line [1]. Most internet research on a specific subject results in wholesale copying from the source, but in this case, the students chose, in a socio-cognitive relation, what they had considered to be the best equipment in the defined context and then justified their choices, thus resulting in greater teaching success.

The results are very encouraging. The achievement of objectives was real, the students in the final examination were able to base their opinions better when they eventually came to buy a new hardware. On the other hand, it also revealed a strong participation in all the activities and an increasing familiarization in the technological context. This scene looks promising regarding the viability of future projects. The learning process combined with traditional practical methods and distance education also looks as promising. To the teacher the challenge lies in finding new ways of balancing traditional learning and the computer-assisted learning, to look into the abilities to develop the available media, the academic alternatives and the students' characteristics in order to choose the combination that will be able to produce more efficient results.

In this experiment it was vindicated, as in a traditional classroom the work presented and signed by the group might well have been produced by the one member who showed greater leadership charisma. It is foreseen in the future to change this experiment in order to divide the tasks in such a way that the work of each group will be created on the Internet so as to get the formal register of personal opinions, to determine if the Internet is a way of freeing the opinions of the more reticent, less forthcoming, students. In educational institutions, the fact that the teacher asks for a group work does not by itself mean that there will be different contributions. A greater interactivity and motivation is important for the task. Collaborative learning environments are excellent for the learning process because they promote the exchange of ideas, the joint resolution of problems, the breaking and reconstruction of mental structures, respect for the other community members and the feeling of joint responsibility for the text which belongs to everyone.

Collaborative writing made it possible to make explicit the knowledge and to construct the collective memory of the community practice learning.

As a challenge the question remains: How can the technologies support the activities of the practical learning communities? It is necessary to develop research projects that are based on these reflexive practices and that promote the effectiveness and quality in the dichotomy of teaching and learning.

References

1. Beaudin B (1999) Keeping Online Asynchronous Discussions on Topics, Journal of Asynchronous Learning Networks, 3(2), November 1999
2. Freitas L, Freitas C (2003) Aprendizagem Cooperativa – Edições Asa Porto.
3. Johnson D, Johnson, R (1995) Academic Controversy. University of Minnesota, U.S.A. Accessible in :http://www.co-operation.org/pages/ academic.html
4. Karayan S, Crowe J (1997) Students Perceptions of Electronic Discussion Groups, T.H.E. Jounal, 24(9). Accessible in: http://www.thejournal.com/ magazine/vault/a1367.cfm
5. Miranda L, Morais C, Dias P, Almeida C (2001) Ambientes de aprendizagem na web: Uma experiência com fóruns de discussão. II Conferencia Internacional Challenges'2001/Desafios'2001. Universidade do Minho. Portugal
6. Ramos A, Freitas C (1999) Gostei, aprendi, diverti-me, perspectivas dos alunos acerca da utilização educativa das tecnologias. I Conferencia Internacional Challenges'99/Desafios'99. Universidade do Minho. Portugal.
7. Renato Rocha S (2005) Uma proposta construtivista para a utilização de Tecnologias na Educação. Educação, aprendizagem e Tecnologia – Um paradigma para professores do século XXI. Sílabo editions

The 'Contract' as a Pedagogical Tool in e-Learning

Lina Morgado, Alda Pereira, António Quintas-Mendes

Universidade Aberta, Portugal
lmorgado@univ-ab.pt; amp@univ-ab.pt; quintas@univ-ab.pt

1 Towards a Pedagogy of e-Learning: A Model

The development of a pedagogical model for post-graduate online learning couples with a strategy to dynamize a new generation of distance education. This pedagogical model was designed and implemented in a specific context – a distance higher education institution. It is a model rooted in distance education which proposes a transition to online education.

The elaboration of this pedagogical model for post-graduate e-learning rests on a set of ten principles that define its architecture, and on the conviction that e-learning can constitute an adequate response to the needs of Knowledge Society and lifelong learning when it brings together a Pedagogy and the potentialities of Technology [15, 17]:

1. **Distance Education and e-Learning** – this pedagogical model sets itself in the distance education domain and reflects the need for promoting changes of a pedagogical nature in the transition to online education.
2. **Learner-centred instruction** – the proposed model follows the recommendations on the education of individuals towards the Knowledge Society, seeking to embody the vision of a learner-centred instruction.
3. **Transition Model** – this is a transition model. It is essentially an e-learning asynchronous model, combining the paradigm of flexibility and openness that has characterized distance education and the characteristics and potentialities of e-learning.

4. **e-Learning Pedagogy** – the proposed model entails a vision centred on an e-learning pedagogy. It therefore contemplates five essential pedagogical elements of online learning [8, 9]: structuring of discussions; collaborative activities; assessment re-design; interactive learning materials; design of a specific pedagogy.

5. **Interaction** – Interaction assumes a central role in this model. It no longer refers exclusively to student-content and student-teacher interaction, typical of the earlier generations of distance learning [10–12], but gives also relevance to student-student. Furthermore, this model takes on the assumption that online interaction is (almost) exclusively based on written communication.

6. **Re-socialization of actors** – In the context of distance education, both students and teachers, as well as other mediators in the learning process (the *basic species* [14] in the ecology of the virtual classroom), have been socialized according to models heavily based on self-learning. In the context of a pedagogical change such as this model entails, it is important to create supporting mechanisms for the various actors so that a *re-socialization for interaction* may take place. It should not, however, be merely added to the course contents, but constitute the integral component of the learning experience through the design of significant activities, helping to overcome resistance to new forms of learning, to technology and to a new kind of pedagogical relation.

7. **Being a virtual student** – Although some of the challenges faced by the online student are the same as those faced by the distance student – self-motivation, self-direction, autonomy, independence, organization and time-management, self-discipline and adaptability, active approach to learning – there are others specific to online learning. E-Learning contexts redefine not only the ways in which the individuals perceive themselves and others (fellow students and tutor), but also the way in which they perceive interaction.

8. **Being an online tutor** – The results of the research conducted [11, 13, 18] identify the need to differentiate between online tutoring and face to face tutoring or the traditional tutoring practices in distance education, basing itself on the specific characteristics of a new communication context, on reflexiveness, on the particular nature of interactions and on asynchrony. The continuing training of tutors (before and during the process) is thus assumed as a fundamental element in this model, carried out through the creation of support mechanisms which function as anchors in the implementation of the instruction process and as instruments in the development/perfecting of tutoring-specific skills as well.

9. **Quality in teaching and learning** – This pedagogical model presupposes the restatement of the principle of quality in the teaching and learning process. Important priorities thus include the incentive and support of self-responsibility in learning and the active participation of all actors, and the promotion of reflection based on the increase of personal interaction. The creation of a quality system to evaluate the courses is an important factor to assure this principle.

10. **Evaluation of the model** – The implementation of this pedagogical model is viewed as a continuous work in progress, therefore subject to improvement. It thus requires a permanent research and evaluation process which allows for the providing of feedback to the system.

2 The Pillars of the Pedagogical Model

This model is built upon two structuring pillars which interconnect: *self-directed learning*, rooted in the field of distance education and in the adult learning theories [1]; and *collaborative learning*, rooted in the constructivist and socio-constructivist paradigms [6, 2, 3].

Self-directed learning assumes that the student be autonomous and responsible for self-directing the personal learning process, according to the suggestions of the teacher/tutor. Collaborative learning sees learning as resulting from working together with other people, with shared goals and values, thus putting individual skills to the service of the group.

According to these principles, the teaching and learning model follows this structure: a module or discipline is designed upon sequences which include a phase of independent, autonomous study, with asynchronous discussions organized and moderated by the students themselves, ending with asynchronous discussions moderated by the teacher/tutor on previously defined topics.

The management of teaching and learning time should take into account the students' individual characteristics and the desirable student-teacher and student-student interaction levels. The integration of autonomous learning experiences, based on learning resources (materials), teacher/tutor-guided learning experiences, and collaborative learning experiences should make room for the diversity and specificity of each individual student's learning processes.

3 The Indispensables of the Pedagogical Model

The model's basic elements are: 1. Learning Contract; 2. Learning Materials; 3. Assessment; 4. Course Organization.

1. **Learning Contract** – The *Learning Contract* constitutes a core pedagogical instrument in this model, and its elaboration is the teacher/tutor's responsibility [7, 21, 22]. This contract is made available to the students (and negotiated with them) in the online environment (virtual classroom) at the beginning of the module/discipline, establishing its *geography* (descriptive plan or detailed *map*). It thus provides a detailed description of the whole teaching and learning process, acting as an orientation guide for both the student and the teacher/tutor.

2. **Learning Materials** – The *Learning Materials* are divided in two categories: those of a theoretical nature and those of a more practical nature. The former constitute reference materials (RM) and should be organized to enable the theoretical study of subject-matter; the latter comprise the *Online Student Guide*, the *Course Guide* and the *Learning Contracts*, supporting methodological and evaluative purposes, and performing also as important support devices to the learning process [16].

3. **Assessment** – The type of assessment to apply and the corresponding instruments are devised by the teachers/tutors in charge of each module/discipline when they elaborate the learning contracts. The students should be informed right from the start, clearly and unequivocally, of all aspects related to assessment.

4. **Course Organization** – The *Course Organization* is designed according to three differentiated temporal cycles and obeys a principle of balance regarding the distribution of activities among the trimesters. Each course is structured and organized in a set of cycles: the online familiarization cycle, the learning activities cycle and the final summative assessment cycle.

All the courses have a coordination and student support structure.

4 The Learning Contract as an Instrument to Mediate Learning

4.1 The Communication Process as "Contract"

The interpersonal communication processes are ruled by contracts with more or less explicit rules – the communication contracts [18, 4]. These allow for the understanding of the relations between the activity of the individuals in context (situated activity) and the construction of shared meaning. This construction is marked by cultural variables which go beyond the characteristics of any didactic interaction. It is thus in this light that the individuals' behaviour should be understood.

Their behaviour is not only influenced by the characteristics of the situations, but also by the interpretations that the individuals themselves make of them, i.e. by the definition of the situation, in what Wertch [23] describes as the mode in which the objects and events in a situation are represented and defined. These objects and actions/behaviours might or might not be present in the spacio-temporal context of the interlocutors and might be concrete or abstract, depending heavily on the status and roles of the interlocutors, their personal experiences and the socio-instructional context in which the interaction takes place.

Connected with the definition of the situation comes the concept of *intersubjectivity*, a key element in the communicative processes. Intersubjectivity arises when the interlocutors share some aspect of their definitions of situation. This coincidence can be produced at different planes, at different levels of intersubjectivity [23]. The degree of intersubjectivity that is created, maintained and reestablished in learning communities shows that communication transcends the private worlds of the participants, setting up what we might call "states of intersubjectivity" [23].

4.2 The Teaching and Learning Process as "Contract"

Adopting the perspective that each context is ruled by a specific contract, composed of explicit and implicit rules, means that it's the acknowledgement of these rules[1] that makes individuals adopt certain behaviours relatively to the tasks (and choose the solving strategies) [5].

---

[1] There are, however, different kinds of contracts, such as pedagogic, communication and experimental contracts, for example.

In this light, the interactions between teacher and student are marked by rules of a contractual nature which are mostly implicit. On the other hand, the relationships between these two interlocutors (teacher and student) and knowledge are also mediated by a contract – the didactic contract [4, 5, 19, 20].

This didactic contract "forces" the teacher to teach and the students to learn the subject-matter/knowledge defined by the institution (curricula, contents), and requires that its acquisition be verified (evaluation/assessment). Thus, the didactic contract is formed by the reciprocal expectations of both the teacher and the students regarding the subject-matter/knowledge, leading to the formation of social representations which the teacher and the students elaborate on subject-matter/knowledge, specific and complementary roles involved in the group-class and the didactic relation [19].

4.3 The "Learning Contract" as an Instrument to Mediate Learning

The "Learning Contract" [LC], cornerstone of the proposed pedagogical model, is thus inspired in the idea of the contract as ruling and mediating the communication processes and the teaching and learning processes, and as facilitator of adult learning.

The discussion of this issue in the online environment is of great pertinence to the extent that, in our opinion, the communication context and the didactic context have specific characteristics that make implicit rules and "what is not said" bear a greater dimension than in face to face contexts. On the other hand, the nature of distance interaction and of asynchronous communication based on writing calls for an awareness as to what is expectable on the part of the actors in the interaction. Thus, rendering very explicit the whole communication process, the didactic process, and the student's learning process can, on the one hand, contribute to the attainment of what the model sets itself to achieve and, on the other hand, establish the "anchors" and the support of the online tutoring and learning processes.

4.4 The "Learning Contract" as Negotiation of the Teacher/Tutor's Action

As one of the structuring elements of this pedagogic model, the "Learning Contract" [LC] emerges as a powerful pedagogical instrument in the teacher/tutor's action. This *contract* does not involve the more common conception of transmission of information to the student. On the contrary, it entails a more cooperative view, a dialectical approach to the learning process which values independent learning and the students' control over their own learning process.

We thus consider that the "Learning Contract" should be thought out and designed as a pedagogic contract which renders explicit the responsibilities and duties of the students and the teacher/tutor, serving as a "navigational map" for both. If in the last analysis it sets up a contractual relation between the institution and the student, it is up to the teacher/tutor to negotiate the subsequent involvement of each of the parties.

By establishing the fundamental guidance to a discipline/module, the "Learning Contract" is, in our view, a solid foundation for success, be it of the teaching experience or of the learning experience.

Furthermore, the *contract* defines the degree of structure needed in distance education (which varies according to the pedagogic model adopted) but, at the same time, allows for a level of flexibility that makes it adjustable to individual situations, characteristics and formative needs.

In this model, the "Learning Contract" describes what the student will learn in the context of a learning group (group-class), serving as an instrument of communication between the teacher/tutor and the student and defining the structure of the module/discipline, the degree of flexibility, the responsibility of each actor (students and teacher/tutor) and, lastly, the degree of control that the student has over a learning process which is self-directed and socially contextualized within a group.

As in any common contract, all elements likely to be discussed are present. It is a guide for the contents, the structure of the module/discipline, the proposed activities, the work methodology and the assessment strategies, where these components should be presented in the most explicit and detailed manner, since it constitutes the core reference for the student. Seen in this light, the "Learning Contract" also allows for making expectations explicit right from the start: this will help students adequate their expectations, making them more realistic and better adapted, while helping the teacher in their management. This aspect has been widely studied in face to face contexts and is also of great relevance to online education.

From the students' point of view, this "Learning Contract" [LC] also acts as a map that guides them relatively to what the module/discipline involves, what they should do, how and when, where to look for assistance and support, ad so on. Therefore, the LC should include the following elements: objectives and competencies, structure, virtual classroom, organization, participation level, pace, assessment and general information.

5 Analysis of the *Learning Contracts*

The empirical study conducted on the learning contracts involves three post-graduations implemented in the form of e-learning. These post-graduations have different characteristics according to the target audience and the level of training and depth to attain: two are long, comprising 3 trimesters and 12 modules/disciplines; the other is shorter, comprising 2 trimesters and 6 modules/disciplines, and is targeted at non-specialists.

We wanted to analyse which elements had been included by the teachers/tutors in their "Learning Contracts" with respect to: 1) definition of objectives; 2) structure of the module/discipline; 3) methodology; 4) organization of the virtual classroom; 5) type of interaction; 6) level of participation; 7) type and characteristics of the activities (e-activities); 8) type of assessment.

It is not possible to present quantitative results yet, since the data are still being processed, but some tendencies can already be noted:

- All the analysed contracts try to state general goals to be attained and, in some cases, more specific objectives;
- All the contracts structure the module/discipline through the sequencing of activities and tasks;
- Globally speaking, the methodologies to be used in the teaching and learning process are described;
- With respect to the organization of the virtual classroom, the majority of the contracts is very general, failing to specify the type of areas which are favoured;
- As for the type of interaction, there is a tendency to favour a "many-to-many" asynchronous interaction. There is also an observable tendency for the discussion forums and small teams to assume some relevance in the contracts proposed by the teachers/tutors;
- The levels of required or desirable participation are made explicit in the majority of the contracts, though not thoroughly. However, there is a tendency towards more detail in the modules/disciplines of the 2nd or 3rd trimesters;
- There is a great variety of activities, although individual work, discussions among students and teacher/tutor moderated discussions are present in the majority of the contracts analysed;
- The type of assessment proposed also shows great variety, though the most common are continuous assessment based on the participation in group discussions (small groups or class) and assessment of individual work – projects, working papers, essays, portfolios and exams;

- Finally, with respect to the evaluation criteria, several modalities are present, with a tendency towards making the criteria explicit and detailed (some times exhaustively).

6 Conclusions

Although the data are not final yet, the study shows an apparent adherence of the teachers/tutors to the "Learning Contract". It also shows a tendency on their part to deepen the use of this instrument as a mediator for learning. From the point of view of their work, there is clearly a tutoring plan, which allows them to pinpoint, among other things, the moments with a higher workload, when they should be available, the pace to impose or the intensity of the work required from the students.

Acknowledgments

The authors want to thank the collaboration provided by all the teachers and tutors involved in this study, as well as the coordinators of the respective courses.

References

1. Brookfield SD (2001) Understanding and facilitating adult learning. Open University Press, Milton Keynes
2. Dillenbourg P, et al (1996) The evolution of research on collaborative learning. In Spada E, Reinman P (eds) Learning in humans and machines: towards an interdisciplinary learning science. Elsevier, Oxford, pp 189–219
3. Dillenbourg P (1999) Introduction: what do you mean by 'collaborative learning'? In Dillenbourg P (ed) Collaborative learning: cognitive and computational approaches, Pergamon/EARLI, Oxford, pp 1–19
4. Elbers E (1986) Interaction and instruction. European Journal of Psychology and Education, 1: 77–90
5. Gonzalez AJ (1998) Context, signification, contract: some conceptual and methodological propositions based on the work of Vygotsky (in Portuguese). J Análise Psicológica XVI, 4: 581–598
6. Kaye A (1992) Learning together apart. In Kaye A (ed) Collaborative learning through computer conferencing. The Najaden Papers, Springer-Verlag, Berlin-Heidelberg, pp 1–25.
7. Knowles M, Holton E, Swanson R (2001) Andragogy (in Portuguese). University Press, Oxford

8. Mason R (1998) Models of online courses. ALN Magazine 2: 1–10
9. Mason R (2003) Models and methodologies in distance education. J Discursos Perspectivas em Educação 1: 91–103
10. Moore M (1989) Three types of interaction. The American Journal of Distance Education 3:1–6
11. Morgado L (2003) The new challenges of the distance tutor: the return to the classroom paradigm (in Portuguese). J Discursos Perspectivas em Educação 1:77–90.
12. Morgado L (2004) What does the tutor do in the virtual classroom? An analysis of tutoring acts (in Portuguese). In Elearning in Higher Education Conference, Aveiro
13. Morgado L (2005) New roles for the teacher/tutor in online pedagogy (in Portuguese). In Vidigal R, Vidigal A (eds) Education, learning and technologie, 1st ed., Sílabo Editions, Lisbon, pp 95–120
14. Nardi BA, O' Day VL (1999) Information ecologies: using technology with heart. The MIT Press, Massachusetts
15. Pereira A, Mendes AQ, Mota J, Morgado L, Aires LL (2003) A contribution for a pedagogy of post-graduate online education: a model (in Portuguese). J Discursos Perspectivas em Educação 1:125–152
16. Pereira A, Mendes AQ, Mota J, Morgado L, Aires L (2004) Instruments to support online teaching and learning: Online teacher/tutor's guide and online student's guide (in Portuguese). J Discursos Perspectivas em Educação 2:193–220
17. Pereira A, Mendes AQ, Mota J, Morgado L, Aires LL (2005) A pedagogical model for e-learning in post-graduate education (in Portuguese). In Dias P, Freitas CV (eds) IV International Conference of information and communication technologies in Education Challenges'05, pp 303–318
18. Rommetveit R (1979) Deep structure of sentence versus message structure: Some critical remarks on current paradigms and suggestions for an alternative approach. In Rommetveit R, Blakar, RM (eds) Studies of language, thought and verbal communication. Academic Press, London
19. Salmon G (2000). E-moderating. Kogan Page, London
20. Schubauer-Leoni M, Perret-Clermont A-N (1988) Répresentations et significations de savoirs scolaires. European Journal of Psychology of Education, Hors Série: 55–62
21. Sorsana C (1998) Psychologie des interactions sociocognitives. Armand Colin, Paris
22. Stephenson J, Laycock M (2002) Using learning contracts in higher education. Kogan Page, London.
23. Wertsch JV (1985) Vygotsky and the social formation of mind. Harvard University Press, Cambridge

Development of a Personalized e-learning Experience Based on IMS Standard Technologies

Pilar Sancho[1], Ivan Martinez-Ortiz[2], Baltasar Fernández-Manjón[3], Pablo Moreno-Ger[3]

[1]Universidad Complutense de Madrid pilar@sip.ucm.es
[2]Centro de Estudios Superiores Felipe II imartinez@ccsfelipesegundo.com
[3]Universidad Complutense de Madrid {balta, pablom}@fdi.ucm.es

1 Introduction

Internet and web technologies applied to computer-based learning applications have made feasible the construction of very complete educational environments with new and promising features. In the context of Spanish higher education, many public and private institutions are making great investments in on-line applications that complement, and sometimes substitute, classic education. One of the institutions that have heavily bet on learning technology is the Universidad Complutense of Madrid.

Nevertheless, experience has shown that results are not as good as could be expected. For the last few years, Spanish higher education has been characterized by a gradual decrease of student performance and motivation. This phenomenon is particularly acute in the cold environment of computer-based instruction.

In this sense, the possibility of adapting the learning experience to some basic student characteristics appears as a promising way to decrease student frustration and enhance performance:

1. The perceived difficulty of the learning task should fit the students' previous knowledge and their intellectual capabilities. According to [2], self-efficacy judgments get lower when students perceive the required mental effort for performing a learning task as being

excessively high. This may lead to the cancellation of the learning process due to student frustration.

2. The learning strategy and the learning style of the student should be congruent. Research shows [14] that students have a clear preference for learning environments that allow and promote their habitual approaches to learning (learning styles).

Our long term goal in the <e-aula> project is to generate just-in-time personalized learning. Courses will be created by the assembly of atomic learning assets into coherent learning activities based on the following learner cognitive particularities:

- learning styles
- cognitive abilities
- previous knowledge

On the other hand, content interoperability and platform independence are basic requisites of today's educational applications. There is a great effort going on to standardize educational technologies; including content packaging [6] and metadata [5], instructional design [7] and student information [8]. But under current standards and practices, it is difficult to harvest the information required for the adaptation of the learning process to individual characteristics [11]. Therefore the question is: how can we adapt the pedagogical e-learning strategy to best fit an individual in a standard way or, at least, in a standard compatible way?

In this work we propose an approach to constructing dynamically personalized learning courses based on today's popular e-learning standards: Learning Object Metadata [5], IMS Learning Design [7] and IMS LIP [8].

The idea is to compose dynamic learning activities by selecting learning objects at runtime and combining these activities into different units of learning using IMS LD specification. We aim to generate a personalized course by using several learning design patterns implemented according to IMS LD for the different learner profiles.

2   The <e-aula> Approach for Personalization

According to [1] the adaptation logic of a personalized learning system can be defined by the following terms:

- The determinants, the aspects of the learning experience which drive the adaptation. What is the adaptation based on?
- The constituents, the aspects of the learning experience subject to adaptation. What is being adapted?

- The rules, the logic that defines what constituents are selected for adaptation. How are the constituents selected and sequenced?

2.1 What is Adaptation Based on?

As mentioned in the introduction, personalization in <e-aula> addresses three of the students' particularities concerning the learning process:

- Cognitive abilities. When the task is perceived as extremely difficult or even impossible, the mental effort stops and attention is automatically re-focused on novel and different goals because students perceive that they are not able to meet the requirements of the learning environment. To avoid this, the tasks designed for students should be congruent with their intellectual capabilities. For example, learners with low working memory capacity should receive smaller units of instruction.
- Previous knowledge. Many studies have shown that students' ability to understand something new depends on what they already know. Educators cannot build expertise by having learners memorize experts' knowledge. New knowledge must be built on the foundations of already existing frameworks.
- Learning styles. Our long term aim is to implement an e-learning adaptation of Vermunt's pedagogical theories [15]. Nevertheless, Vermunt's adaptation seemed too complicated for a first attempt as it requires a very complex user modelling process. Within Vermunt's framework, four learning styles are defined: meaning-directed, application-directed, reproduction-directed and undirected. Each learning style is said to have distinguishing features in 5 areas [3]. The resulting 4×5 matrix is shown in Table 1. In addition to the complexity of the classification, Vermunt categories are not fixed, and cannot be matched to a learning profile as he considers that students vary their learning habits in response to many factors including the context, stimuli and self-consciousness.

  Therefore, we have developed a first pilot experience as a case study to determine the standards' capacity of personalization and their possible weaknesses, implementing a system based on Felder-Silverman's model for learning styles. It is a simpler model that provides a simple five-way (see Table 2) classification mechanism for learning style estimation based on the administration of a well-known 44 item questionnaire. In addition, it was originally conceived for the same field as our pilot study: Engineering Education.

Table 1. Vermunt's learning styles [15]

	Meaning-directed	Application-directed	Reproduction-directed	Undirected
Cognitive processing	Looks for relationships between key concepts/ theories: builds an overview	Relates topics to everyday experience: looks for concrete examples and uses	Selects main points to retain	Finds study difficult: reads and re-reads
Learning orientation	Self-improvement and enrichment	Vocational or "real world" outcomes	Proves competency by getting good marks	Ambivalent; insecure
Mental model of learning	Dialogue with experts stimulates thinking and engagement with subject through exchange of views	Learns in order to use knowledge	Looks for structure in teaching and texts to help take in knowledge and pass examinations. Does not value critical processing or peer discussion.	Wants teachers to do more. Seeks peer support
Regulation of learning	Self-guided by interest and their own questions; diagnoses and corrects poor understanding	Thinks of problems and examples to test understanding, especially of abstract concepts	Uses objectives to check understanding; self-tests; rehearses	Not adaptive

Table 2. Learning dimensions and styles in Felder-Silverman model [13]

Learning Dimension	Learning Style 1	Learning Style 2
Perception	Sensing: Concrete and practical, oriented toward facts and procedures.	Intuitive: Conceptual and innovative, oriented toward theories and meanings
Input	Visual: Prefers visual representations: pictures, diagrams, flowcharts.	Verbal: Prefers written and spoken explanations.
Organization	Inductive: Prefers representations that proceed from the specific to the general.	Deductive: Prefers presentations that go from the general to the specific.
Processing	Active: Learns by trying things out, and working with others.	Reflective: Learns by thinking things through, generally working alone.
Understanding	Sequential: Linear and orderly, learns in small incremental steps.	Global: Holistic and system wide thinkers, learns in large steps.

2.2 What is Being Adapted?

The system is implemented according to IMS Learning Design Standard [7] and to IEEE Learning Object Metadata Standard [5].

The <e-aula> adaptation constituents are two: at a first level the learning activities and the learning design (construction of a Unit of Learning) and at a second level, the learning objects. The first level deals with students' learning styles. The adaptation at the LO level fulfils the previous knowledge and the cognitive abilities personalization goals.

2.2.1 First Adaptation Level: Learning Activities and Learning Design

Learning Design is a framework that aims at "modeling units of learning" [9]. In IMS LD a unit of learning (UoL) refers to a complete, self-contained unit of education or training. The creation of a UoL involves the creation of an instructional design and also the bundling of all its associated resources. Learning designs created using the LD specification are managed as packages using IMS Content Packaging [6] to facilitate the sharing of the learning design between different platforms and tools [10].

The learning design, which is the root element, contains objectives, prerequisites, components and the method of teaching. A method is formed by a play (the way the method is executed) and conditions (if-then-else statements), see Fig 1.

In our system, each unit of learning is a learning topic and it is dynamically constructed for the type of learner interacting with the environment. A UoL contains (among other elements, see Fig. 1) the activities to be performed by the different roles to reach the intended learning goal and the method that defines the sequence of performance.

A learning activity in <e-aula> is defined in terms of two elements:

1. The context within which the activity occurs. The context includes the topic to which it is applied, the level of difficulty, the environment in which the activity takes place and the associated resources, i.e. the learning objects.
2. The "type of task" which the concrete activity specifies. The concept "type of task" is similar to a class in object-oriented programming paradigm or to an abstract data type: it has a set of common properties, a restricted set of possible values and a set of methods that can be performed by the objects of the class (the concrete activity). For our model, we have defined the following types of tasks, taken from the framework presented in [4]:

- Assimilative:
  - Visual
  - Verbal
- Information handling
- Adaptive
- Communicative:
  - Discussing
  - Presenting
  - Debating
- Productive
- Experiential

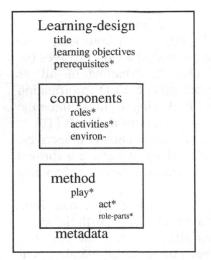
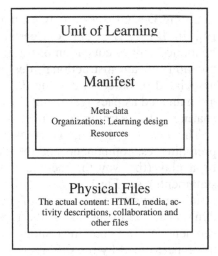

Fig. 1. The basic structure of the learning-design element and a Unit of Learning [10]

The method (i.e. the defined learning strategy for a certain learner) is defined in terms of patterns: a predefined play, implemented using IMS LD specification, with tasks associated with different roles (see Table 2). We are currently using only 2 of the 5 dichotomies defined in the model: the preferred input channel (visual/verbal) and the preferred processing method (active/reflexive). Therefore, four different learner types are managed by the system: active/visual, active/verbal, reflexive/visual and reflexive/verbal. The learning design pattern defines the types of tasks to be performed for every type and the sequence according to which the tasks are performed. For example:

An active/visual learner is supposed to prefer learning by doing things, by interacting with other learners and to perform better with visual resources such as diagrams, charts and images. Therefore peer to peer communication with teachers and interaction with other students' tasks are included in the pattern: mainly of the assimilative visual, experiential, information handling and communicative type.

2.2.2 Second Adaptation Level: Learning Objects

To cope with our personalization objectives and still maintain a cost effective system, the LO adaptation is performed at two different levels of granularity:

1. Intra learning object level. This is the way the system adapts information to suit the prior knowledge and the knowledge capabilities of the learner. In <e-aula> all the basic course contents are represented in XML and not in HTML as is done in most e-learning systems [12]. When a specific content is accessed in the webscrver an XSL transformation is applied to the content, obtaining the document that is delivered to the web client. This document is usually a fully featured HTML page, although the transformation is dynamically selected, which makes it possible to generate alternative outputs such as a PDF file for printing or a simplified HTML for mobile devices. In addition, our marked LOs contain information about the level of detail of each section, allowing adaptation of the content itself. The transformation can filter out all the sections with a level of detail considered excessive at a particular moment.

2. Inter learning object. LOs are dynamically recovered from the repository for a specific UoL (i.e. for a learning topic). To make this goal feasible, the metadata record associated with a learning object includes context domain information. We propose the use of a context domain ontology to capture the context of the knowledge domain the LO belongs to. This kind of representation offers the usual advantages of ontologies: it can provide humans with a shared vocabulary and can serve computers as the basis for semantic interoperability.

2.3 The Adaptation Process in <e-aula>: Learning Design Patterns

The process of delivering the dynamically generated UoL for a learner involves the following steps (see Fig. 2):

1. When a student signs up in the system, the system classifies him or her into a certain profile by means of the results obtained from a questionnaire (we are currently using the 44 item questionnaire defined by Felder-Silvermann to determine students' learning styles).

The different profiles include information about the student's learning style, the student's background knowledge and the learning topic to be delivered.

2. The system matches the learner profile to a certain learning pattern.

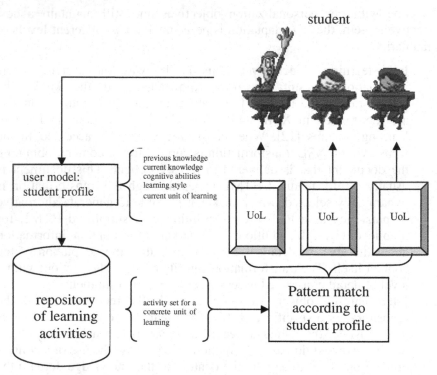

Fig. 2. Dynamic generation of Units of Learning in <e-aula>

3. For every "task" specified in the pattern, which works as a class in OOP, the system constructs the corresponding activity by bundling an LO to an environment..This is possible because of the rich LO and activity metadata records stored in the repository. These records, as previously explained, include contextual and pedagogical information formalized by ontologies.

4. The UoL is then completed and delivered to the student. In the last step, a filter of the LO content is applied in order to adapt it to the learner's previous knowledge.

3 Conclusions and Future Work

Adaptive systems appear as a promising way to enhance student performance in e-learning environments. Technology is beginning to permit the implementation of new pedagogical theories which have demonstrated good reliability in classical educational environments.

In <e-aula> we are trying to determine whether current standards and practices are capable of supporting learner-centred educational models, with different adaptive capabilities (cognitive abilities, previous knowledge and learning style). We have started with a pilot implementation that supports the basic adaptive features based on the Felder-Silverman model.

The conclusion of this experience is that basic information (including context domain and pedagogical information) needed for adaptation cannot be easily harvested under current standards and practices. Therefore we have enriched metadata records at different granularity levels with ontological representations and we have represented contents in XML in order to increase efficiency and maintain functionality.

Our proposal of learning design patterns has proven to be a good approach to the dynamic construction of units of learning, for they combine flexibility and cost-efficiency. A more complex model will be constructed in the future to support a constructive environment adapted for the four different habits of learning proposed by Vermunt.

References

1. Brusilovsky P (1999) Adaptive and intelligent technologies for web-based education. Kunstliche Intelligenz, Special Issue on Intelligent Systems and Teleteaching, 4
2. Clark RE (2001) New directions: cognitive and motivational research issues. In RE Clark (Ed.), Learning from media: Arguments, analysis and evidence (pp. 263–298). Greenwich: Information Age Publishing
3. Coffield F, Moseley D, Hall E, Ecclestone K (2004) Learning styles and pedagogy in post-16 learning. Learning Skills Research Centre
4. Conole G, Fill K (2005) A learning design toolkit to create pedagogically effective learning activities. Journal of Interactive Media in Education. JIME
5. IEEE LOM (2002) Draft Standard for Learning Object Metadata IEEE P1484.12.1/D6.4. http://ltsc.ieee.org/wg12/par1484-12-1.html
6. IMS CP (2004) Content Packaging Specification. Version 1.1.4. Final Specification. IMS Global Learning Consortium. http://www.imsglobal.org/content/packaging/index.html

7. IMS LD (2003) Learning Design Specification. Version 1. Final Specification. November IMS Global Learning Consortium. http://www.imsglobal.org/learningdesign/index.html.
8. IMS LIP January (2005) Learner Information Package Specification. Version 1.0.1 Final Specification. IMS Global Learning Consortium. http://www.imsglobal.org/profiles/index.html.
9. Koper R (2001) Modelling units of study from a pedagogical perspective. The pedagogical meta-model behind EML. OTEC working paper. http://dspace.ou.nl/handle/1820/36.
10. Olivier B Tattersall C (2005) The Learning Design Specification. In R K- C Tattersall (Eds.), Learning design a handbook on modelling and delivering networked education and training. Springer-Verlag Berlin Heidelberg, pp. 21–40.
11. Rodriguez O, Chen S, Shang Y (2003) Open learning objects: The case for inner metadata. The Journal of Computing in Small Colleges. Volume, 18. Issue 4. 56–64.
12. Sancho P, Manero B, Fernández-Manjón B (2004) <e-aula>: a personalised learning system based on educational standards and mark-up languages. In proceedings of IAESTED 04. Innsbruck, February 2004.
13. Sharda N (2003) Meta-learning with semantic web technologies. IEEE Learning Technology, Volume 5, Issue 4, IEEE Computer Society Learning Technology Task force.
14. Vermetten YJ, Vermunt JD, Lodewijks HG (2002) Powerful learning environments? How university students differ in their response to instructional measures. Learning and Instruction, 12, 263–284.
15. Vermunt J (2003) The power of learning environments and the quality of student learning. In E De Corte, L Verschaffel, N Entwistle, JJG Van Merriënboer (Eds.), Powerful learning environments: Unravelling basic components and dimensions. (pp. 109–124). Oxford: Elsevier Science.

e-QUAL: e-Learning with Quality. Proposal for an Evaluation Model on the Quality of e-Learning Courses

Célio Gonçalo Marques[1], João Noivo[2], Mário Veríssimo[3]

[1]Instituto Politécnico de Tomar
Quinta do Contador, Estrada da Serra, 2300-313 Tomar, Portugal
celiomarques@ipt.pt
[2]Universidade do Minho
DSI, Campus de Azurém, 4800-058 Guimarães, Portugal
[3]NRC-APPC
Rua Garcia de Orta, Vale das Flores, 3030-188 Coimbra, Portugal

1 Introduction

The goal of this study is to address e-learning quality by analysing the main specific approaches to the process, recommendations and lists of good practices. Based on this information we present a model, called e-Qual, to access the quality of e-Learning courses. Considering that the complexity of such models can lead in many cases to its reduced use, the e-Qual model should be simple and flexible to allow the analysis of different pedagogical models.

The adoption and the integration of e-Learning vary significantly from country to country. The ROI issue is not taken for granted; e-learning is, not only focused on technology, but it is mainly centred in an individual-oriented learning; the quality of many e-Learning programmes and courses can be classified as "not satisfactory"; high-quality e-Learning programmes and structures presuppose a significant investment on resources in what concerns evaluation, design, development, contents and management; etc. [1].

In this discussion about quality, it becomes clear that e-Learning has to be oriented towards learners [4, 8].

In [2] Ehlers and colleagues refer to the open nature of quality as both a normative definition and a relation between supply and training needs.

2   e-Qual Model

The e-Qual model derives from the analysis of reference frameworks presented through projects such as Open eQuality Learning Standards [5], SEEQUEEL – Sustainable Environment for the Evaluation of Quality in eLearning [6], Innoelearning [9], MECA-ODL [3], Quality On the Line [7] and the several lists of good practices and is based on structural simplicity and flexibility for the analysis of different pedagogical models.

The need to consider the contributions from several reference frameworks, already mentioned, and also to overcome the conceptual complexity and some lack of flexibility of some of them are the reasons for the creation of a new model.

The structure of our model is the result of an adaptation of the structure of the *Open eQuality Learning Standards* and includes four areas: Learning Contents, Learning Management System (LMS), Processes and Results.

The two first areas concern the necessary resources for the implementation of an e-Learning course (Learning Contents, Learning Management System). The third area deals with the processes ensured by the staff (administrative, technical and pedagogical). The last area is related with the results, in particular with learners' satisfaction, which is the main aspect to be considered as far as quality is concerned.

Within the four areas 16 items have been identified, which are to be classified according to a 0–10 scale. The flexibility of the classification chart lies in the attribution of a weight to each item, which varies from 0 to 3 according to the pedagogical model adopted. Therefore, the score obtained depends on the punctuation of each item and respective weight.

The course analysis can be done in a global basis or by area.

The Learning Contents comprise four items: Written Contents, Multimedia Contents, Complementary Bibliographical Sources and the Content Management System.

In this area all the content-related aspects are analysed. The two first items refer to the materials made available while the third item addresses the content markers used to deepen topics. The last item, in turn, deals with the way contents are acceded.

In the second area the Learning Management System, a fundamental infrastructure for learning performance, is assessed in three items: the Common Space of the Learning Community, the Asynchronous Communication Tools and the Synchronous Communication Tools.

The aspects included in these items reveal themselves as determinant in the implementation of a real learning community which characterises the quality e-Learning courses.

The Process area focuses on the staff fostering learning processes. The five items to be classified are: Administrative Management (administrative staff); Technical Management (technical staff), the Management of Contents Transfer (trainers/tutors), the Management of Learning Communities (trainers/moderators) and the Learners Evaluation.

The e-Learning added two different actors and their performance affected learning quality. The significance of tutors and/or moderators depends on the pedagogical model adopted. In the case of individual-centred contents tutors acquire a more important role. In the case of the learning community, on the other hand, moderators become the most important actors.

In the results area, the last to be analysed, four items were identified: Knowledge and Skills Acquired, Training Recognition, Learners Satisfaction (clients) and Business.

Knowledge and acquired skills are the most quantifiable and measurable result providing an objective idea of training quality.

Training recognition is an important aspect for the client and must be viewed as so in this assessment.

Learner's satisfaction is no doubt the most sensitive item in quality terms because true satisfaction is only achieved when it is not perceived by the client.

The last item relates with the sustainability of the e-Learning activity and reveals determinant since a "non-profitable" business ends up by failing, no matter the quality shown.

3 Description of e-Qual Model

This chapter describes some important points to consider in the classification of items. The evaluator's sensibility in each of the referred points, the evaluator's perspective (producer, distributor or learner) and the course goals will determine their importance within each item.

1 - Learning Contents

   1.1. Written Contents: reliable (recognized authors in the area) and updated; include real experiences; interactive; module-based; reusable;
   1.2. Multimedia Contents (presentations, animation, simulation, audio and video): reliable (recognized authors in the area) and updated;

with technical and aesthetic quality; in accordance with the standards and usability; adequate to technical limitations (e.g. the bandwidth) of trainers; interactive; include real experiences; module-based; reusable;

1.3. Complementary Bibliographical Sources: Web addresses/Virtual libraries; books;

1.4. CMS - Content Management System: coherent structure according to a learning theory; adapted to learning needs; independent of browsers and plug-ins; system customization; easy tracking, visualisation and download of contents; electronics security to ensure the integrity and validity of the contents made available.

2 - LMS – Learning Management System

2.1. Common Space of the Learning Community: relevant administrative and pedagogical information; introduction of the learners; activities timetable; news;

2.2. Asynchronous Communication Tools: e-mail; mailing lists; newsgroups; forums; blogs; wikis;

2.3. Synchronous Communication Tools: chat; documents transfer; whiteboard; documents share; audioconference; videoconference.

3 - Processes

3.1. Administrative Management (administrative staff): course marketing and publicity; presentation of course duration, aims and pedagogical methods; guarantee of pre-requisites of formal and informal learning; guarantee of an acceptable learners/staff ratio; enrolment procedures (on-line or in presence); different types of payment (bank transfer, credit card, cheque, currency, etc.); administrative support;

3.2. Technical Management (technical staff): technical support in the use of CMS or LMS;

3.3. Management of Contents Transfer: availability of the trainer/tutor; effective access to the available contents;

3.4. Management of Learning Communities: intervention of a trainer/moderator; effective use of communication tools;

3.5. Learners Evaluation: quantitative and qualitative evaluation;

4 - Results

4.1. Knowledge and Skills Acquired: knowledge acquired; learning skills;

4.2. Training Recognition: accreditation by professional organisations; recognised credit by teaching institutions aiming the completion of academic degrees; equivalence to similar courses accomplished in a "presential" setting; national and international recognition of training;

4.3. Learners Satisfaction (clients): learning outcomes satisfaction (efficiency); satisfaction regarding the money, time and energy spent (efficiency); satisfaction regarding the contents available; satisfaction regarding the contexts created;

4.4. Business: Return of Investment (ROI).

4 e-Qual Model Application

In order to validate e-Qual Model the 16 main items have been applied in three courses promoted by accredited organizations, namely, Excel 2000-Level 1 from ElementK (http://www.elementK.com), Project Management Essential from NETg (http://www.netg.com) and Training from Prof 2000 (http://www.prof2000.pt).

Two of the organizations at stake are international and one of them is national and they certainly have different aims and ambitions and, of course, resources.

In this study the choice of courses derived from no pre-defined criteria but the possibility of "attending" them.

The results allow comparing courses either in a whole basis or by area: Learning Contents, Learning Management System (LMS), Processes and Results (Table 1).

A global appraisal allows the following classification: "Excel 2000-Level 1" (7.1), "Project Management Essential" (6.5) and "Training" (6.5).

This classing serves as a directive for the learner who intends to choose one of these three e-Learning courses. Another important aspect of e-Qual model is its flexibility to comprise the different perspectives of the ones interested in the e-Learning evaluation. The mechanism used to transact this flexibility is the weight attributed to each of the 16 items.

Table 1. Application of e-Qual model

	Excel 2000 Level 1	Project Management Essential	Training
1. LEARNING CONTENTS			
1.1 Written Contents	8	8	8
1.2 Multimedia Contents	7	7	5
1.3 Compl. Bibliographical Sources	6	7	6
1.4 Content Management Systems	8	6	6

Average	7.3 (73%)	7.0 (70%)	6.3 (73%)
2. LMS			
2.1 Com. Space Learning Community	8	6	8
2.2 Asynchronous Com. Tools	7	6	7
2.3 Synchronous Com. Tools	5	5	5
Average	6.7 (67%)	5.7 (57%)	6.7 (67%)
3. PROCESSES			
3.1 Administrative Management	8	6	6
3.2 Technical Management	7	6	6
3.3 Management Content Transfer	8	6	6
3.4 Manag. Learning Communities	6	5	5
3.5 Learning Evaluation	7	8	6
Average	7.2 (72%)	6.2 (62%)	5.8 (58%)
4. RESULTS			
4.1 Knowledge and Skills Acquired	8	8	8
4.2 Training Recognition	7	7	9
4.3 Learners Satisfaction	7	7	7
4.4 Business			
Average	7.3 (73%)	7.3 (73%)	8.0 (80%)
GLOBAL	7.1 (71%)	6.5 (65%)	6.5 (65%)

Thus if the learner gives more importance to the contents and the support for doubts clarification from his trainer, items 1.1, 1.2, 1.3, 1.4 e 3.3 should be evaluated with the maximum score/weight.

On the other hand, if the learner favours the learning community, where the interaction with other learners allows the experience and information exchange, then the items to be favoured with the maximum weight will be 2.1, 2.2, 2.3 and 3.4.

A learner who looks for quality contents obtains the classing "Excel 2000 – Level 1" (7.3), "Project Management Essential" (6.8) and "Learning" (6.6).

And a learner who looks for experiences and exchange of information with other learners has a different indication of the e-Equal model, the "Training" course (6.7) presenting a better classification than the "Project Management Essential" course (6.4).

Due to its quality in all the areas, the classification "Excel 2000 – Level 1" reveals to be the favourite, irrespective of the perspective adopted by the learner.

5 Conclusions

e-Learning quality is a topic that has been gaining importance to all actors involved, from researchers to learners.

Quality approaches have different perspectives according to its methodology and implementation. Therefore, any quality approach will have to be open to different values, interests and objectives.

e-Learning, as a wonderful opportunity of working out the information in knowledge, will only grow in a sustainable way if it is based on quality.

Quality is a process under permanent evolution and transformation, as technology itself, organisations and people – in one word society.

In the context of this changing process, the concept of quality should be more and more learner-centred without disregarding the other actors involved, obviously.

The e-Qual model has confirmed its flexibility in the described application as different results have been obtained with different learning approaches.

Two aspects that should be emphasized are the detail and the tuning of topics considered in each item classification and the gap for marks and weights. These aspects can be improved based on the results analysis from a more detailed application of the model. At this point evaluators with different sensibilities will be able to attribute distinct classification to each item.

References

1. Dam N (2004) The E-Learning Fieldbook: Implementation Lessons and Case Studies from Companies that are Making e-Learning Work. McGraw-Hill, New York
2. Ehlers U, Hildebrand B, Tescheler S, Pawlowski, J (2004) Designing Tools and Frameworks For Tomorrows Quality Development. In: EQO Workshop@ICALT 2004 Quality in European E-Learning. EQO, Joensuu, Finland
3. Fundación Universidad-Empresa de Valencia (2002) Meca-ODL - Methodological Guide for the Analysis of Quality in Open and Distance Learning Delivered via Internet. Projecto Sócrates-Minerva da Comunidade Europeia
4. Husson A (2004) Comparing Quality models adequacy to the needs of clients in e-Learning. In: EQO Workshop@ICALT 2004 Quality in European e-Learning. EQO, Joensuu, Finland
5. LIfIA, EifEL (2004) Open eQuality Learning Standards. Joint eQuality Committee of LIfIA (Learning Innovations Forum d'Innovation d'Apprentissage) and EIfEL (European Institute for e-Learning)
6. MENON Network EEIG (2004) SEEQUEL Core Quality Framework. Projecto SEEQUEL – Sustainable Environment for the Evaluation of Quality in e-Learning. eLearning Initiative, Comissão Europeia

7. Phipps R, Merisotis J (2000) Quality on the Line: Benchmarks for Success in Internet-based Distance Education. IHEP - Institute for Higher Education Policy, Washington
8. Ruttenbur B, Spickler G, Lurie S (2000) E-Learning – The Engine of the Knowledge Economy. Morgan Keegan & Co, New York
9. Sociedade Portuguesa de Inovação (2003) Empre-Learning: Promoção de Estruturas de e-Learning Inovadores, em Língua Portuguesa, que Permitam o Aumento de Competências e Aumentem a Empregabilidade. Sociedade Portuguesa de Inovação, Porto

Pedagogical Approaches for Online Environments

Luísa Miranda[1], Carlos Morais[1], Paulo Dias[2]

[1]Polytechnic Institute of Bragança
[2]University of Minho, Portugal
lmiranda@ipb.pt

1 Introduction

Assuming that Web-based Information and Communication Technologies are resources for support to the teaching and learning process, this article refers to a few pedagogical approaches which may be contextualized in methodologies supported by online learning environments, with the main aim of motivating reflection and the will to go deeper into strategies that can take advantage of those technological innovations which are fitted into pedagogical models allowing online education to be used and rendered profitable in service to training and educating people over the course of their lives.

Many are the intervening parties, the means and the contexts which could influence the formal teaching and learning process; however, we will point out that the main intervening parties include teachers and students, and the main means of supporting the teaching and learning process include information and communication technologies, most notably the Internet and the resources that are associated with it, by contextualizing such means and intervening elements in the act of teaching and learning in learning environments, in which we foster interactions of a varied nature conducive to the teaching and learning process and, consequently, to knowledge-building.

Discussion can be focused on creating models for online education which connect the intervening elements with the support means and the relationships between both, as structures are defined that can respond to educational objectives and perspectives. With a constructivist model as a reference, student-centred teaching and learning strategies are upheld and, as such, we seek to build learning environments that will embody such strategies.

The task of building of a student-centred online learning environment is quite complex. According to Palloff and Pratt, in order for an online learning environment to be truly student-centred, teachers need to understand who the students are and how they learn, to be attentive to topics students bring to the learning environment and to the type of support they need, and to respect students' role in the learning process [13].

In the field of online education, we notice a continuous debate going on about potential students who feel drawn to this method of teaching. It has been confirmed that the online student is no longer just adults – attending traditional correspondence courses aiming to bring about professional development – , but also young people. This fact has aroused the interest of a large number of institutions, which offer courses in the form of blended learning models, a combination of face-to-face and online learning systems, or totally online, which offer flexible and choice options that are more and more adaptable to the objectives and interests of students from the various age groups. Online education attracts people of all ages and cultures, who live anywhere in the world.

We will be dealing with several topics for reflection on the pedagogical approaches for online learning environments; in particular, such topics will include: contextualizing online learning environments, learning metaphors, most prominently those bearing the following designations: acquisition metaphor, participation metaphor, and metaphor for creating knowledge, as well as the pedagogical approaches of Duart and Sangrà and that of Terry Anderson for developing online education.

2 Contextualizing Online Learning Environments

Given the potential of Web-supported resources for creating online learning environments, we consider that the learning environment concept, on top of physical and time-related areas, involves the availability of resources and strategies based on sharing and joint collaboration between the intervening parties involved in the educational process.

We can consider that online environments constitute an institutionalized teaching and learning context where the main intervening parties in the knowledge-building process, both student and teacher, are not present in the same physical area at the same time, and the development of communication and interaction is supported by technological resources.

Overcoming physical distances and bringing people closer together, in psychological terms, in the way they feel, work or carry out projects in a collaborative and shared manner, all constitute aims to be achieved as part of the teaching and learning process, by fostering pedagogical approaches that ensure efficiency and quality in learning and teaching. We have witnessed the development of pedagogy that is suited to correspondence teaching which has been interpreted and brought about distinct pedagogical models, as new technologies were being applied [15].

Courses in online environments can take on various formats, depending on the objectives with which they are used, the contexts in which they are implemented and the resources they make available. The diversity and amount of formats make it difficult to define a categorization that will be easily accepted. However, Mason points out a certain type, taking into account the use of the Internet, which ranges from courses making only secondary use of the Internet to courses that take place solely online, thus suggesting that the different models of online courses fit into one of the following categories:

- courses with irrelevant use of the Web: where the Web is an extra, optional resource for presenting materials or a means of communication;
- courses with integrated use: where a large part of the contents or activities is online;
- courses solely online: where the course contents and all communication with and support given to the student are online [8].

Online courses, generally the most visible side of online education, should, among other aspects, contribute toward improving learning environments, while fostering access to information and to communication, providing interaction between people and between local, regional, national and international institutions, with the aim of exchanging ideas, sharing cultures, projects, comparing problems and contributing toward solving them.

The type of online courses involves particular characteristics in pedagogical approaches that we intend to develop, although, as suggested by Morgado, despite the high number of online teaching experiences described in literature, it is not always possible to identify those conceptual models that guide such experiences [10].

In order to justify online courses in pedagogical theories, and especially in alluding to the development of online learning resources, Ally points out that the behaviourist, cognitivist and constructivist theories have contributed toward designing online resources and toward developing these same resources, and Ally also adds that behaviourist strategies can be used for teaching facts, cognitivist strategies for teaching principles and processes, and constructivist strategies for pinpointing problems in real-life situations and contextualizing learning [1].

The early computer-supported learning systems were designed on the basis of behaviourist approaches, generally oriented toward carrying out automated tasks and learning support services which rest on models for transmission of information. With the evolution of the potential associated with information and communication technologies and with the latest learning theories, we moved to models that regard the student as the centre of learning.

In reply to concerns pertaining to the means used for teaching, learning and characterizing strategies that are conducive to fostering and acquiring knowledge, we will address a few of the characteristics of this problem, as they fit into learning metaphors.

3 Learning Metaphors

The concept of metaphor allows for various interpretations; however, it always represents an effort to create models that will make it easier to understand topics at the expense of concepts that are mastered.

In a pedagogical scenario with a wide variety of approaches, where there are theories that stress factors of a social, cultural or cognitive nature, Sfard points out two alternative means of understanding learning, giving them the designation of acquisition metaphor and participation metaphor [16].

The acquisition metaphor conceptualizes learning as an individual process for acquiring knowledge, and it can take on the form of a traditional receptive process or of an active and constructive process, how they stand up for constructivist theories that are concentrated on individual learning processes. Learning is considered in terms of knowledge structures which exist in the mind of each student, where the human mind can be considered to be a receptacle of knowledge, and learning is a process that enables the accumulation of knowledge in such a receptacle.

With the participation metaphor, learning is represented as a participation process in various cultural practices and in shared learning activities. In this regard, Palonen and Hakkarainen refer that the participation metaphor emphasizes the role of social communities in the learning and knowledge-building process [14]. Thus, the focus of learning is on activities and on doing things and not so much on knowledge as such, and it is also considered that learning is a process for participating in social scenarios [12].

Bartolomé notes that today's society emerges with the notion of participation, contrasted with the classic, one-directional discourse of the perfect class, the manual, the textbook and the classic interpretation of television or of audiovisual materials [4, p. 21]. The same author also suggests that technology evolves with regard to those pieces of equipment which made participation easier between the intervening parties in education, where the Internet and the resources associated with it were considered to be extremely important for such participation.

As a supplement to possible learning scenarios, and considering the two aforementioned metaphors, Paavola et al. suggest a third learning metaphor, which they call a metaphor for creating knowledge [11]. The same authors admit that, in terms of this metaphor, learning is analogous to research development models, in which new ideas, tools and practices are created in a collaborative manner and contribute toward enabling the original knowledge to be significantly enriched or transformed during the process. Thus, the focus of learning is not on the individual mind, as with the acquisition metaphor, nor is it on the social process, as with the participation metaphor, but, rather, in products of mediation as objects and practices developed in a collaborative manner during the learning process.

This learning approach as the creation of knowledge stresses the importance of the processes of mutual interaction and involvement in learning communities, by sharing in solving problems, in defining theories and in assessing results [6].

The creation and development of online learning environments, where learning can be fostered actively and in a collaborative way and based on the interaction between the intervening parties is a challenge for every teacher. The response to such a challenge involves successive planning stages and making various choices before implementing the teaching and learning process.

Each learning environment has to be built while taking into account the way to approach each topic, which can be in terms of the student, the teacher, the type of interactions one wishes to foster, the support means one intends to use, the costs, or in terms of a variety of other forms, while maintaining, in each of these approaches, a coherent whole, which can comprise the structure and the possibility of implementing online courses supported by teaching institutions.

By pointing out pedagogical approaches showing mostly concern for the student, the role of the teacher or of the technology with the aim of building models, we are contributing toward building a theoretical field that can be the supporting basis for practices that are or that could be experienced in the field of online education. In this regard, we point out a few contributions from pedagogical approaches, developed by [7] and by [3] with implications to the theoretical field of online education.

4 Pedagogical Approaches

The development of online education has had quite an impact and has been accepted in institutions of Higher Learning. Since institutions of Higher Learning play an important role in preparing people for life within society and for work, we will not be able to implement pedagogical approaches starting from these institutions if we do not consider their curricula. Zabalza defines curriculum as: integrated formative project [17]. The same author considers: project – as something that has been thought out and designed in whole; formative – as this is aimed at improving the training of people taking part therein; integrated – because curricular projects need unity and internal coherence, and they should consist of a process characterized by a suitable internal structure and a continuity that is able to foster as much personal and vocational development as possible.

By associating pedagogical approaches with the notion of curriculum as an integrated formative project, this is then followed by the approach by Duart and Sangrà and that by Terry Anderson.

4.1 Pedagogical Approach by Duart and Sangrà

By admitting that there is an increasing *virtualization* of teaching institutions, [7], they sought to build a model in which a methodological framework of such institutions is possible, by proposing conceptual models based on three variables: the means (the technology), the teacher and the student, which correspond, respectively, to models centred on means, teacher-centred models and student-centred models.

Models centred on means, resulting from the development of technology, are characterized by their centrality in the use of one of several technological tools. The student and the teacher, the main players involved in fostering the educational process, play a secondary role in this model. The teacher becomes a provider of contents, with the student becoming a user of those same contents, from which self-training should occur.

As an example of a model centred in means, we point out intranets, whose main function includes storing resources and making them available to students and teachers. Other distinctly emphatic situations in means consist of presenting contents using PowerPoint, or even providing contents in personal pages of teaching staff or on specific sites intended for particular subjects or courses from certain institutions. In each of the aforementioned cases, we notice that teachers very often simply place contents, which are received by students as a finished, ready-to-use product.

Although this type of use of technologies can be regarded as yet another means for distributing contents, which is a little different from the means of making photocopies and giving them out to students, we feel that, on top of the contents shown, there is something more than making them available, both in the attitude of the teacher who looked for means to use for reaching students in a simple, innovative and convenient way, but also in the attitude of students who gradually feel they are obliged to use technologies which, although they start off as a simple act of consulting contents, quickly evolve to other formats and perspectives for using computer-related resources, such as in communicating and in presenting information research.

As suggested by Bartolomé, when a teacher fosters conditions in his students in order to use texts from the Internet, he/she is not limited to a simple change in information support, but is implementing a much more profound change into his/her teaching dynamics, where such a change affects the way we get to know the very essence of the knowledge we include [4]. The models centred on means, according to Duart and Sangrà, represent the classic self-training systems, which are modernized using the latest technologies [7].

Teacher-centred models refer us to classic models that are centred more on teaching than on learning, and in which the teacher is the main reference to the knowledge.

Student-centred knowledge is characterized by emphasis and centrality on the student. A student-centred context should also meet the needs of the teacher, the institution, society and, often, the group of students [3].

The independent nature provided by computer-supported technology favours student-centred teaching, thus enabling reflexive construction of knowledge based on the student's skills and objectives [5]. Creating a student-centred approach involves providing different students with different options.

By allowing for a certain centrality in the student's role, we will have to allow for a change in the teacher's role. The latter no longer holds down the exclusive role of transmission of knowledge, to become a facilitator and an orienting guide in the student's learning, as the teacher seeks to respect the student's learning runs. Thus, learning tasks should be mostly developed and oriented, in order to provide a response to the particular interests and concerns of each student.

The three models described are shown as being independent from one another, which gives the impression that it is possible to stress only one of the roles of the means, of the teachers or of the students, which is neither possible nor desirable. In this regard, we are of the opinion that the three models mentioned herein constitute a coherent whole in the teaching and learning context, although they can have different levels of use, depending on the context, the objectives and the strategy outlined for the teaching and learning process.

For Duart and Sangrà, it is possible to identify three variables in the afore-mentioned models, by showing them in a three-dimensional model in which the coordinates can be depicted so as to characterize each teaching institution on its way to virtualization. As adapted from the same authors, the following Fig. 1 illustrates the afore-mentioned three-dimensional model [7].

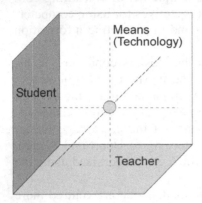

Fig. 1. Balance in a three-dimensional model, adapted from [7]

Among the advantages of the previous model, we point out the possibility of identifying main axes for pedagogical guidelines that we intend to define and implement at each institution, as we stress, on one hand, that students, teachers and the means are the fundamental elements of the educational context; on the other hand, this forces us to think about these three elements in a balanced way, for if we place too much emphasis on one of the axes, we might minimize the others and, consequently, not comply with a curriculum, which we defend as an integrated formative project.

Duart and Sangrà's contribution resulted in the construction of a theoretical organizational model, which can work as a generator of pedagogical models for online education, with a strong common basis, taking into account concerns with students, teachers and means, by fostering, at teaching institutions, combinations of these elements so as to be able to build suitable models of online learning environments that personalize them and respond to their education and training objectives and projects.

4.2 Pedagogical Approach by Terry Anderson

In considering the various teaching and learning formats that can be supported by the Web, Anderson suggests that it is premature to define an online learning theory [3]. However, he feels that the creation of a model is often the first step toward developing a theory. In this regard, he presents an online learning model in which we see a representation of the main variables included in building contexts and in developing learning experiences, where such variables include students and teachers, as well as interactions between them, and with contents.

The model put forth by Anderson rests on two pillars: independent learning, with roots in the field of distance education, and collaborative learning, with roots in the constructivist and socio-constructivist models [3]. The same author considers the Web potential important for building the pedagogical model, as he admits that quality learning should always be student-centred, in knowledge, in the community and in assessment, as we point out the importance of interactive formats.

The concept of interaction is complex, as it allows for various sizes and interpretation, which is sometimes considered to be synonymous with the dialogue taking place in the classroom, between the teacher and the students, or between the students themselves.

In distance education, the concept of interaction is shown by Moore in terms of the following relations: student-student, student-teacher and student-contents [9], where Anderson and Garrison (1998) (apud [2]) added to these the interactive formats rendered by the relations: teacher-teacher, teacher-contents and contents-contents.

In this model, the teacher takes on a driving role, by intervening in creating and updating contents and in learning activities (teacher-content interaction), in the development of activities implemented in the learning community and in individual support to students (student-teacher interaction), in creating opportunities for the vocational development of teachers through communities where they can share problems, discuss ideas and outline teaching and learning strategies (teacher-teacher interaction).

Content-content interaction is rendered in the way contents are programmed to interact with other contents via automated resources, as we point out the example of researching contents on the Internet using search engines, for it is through web agents that contents interact with one another in continuously operating networks, as we obtain search results almost instantly.

Within the context of innovation in the field of online education, the teacher will play a very important role, not just in using innovative interactive formats with the contents, but also as a participant on work teams that are responsible for defining learning objects that offer flexibility and the re-use of online resources that meet both individual and group needs of students.

The model we have just referred can be regarded as an open and flexible model providing the student and the teacher with the possibility of creating environments directed at learning contexts, ease of interaction and opportunities for developing both individual and collaborative work strategies.

As a summary, we point out that the Anderson model shows various ways of learning and teaching on the Web, as we stress the main variables involved in the teaching and learning process and the relationships between them, by putting in perspective the great importance to be attached to the interaction concept and to the various types of interaction that need to be favoured and nurtured in the educational context.

5 Final Considerations

Online learning needs to respond more and more to the demand of different cultures, styles and motivations [1]. The approaches that have been presented help us to reflect on and build and a deeper vision of this very complex field. We point out the importance that the pedagogical aspect gains in online learning environments: while technological innovations help overcome the barriers of space and time, pedagogical approaches can contribute toward reducing psychological and cultural distances.

According to [6, p. 3] "learning activities supported by online environments on the Web are characterized by making training flexible and by developing interactions directed at learning processes, namely in collaborative aspects."

Pedagogical approaches pointed out in the text provide us with strong support elements for the development of online education: while the Duart and Sangrà approach implements a reference in an idealized teaching and learning area, made up of a three-dimensional model with the axes comprising the teacher, the student and the means, the Terry Anderson approach stresses not only the teacher, the student and the contents, but also the various types of relationships and interactions occurring in education contexts.

Because the information and communication society that we live in provides many abundant sources of information, it requires continuous consolidation and updating of the knowledge of citizens. Thus, online education can play an essential role, in order to monitor major changes in contemporary society, where the concept of lifelong education and training, constitutes a constant concern in the individual's sustained development, his/her knowledge and abilities in how to be active and to intervene in the collaborative construction of learning and knowledge networks.

References

1. Ally M (2004) Foundations of educational theory for online learning. In: Anderson T, Elloumi F (eds.) Theory and practice of online learning. Athabasca University, Athabasca, pp. 3–31
2. Anderson T (2003) Modes of interaction in distance education: Recent developments and research questions. In: Moore MG, Anderson WG (eds.) Handbook of distance education. Lawrence Erlbaum Associates, Mahwah, New Jersey, pp. 129–144
3. Anderson T (2004) Toward a theory for online learning. In: Anderson T, Elloumi F (eds.) Theory and practice of online learning. Athabasca University, Athabasca, pp. 33–60
4. Bartolomé A (2005) Sociedad de la información y cambio educativo. In: Dias P, Freitas C (eds.) Actas da IV Conferência Internacional de Tecnologias de Informação e Comunicação na Educação, Challenges 2005. Centro de Competência Nónio Século XXI da Universidade do Minho, Braga, pp. 17–41
5. Crook C (1998) Ordenadores y aprendizaje colaborativo. Ediciones Morata, Madrid
6. Dias P (2004) Desenvolvimento de objectos de aprendizagem para plataformas colaborativas. In: Barrientos X, Zúniga V, Ortiz J, Isaías L, Guerra S, Garza R, Cantú M, Hinojosa S (eds.) Actas do VII Congreso Iberoamericano de Informática Educativa. Universidad de Monterrey, Monterrey, pp. 3–12
7. Duart J, Sangrà A (2000) Formación universitaria por medio de la web: un modelo integrador para el aprendizaje superior. In: Duart J, Sangrà A (eds.) Aprender en la Virtualidad. Editorial Gedisa, Barcelona, pp. 23–49
8. Mason R (2003) Models and methodologies in distance education. Discursos: Novos rumos e pedagogia em ensino a distância 1: 91–101
9. Moore M (1989) Editorial: Three types of interaction. The American Journal of Distance Education vol 3, 2: 1–6. http://www.ajde.com/Contents/vol3_2.htm#editorial
10. Morgado, L (2003) Ensino online: Contextos e interacções. Ph.D. thesis, Open University, Portugal
11. Paavola S, Ilomäki L, Lakkala M, Hakkarainen K (2003) A framework for evaluating virtual learning materials through the three metaphors of learning. http://www.eun.org/eun.org2/eun/downloads/Three_metaphors.doc
12. Paavola S, Lipponen L, Hakkarainen K (2002) Epistemological foundations for CSCL: A comparison of three models of innovative knowledge communities. http://www.newmedia.colorado.edu/cscl/228.html
13. Palloff R, Pratt K (2003) The virtual student: A profile and guide to working with online learners. Jossey-Bass Publishers, San Francisco
14. Palonen T, Hakkarainen K (2000) Patterns of interaction in computer-supported learning: A social network analysis. In: Fishman B, O'Connor-Divelbiss S (eds.) Fourth international conference of the learning sciences. NJ: Erlbaum, Mahwah, pp 334–339

15. Pereira A, Mendes A, Mota J, Morgado L, Aires L (2003) Contributos para uma pedagogia do ensino online pós-graduado: Proposta de um modelo. Discursos: Novos rumos e pedagogia em ensino a distância 1: 39–52
16. Sfard A (1998) On two metaphors for learning and the dangers of choosing just one. Educational Researcher 27: 4–13
17. Zabalza M (2003) Competencias docentes del profesorado universitario: Calidad y desarrollo profesional. Narcea, Madrid

Contextual Online Learning Model: A Proposal

Raquel Pedrosa[1], Joana Valente[1], Filipe Rocha[2], Ana Amélia Carvalho[2]

[1]Edulearn
[2]University of Minho, Portugal
raquel.pedrosa@eduweb.pt

1 Introduction

The Contextual Online Learning Model, to be known as COLM, arose from the need for a model that would provide a facilitating environment for learning in context.

COLM was created on the basis of a theoretical framework centred round adult learning, constructivist learning and social negotiation (which is essential when working collaboratively), learning autonomy and the support or guidance that is needed for those who are learning.

Since adult learners find it difficult to be in a certain place at a certain time, an almost entirely online course was chosen, more specifically, one that would involve a blended-learning regime. Attendance would only be required at the first session – at which the course, the moderator, the students and the COLM are presented – and the final session, involving project presentation and final evaluation of the course.

Flexibility of space and time is today an extremely important variable in choosing the environment in which the learning process will take place. The possibility of learning at one's own pace without having to be in a specific place at a specific time (anytime/anywhere) is conciliated with the modern day needs for learning and training brought about by the globalisation of information through Information and Communication Technologies.

Before we describe the Contextual Learning System, we will explain the theoretical framework underlying it.

2 Theoretical Framework

The studies developed by Malcolm Knowles in the 1970s contributed towards a different view being taken of learning in adults compared to that of children and adolescents, with the term *andragogy* becoming common.

The author [11] defends that adults need to know why they have to learn something, they need to learn by experimenting, they see learning as the resolution of problems and learn better when the contents have immediate use.

These guidelines must be considered when structuring courses or training sessions. The teacher must play the role mainly of learning facilitator, guiding the student towards achieving learning.

Constructivism describes knowledge as temporary, not objective, internally constructed and socially and culturally mediated, with learning as a self-regulatory process of conflict between personal knowledge of the world and new perspectives that the individual has to face [9]. Learning progresses due to the construction of new representations and models of reality and the negotiation of knowledge with others [9]. These representations are dynamic given that the contact with the world implies successive interiorisations and consequent restructuring of the created representation. Nevertheless, as [27] mentions, the most common source of disturbance in cognitive development results from interaction with others, and this social negotiation of knowledge with others is necessary for learning. That is why the creation of *communities* is important. Belonging to the community will provide contact with others, with their points of view and their preconceived beliefs and will trigger off situations of confrontation and negotiation that provide social development and learning. In the community it is equally important to receive assistance as well as to give it. The members of the group understand that they will only reach their objective if the group, the community, reaches it, too [10].

"In communal learning the learners discuss, externalise and interpret information. Dialogic communication and interaction are associated with trust and sharing." [25].

The learner must use concrete experiences in context, looking for patterns, raising questions and constructing his/her models, concepts and strategies.

Constructivists propose a holistic approach, because they consider it inadequate to isolate units of information. Instead, they place importance on context, recognising that facts or components in context are much more significant than the sum of the characteristics of each of its components [20]. This is why learning centred round *projects* [19] has become an increasingly important learning strategy.

The student or learner must receive *support* [3] or guidance from the teacher or educator in order to construct his/her learning.

Autonomy in learning, shown in the studies of [12, 21, 22], is a source of satisfaction and self-esteem in subjects and, as a moral and social ideal, leads the subject to emancipation and change.

Autonomy is shown in the way in which the subject learns and how s/he transfers what s/he learns to wider contexts [14].

The learning environment is influential in the way in which the students learn and in what they learn. In order to encourage autonomous learning, an environment of cooperation and negotiation is necessary in the exploration of knowledge [1].

2.1 Context

As we have already mentioned, the constructivists highlight the importance of context for significant learning to occur, as happens with Situated Cognition [2], Cognitive Learning [6], Situated Learning [13], Situated Action [17] and Anchored Instruction [5], among others. However, within the scope of this study, we will use the term context proposed by [8], which, in our view, presents a dynamic and flexible design that we will now characterise.

The context exists through the learner's *interaction* with his/her surroundings, such as the activities, the others and the space. It is these interactions that organise the context and provide the individual with a constant rearrangement of this context. Taken to the extreme, as the authors say, the context "is what the learner *feels* as the context of the learning experience." [8, p. 8].

The context results from the interactions between the actors of a course that share and construct knowledge. It is in constant change, and therefore can not be located or restricted. The context is dependent on the learner's activities, which do not occur in the context but are part of the context. "Context is what is relevant for the learner to build his/her knowledge, and that may change from moment to moment." [8, p. 9].

We also considered that in this context, the group in interaction will use what Vygotsky calls the "proximal development zone" and will live the particular dynamics of a group [26].

The context of a group begins with the proposal for a project and the students' adherence to this proposal. From then on, the dynamics that will develop are generally unpredictable. "The more open-ended or socially complex the activity is, the less we can predict its development" [8, p. 9].

Finally, the authors say that "the context is what the designer feels relevant for the learning experience of the learner" [8, p. 9]. Thus, the starting context (the theme and the actors' involvement) for the learning process is determined, not by the group but by the course designer or coordinator.

In the following point, we will describe the system to support the interactions to occur with in the context centred learning.

3 Contextual Online Learning Model

Based on theoretical justification and according to what technology allows us today, we propose the contextual online learning model, as shown in Fig. 1, which we will describe throughout the text.

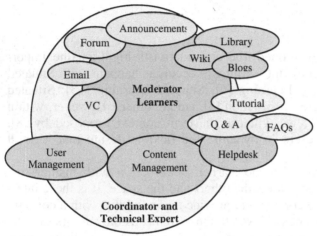

Fig. 1. Contextual Online learning model

The Contextual Online Learning Model supports online learning, except for the first and the last sessions, which must be face-to-face. In this way, it answers the target public's needs for flexibility of place and time. Not only does it therefore promote knowledge of the tools of synchronous and asynchronous communication, but it also promotes understanding of the advantages and drawbacks of each, as well as the available tools of collaboration. These are essential experiences for any citizen in the 21st century to achieve social insertion onto the job market.

Since time is a determining factor, though it is the coordinator that defines the duration of the course, we propose that the course lasts for 10 weeks, with weekly sessions in an after-work schedule online, except for the first and the last sessions, which must be attended on site, as we have said.

A videoconferencing system was chosen as the synchronous communication tool given that it aids visual and auditory interaction in real time, reducing the transactional distance between the participants [15]. The forum, e-mail and wiki were selected as means of asynchronous communication.

In this environment, four kinds of actors were considered: *coordinator* (who promotes the course and its structure), *moderator* (who facilitates learning, provides support material, clarifies difficulties and promotes interaction), the *learners* and the *technical expert* (provides technical support for the learners).

Each course creates its context through the theme and through the intervention dynamic that is determined for the moderator, both proposed by the coordinator.

We bore in mind that "learning is a constructivist activity that the students themselves must perform. From this point of view, the task of the educator is not to dispense knowledge but to give students the opportunities and incentives to construct it." [28, p. 20]. In this sense, the thematic contextualisation of the course provides the opportunity for learning and for sharing ideas and constructing knowledge, facilitated above all through the Forum and the Wiki, by the moderator.

There are contents available to the learner in the library that will allow him/her to broaden his/her knowledge and justify his/her positions. A learner is selected at random and must summarise the ideas presented in the Forum in a concept map [18]. The concept map is represented in the Wiki, available in the system. In the weekly synchronous sessions, which last two hours, the concept map is discussed and the group positions readjusted. Once the representation of the concept has been approved, it is stored in the Wiki, in the Reflection and Construction folder which reflects, as the name itself suggests, the construction of the group.

The Wiki is the support instrument for the collaborative construction of knowledge. It is recommended that folders be created for the concept maps (Reflection and Construction), for the projects (to be designated) and for other thematic discussions that may arise in the heart of the community. The existence of a common space (the wiki), where all the collaborative construction within the scope of the course is placed, allows a better framework for the results and enhances community spirit (where everyone participates for a common knowledge construction), thus constituting a true repository of collaborative knowledge, organised and integrated.

In parallel, individual blogs will be developed that can be commented on by all the participants.

Once the theme of the course is contextualised, the right conditions have been created for the proposal of projects that will be developed as a group.

In the Announcement Table, project proposals are put forward by the learners, which will be negotiated in the videoconferencing space. The Projects are developed in the *Wiki*.

Every week, presentation sessions will be held on project evolution using the whiteboard. During this phase, the moderator activates the forum with questions related to the tools of communication and collaboration. The forum can also be moderated by the groups with themes related to the projects.

We will now explain the technical and pedagogical specifications, the functional specifications and the specifications of the actors' profiles in the contextual learning model.

3.1 Technical and Pedagogical Specifications

As we have already said, *videoconferencing* is the chosen tool for synchronous interaction to allow the most real interaction between participants. In addition to this, it enables collaborative online interaction using various types of basic software.

The *forum* was chosen as the promoter of thematic contextualisation for two reasons. Since it is asynchronous, it enables the learner to reflect upon the theme or issue [4], consulting the material available in the library or on the wiki. As the issues dealt with are generally complex, and in order to prevent distortion of their understanding, they need to be seen or analysed according to multiple points of view [24, 16], each contributing to a multifaceted understanding of the theme in focus. On the other hand, reflection is essential for constructing knowledge.

Issues essential to the theme of the course are placed on the forum every week. In the first five weeks, these deal with the course content and in the following weeks with the tools of communication and collaboration as well as group dynamics. In this way, through reflection and the online session, a community is created that debates themes and shares a purpose: that of learning collaboratively [7]. The five initial sessions are more demanding from the point of view of the individual construction of knowledge and the following five are more focused on the dynamics of each group to see the project through to the end. In order to keep the community spirit alive, the forum continues to be energised but without requiring such high personal involvement.

On the *blog*, each learner makes his/her own personal reflection, which can be commented on by the moderator as a means of learning support. The other learners can also write their own comments, thereby strengthening community ties.

E-mail will be used to contact some of the actors (moderator or learner) which at a given time cannot clarify any information online.

Additionally, this tool becomes quite useful for communication between all the participants in the system, for file sharing and for the construction of collaborative projects. E-mail allows all communications to be recorded in order and is a tool that is generally common to all learners.

The *Wiki* is an excellent tool for thematic discussions, reflections, summaries and construction of knowledge/learning. In the model that is presented, it is suggested that there should be a wiki for the entire course, where the various themes can be expanded through the participation of all, both through interaction in the projects and through the thematic discussions. The person responsible for the concept map includes it in the wiki structure. The groups are responsible for running their space freely on the wiki. The rules will have to be determined in the first synchronous sessions.

Announcements can be posted by the moderator and by the learners, so that this space constitutes one of sharing. According to each profile, the pop-up window records by topic all the new entries in the environment. In this way, the learner immediately has a summary of the movements in the environment, providing quicker access to the information and thus enabling feedback to be given more rapidly.

The *Tutorial* on the system is always available in case any learner needs to review any information.

The *Library* provides the support contents for the course in various formats, but material can also be placed there by the learners. It therefore constitutes a true repository of knowledge that can be shared.

3.2 Functional Specifications

Below we briefly describe the main points of the functionalities that constitute the COLM.

a) The *user management* covers the enrolment and profile management zones.

The enrolment process can be done through the submission of an individual enrolment proposal in the system (courses open to the Web) or by loading a data file (institutional). In the case of the individual enrolment process, the candidate submits his/her data and is later notified of how the application evolves. With regard to institutional cases, the access data is provided automatically via e-mail. This flexibility of the process enables different types of publics to be registered.

Profile management is the responsibility of the course coordination, which attributes the profile of moderator or learner as the course is defined and enrolments validated. It is also responsible for activating or deactivating tools at the request of the Moderator. It is also in charge of monitoring the action of the moderator in the environment.

The Moderator profile involves the authorisations of visualising in any tool, as well as that of altering the profile authorisations. It controls participations in the videoconferencing tool and has the authority to attribute this function to learners within the scope of the project planning sessions. It can also create sub-folders in the library and in the wiki.

In the case of the learner, we consider that s/he must have authorisation to edit the collaboration tools, insert documents and use the communication tools as well as moderate videoconferencing sessions and create sub-folders in the library.

b) *Content management* - The publication of contents produced by the groups is their responsibility. The moderator publishes, in the appropriate places (library, wiki, Forum, etc.), the requests for information and the suggestions for reading adapted to the context(s).

The *library* is organised into folders: one for contents and another for course projects. The creation of sub-folders is also possible after validation by the moderator.

c) *Customisation* - The technological support platform for the COLM must allow customisation of the general learning environment so that the graphic environment can be contextualised to the theme of the course or the institution that promotes it, namely in terms of the choice of scenarios (colours, text type, menus and integration of institutional image).

It must be possible for the course designer to run the navigation options, including network or hierarchical browsing, depending on the options outlined in the access to contents criteria and taking into account the context or the learning contexts. We suggest a network navigation that allows more interactive and discovery exploration. Both can be used depending on the learning contexts and the creative approaches used.

d) *Communication* - The *forum* must have a hierarchical structure and it must be possible to annex files when inserting messages. As new insertions of messages are made on the Forum, they are automatically directed to the participants. The tool must allow the forums to be printed and it must be possible to save them in text format.

Each message can be classified by all the actors. The forum space must allow different themes to be included for discussion, closing some and initiating others. In a first stage, it is the moderator who launches the themes for discussion and activates them. In a second stage, when new projects are launched, the learners or groups of learners can also launch new themes for discussion.

The *videoconferencing* involves a video system that includes a chat space and enables *private* messages, as well as a whiteboard [application sharing (visualising and editing) and sending of documents]. It is possible to manage participation in the sessions through a "hands up" type of mechanism. It must enable recording (optional) of the sessions for later consultation.

The model must allow rotativity of the mediators, whose rules are discussed by all the actors in the joint initial session (1st session attended).

In terms of video/audio functionality, all those online must always be able to see the orator.

E-mail service for sending and receiving messages (which can be configured with already existing accounts or allow accounts to be created), as well as the sending of an automatic announcement of all the insertions in the system's collaboration tools.

The *blog* is a personal space in which any kind of annex can be placed. It must allow comments on the author's messages to be inserted. Divulgation on the net is optional.

The *wiki* must have its normal functionalities of linking pages, folders management, authorisations for editing and profiles of use.

The *announcements* can be edited by all the participants and allows important message to be divulged throughout the course. New messages, as well as new contents inserted since the last access, are indicated via a pop-up window that appears when the environment is accessed.

d) *User support* - The *tutorial* consists of animated demonstrations of the system's functionalities. These animations are granular and in swf format, but are also available in pdf format for printing.

The *helpdesk* service is provided by phone between 9am and 7pm. After this time, it is suggested that the Q&A functionality be used. Access to the FAQs should be always available.

This service is provided by a technician, a specialist on the platform. Ideally, this technician should know all about the learning contexts.

The *FAQs* functionality allows questions and answers to be inserted, compiled and edited.

Questions and Answers - As a question is sent, a search is made in the FAQ suggesting an answer: if this does not solve the question, it can be sent to the person responsible. Once the learner's questions are answered, the person responsible can forward the question/answer to the FAQ so that the FAQ can be compiled.

3.3 Specifications of the Actors´ Profiles

We consider four types of actors, namely the coordinator, the moderator, the learners and the technician, whose profiles we will now characterise.

The *coordinator* defines the thematic context of the course, the assessment and the dynamics of the moderator. S/he can also choose the tools of communication and collaboration that s/he considers relevant to the course context.

The *moderator* is responsible for the group dynamics; s/he activates the forums, the online sessions and the wiki structure, writes the comments to each learner's contributions to the forum, indicating the most complete aspects and the aspects to reconsider; s/he comments weekly on each learner's blog; s/he defines the schedule for presenting the project proposals in the 5th week; clarifies the learners whenever requested by videoconference or e-mail. S/he is a specialist in the theme of the course and has skills in using the tools of e-learning and in e-moderating.

The feedback that the moderator must give each learner related to the answers to the questions raised in the forum is crucial in supporting the construction of each person's knowledge. This support [3, 23] also extends to the comments to be made on the blogs and the projects.

The moderator must provide an hour every day for interaction through videoconferencing in order to clarify learners' questions, particularly during the project development phase.

The moderator makes the assessment defined by the coordinator, which may mean analysing participations from the learners in the forums, blogs, wiki and project.

The *learner* must be a determined, autonomous person who wants to search for information and likes learning collaboratively or feels the need to learn by learning collaboratively. S/he plays an active role in his/her learning and that of others, even moderating momentarily the synchronous session, particularly during the presentation and discussion of the group work. S/he plays a crucial role in the dynamic to be given to the course and to the learning context of group-class and to the group-project.

The *technician*, who is a specialist in the platform and knows the course, supports the helpdesk, the Questions sent and the FAQs. S/he plays a mainly technical support role, but is highly relevant in the learner's integration into the COLM.

4 Conclusion

The proposed model is based on a theoretical framework, on the experience of the members of the group and on the reflection on learning contexts.

The courses structured in the COLM and following the principles explained will enable mastery of the use of synchronous and asynchronous communication tools; they will allow the manipulation of the tools of collaboration; experimentation and identification phases of group dynamics; collaborative production of a project; and control of the specific themes of each course.

We believe that with the dynamics created in COLM, some of its learners will continue to interact after the end of the course, given that the context evolves and is recreated in new contexts.

References

1. Abercrombie M. (1979) Aims and Techniques of Group Teaching. R.H.E
2. Brown, J., Collins, A., Duguid, P. (1989) Situated cognition and the culture of learning. Educational Researcher 18, 1: 32-42
3. Bruner, J. (1973) Going Beyond the Information Given. Norton, New York
4. Carvalho A., Pinto C., Pereira V. (2004) Desenvolver a Flexibilidade Cognitiva através da Desconstrução e da Reflexão. In Actas E-LES' 2004 – E-Learning no Ensino Superior. Universidade de Aveiro, Aveiro
5. Cognition and Technology Group at Vanderbilt (1993) Anchored Instruction and Situated Cognition Revisited. Educational Technology 33, n° 3: 52–70
6. Collins, A., Brown, J., Newman, S. (1989) Cognitive Apprenticeship: Teaching the Crafts of Reading, Writing and Mathematics. In L. Resnick (ed.) Knowing, Learning, and Instruction. Lawrence Erlbaum Associates, Hillsdale, New Jersey
7. Dillenbourg P. (1999) Introduction: What do you Mean by: "Collaborative Learning". In Dillenbourg P. (ed.) Collaborative Learning: Cognitive and Computational Approaches. Pergamon, Amsterdam, pp. 1–19
8. Figueiredo A., Afonso A. (2006) Context and Learning: A Philosophical Framework. In: A. Figueiredo, A. Afonso (eds.) Managing Learning in Virtual Settings: The Role of Context. Idea Group Publishing, Hershey, PA, USA
9. Fosnot C. (1996) Construtivismo: uma teoria psicológica da aprendizagem. In: C. Fosnot (ed.) Construtivismo e Educação. Instituto Piaget, Lisboa, pp. 23–58
10. Johnson D., Johnson R. (1996) Cooperation and the Use of Technology. In: D. H Jonassen (ed.) Handbook of Research for Educational Communications and Technology: A Project of the Association for Educational Communications and Technology. Simon & Schuster Macmillan, New York, pp. 1017–1018
11. Knowles M. (1984) The Adult Learner: A Neglected Species (3rd Ed.). Gulf Publishing, Houston, TX
12. Knowles, M. (1975) Self-directed learning – a guide for learners and teachers, Englewood Cliffs, NJ: Prentice Hall
13. Lave J., Wenger E. (1991) Situated Learning: Legitimate Peripheral participation. Cambridge University Press, Cambridge
14. Little, D. (1991) Learner Autonomy. Definitions, Issues and Problems. Autentik Language Learning Resources, Dublin
15. Moore M. (1993) Theory of Transactional Distance. In: D. Keegan (ed.) Theoretical Principles of Distance Education. Routledge, London, pp. 22–38
16. Morin E. (1990) Introdução ao Pensamento Complexo. Instituto Piaget, Lisboa

17. Norman D. A. (1993) Cognition in the Head and in the World: An Introduction to the Special Issue on Situated Action. Cognitive Science 17, n° 1: 1–6
18. Novak J., Gowin D. B. (1984) Learning How to Learn. Cambridge University Press, Cambridge, UK
19. Powell, P. (2003) Qualidade e Inovação no Ensino: a aprendizagem cooperativa e por projectos como metodologia de ensino aprendizagem. Aacção de formação realizada na Universidade do Minho de 28 de Janeiro a 6 de Fevereiro
20. Pozo, J. (1994) Teorías cognitivas del aprendizaje. Morata, Madrid
21. Rogers, C. (1977) Liberdade Para Aprender. Interlivros, Belo Horizonte
22. Rogers, C. (1985) Tornar-se pessoa. Moraes Editora, Lisboa
23. Salmon G. (2003) E-Moderating: The Key to Teaching and Learning Online. Routledge, London
24. Spiro R., Coulson R., Feltovich P., Anderson D. (1988) Cognitive Flexibility Theory: Advanced Knowledge Aquisition in Ill-Structured Domains. In: Tenth Annual Conference of the Cognitive Science Society. Erlbaum, Hillsdale, NJ, pp. 375–383.
25. Tella S., Mononen-Aaltonen M., Kynäslahti H., Nummi T., Passi A., Ristola R., Sariola J., Vahtivuori S.,Wager P (1998) Towards a Communal Curriculum: Strategic Planning and the Emerging Knowledge of Media Education. Media Education Publications 8, Media Education Centre, Department of Teacher Education, University of Helsinki., pp. 1–83
26. Tuckman B., Jensen M. (1977) Stages of small group development. Group and Organizational Studies 2: 419–427
27. von Glasersfeld E. (1989) Cognition, Construction of Knowledge, and Teaching. Synthese 80: 121–140
28. von Glasersfeld E. (1996) Introdução: aspectos do construtivismo. In: C. Fosnot (ed.) Construtivismo e Educação. Instituto Piaget, Lisboa, pp. 15–21

School Web Pages and Writing: From Product Exhibition to Knowledge Construction

Luís Barbeiro

School of Education, Polytechnic Institute of Leiria, Portugal
barbeiro@esel.ipleiria.pt

1 Introduction

Word processors have put at our disposal not only a great versatility concerning the writing process, but also new resources to give shape to the graphic design of the written product. This way, besides the motivational factor associated to the use of this technology, the relationship with writing has changed, concerning the process, the visual aspect of the written product and the functions attributed to students' texts.

During the process of writing a text, reformulation and revision have become possible throughout the whole process, without any signs of changes made and without the need of copying the whole text over again. This possibility potentiates the recursive nature of the writing process [8, 9], in other words, the reactivation of planning and composing components, while revising the portion of text already written. Consequently, it favours the introduction of new elements that were not initially considered and the elimination of others that did not turn out to be consistent [1, 4].

In relation to the written product, the joint use of the computer and then printer makes the text available on paper. The immensity of graphic resources brought forward with the computer, made it possible, without resorting to the art of typography, to move the students' texts closer to the texts written by professionals in terms of visual design [11]. This formal progress opened new horizons in the construction of a relationship between students and writing, based on the diffusion of their texts in the community.

In a second moment, the one that we are at, besides the printer and the diffusion of texts using paper, a new means of diffusion came about: the Internet. In this text, we will analyse the new prospects and the new challenges that this means activates in relation to writing and in relation to the contribution of writing to the construction of knowledge.

The availability of access to the Internet in schools has been the main objective of some important projects in recent years. In Portugal we can point out in this domain "The Supervision of the Educational Use of the Internet in Public Elementary Schools Program" or Internet@EB1, developed from February 2002 on. The aim of this programme consisted in increasing the educational use of the Internet among teachers and students of elementary schools (grades 1 to 4) [7].

The Internet has great potential in various dimensions of the educational process: the access to information provided on the web, the communication among schools and with other educational partners, through e-mails and chats, and also the active participation of students with contributions that are put at everyone's disposal on the school web page.

Web designing of school web pages constitutes a fundamental pillar of the project. As it can be read on the evaluation report of the program (2004), the number of elementary schools with web pages was 709 before the program, and reached the number of 6,032 new pages at the end.

After designing the web pages, the new challenge will be to integrate them in the educational process. The question is to know up until what point its power is being put to use. Specifically, in what concerns writing, school web pages have a great potential for the diffusion of students' texts. This way they present an opportunity to develop students' sense of audience and to activate students' resources to represent knowledge.

Our aim is to characterize the school web pages, as a means of publishing the students' texts and as a way of activating the contribution of writing to the process of learning.

2 Method

To be able to grasp the great educational potential being put to use, through the presence of written texts in the school web pages, we analysed a group of elementary school web pages that participated in the Internet@EB1 program. We chose elementary schools because, in the first place, they were the specific addressees of the referred program, which included both the construction and the maintenance facets of their own web pages. In second place, the existence of a generic teacher, that controls the teaching and learning process in different areas, may enhance the articulation between writing and the learning process in other domains. In Portugal, after the fourth grade of elementary school, the fact that there are teachers for each subject may give rise to different perspectives concerning the learning strategies, if there is not a profound coordination among teachers, in terms of the projects to be developed. Moreover, the work developed in the first four years of schooling takes roots in the work that will be developed afterwards especially in terms of the discovery of the functions associated to writing.

The study fell upon a sample of schools from the central region of Portugal. The sample included the total number of schools with a web page belonging to five municipalities of a district from this region, constituted by 212 schools from a total 231 in the five municipalities. These municipalities vary in terms of size, ranging from a big to a small dimension, and they cover different social, economic and cultural realities, including urban, industrial and predominantly rural areas. The schools not included in this study were so because they did not have an active web page at the moment the study was being carried out. There are 547 elementary schools (grades 1 to 4) in the whole district.

The data was gathered by visiting the school web pages between the 10th and 14th March 2005. The contents were available from the school year 2002/2003 onwards, year in which the Internet@EB1 was implemented. However, it is not always possible to identify the school year which the web contents refer to.

This study considers the presence of texts written by students in the school web pages and relates them with two main pedagogical perspectives: the exhibition of the products created in the learning process and/or the expression of the learning process itself. The indicators considered were the number of texts and their categorization according to the textual genre. The categories mobilized in the genre analysis included stories, expressive texts, reports, expository texts, related to specific contents of the school subjects, besides other genres such as the presentation of the school or the neighbourhood, news articles, and so on.

3 Findings and Discussion

Considering the total 212 web pages under analysis, we found 762 texts produced by the students themselves (the teacher's role, even if very important for the final version of the text, does not hinder the student's authorship to the exterior). The number of texts in each school is significantly different. A fourth of the schools did not present any sort of text from the beginning.

A significant number of other schools, about a third, presented very few texts (1 to 3). In many cases, the publication was limited to the first postings made with the first impulse of the program. Only in a minority of cases do the students post their texts regularly. The highest number of texts is 38, the majority of which (35) concern the school year 2004/05 (between October and March) and are due to the particular interest of a teacher who created and stimulated the posting of texts on a blog.

The relevance given to events that do not belong to the student's daily routine constitute one of the most important motivations for the publication of texts on the school web pages. In this way, school trips, activities concerning festivities and celebrations such as the "Magusto" (in which a fire is lit to roast chestnuts), a carnival parade, and so on, are generally a motive to produce written texts. These texts find a natural place for publication on the school web page. The report/ description of events as the ones mentioned above constituted the most frequent genre (29%).

The texts with an expressive nature constituted the second most frequent and most diffused type of text (21%). They mainly include poems or prose that describe likes and personal views in relation to diverse themes such as the seasons of the year, school, Christmas, friendship, violence, war, natural catastrophes, pollution, Nature, Father's Day, Mother's Day, Children's Day, and so on. The next genres are stories created by children (14%), expository texts (13%) and texts presenting the school or the class to the visitors (10%). The less frequent genres include short news articles announcing forthcoming events (4%), reports of experiments and formal or informal learning experiences (3%) and some other genres, such as letters (for example, letters to Santa Claus) rhymes, lyrics invented by children, etc.

The diffusion of texts can be made considering primarily the perspective of the product. In this perspective, the inclusion of the texts on the web page corresponds to the manifestation of the result of a learning process, in other words, to the diffusion of the obtained product. This perspective stands out in the publication of stories and expressive texts produced by the students.

One of the advantages of the school web page is that it allows students to publish texts of genres associated, in our society, to the status of a real "author". This is a dimension that is present in many expressive texts, namely poetic texts, and which is relevant in the case of stories, too. Through the school web page, the student's creative texts are not confined to the class; they can reach a vaster community. This way, students experience the role of an "author", a "writer". Rather than be a social status only of a few, the status of a "writer" can be primarily a feeling experienced in relation to language [2]. The learning community that the school itself constitutes can offer that experience, that feeling of authorship, when diffusing the student's texts in a community, be it through books, the school newspaper, or now through the school web page.

On the other hand, texts and the school web page can show what happens in school life, concerning not only the major events, reflected in news and reports, but also the events through which the process of learning takes place on a daily basis. According to this perspective, learning is an activity that mobilizes mediating tools: resources, tasks, actions, and so on [6, 10]. This activity and the role the different elements in knowledge reconstruction can be made explicit through language. The act of making explicit the elements and actions of the learning activity is, in itself, an instrument of learning. Major events, such as trips, calendar festivities and so on, have their own relevance in school life. Naturally, the texts describing them find their place in the school web page. When the decision made is to post texts referring to the daily activity of learning, it is the activity of knowledge reconstruction itself that is valued.

Among the variety of genres referred to, we can find some texts whose main purpose is to express the knowledge acquired in the different school subjects.

The texts that express knowledge here considered can take the form of expository texts, narrative texts that explicitly present the knowledge that is being studied and descriptions of the learning process.

In relation to texts that express knowledge, the diffusion of the product itself also stands out. This happens in the case of expository texts and narrations that present knowledge. In the first case, the textual product concerns the expression of a declarative knowledge related to the themes that are being studied. This kind of texts is similar to expository texts of an encyclopaedic nature. In the second case, the knowledge is activated and expressed inside the narrative that is produced to represent that knowledge. The students write stories and plays that put to use the contents learned. Besides these cases, in which relevance is given to the final text as a manifestation of knowledge, emphasis can also be put on the expression of the process itself through which the students build their knowledge. In this case, we are in the presence of learning descriptions, which are very similar to learning diaries.

These three categories that are linked to the expression of knowledge attain different levels of frequency. The texts with an expository nature prevail widely, in comparison to texts that represent knowledge using narratives or that adopt the perspective of making explicit the process of learning, as we can see in the graph of Fig. 1.

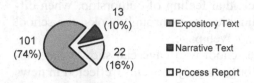

Fig. 1. Expression of knowledge

Concerning the expository texts, after performing the necessary research, the students write texts that fall upon themes dealt with in their different subjects: the seasons of the year, the respiratory system, the Romans, the water cycle, etc. The Internet is a means of research, presenting a variety of sources of information, besides the ones provided in the classroom. It also enables the extension of resources and modes of representation, namely images. Besides language, students' expository texts often include images and scanned drawings, reinforcing the multimodal nature of written documents [10].

In relation to the narratives that seek to illustrate knowledge, we found, for example, stories that give life to the water cycle, resorting to the adventures of a water drop, a story that centres around learning about the digestive system resorting to the adventures of a piece of bread, and a story that narrates the life of a chestnut, employing the perspective "If I were a chestnut…". These stories constitute, in an equal manner, a textual product that, as such, is linked to narration and knowledge representation.

In the expository texts, the students' work is mainly oriented to the search for information in varied sources. Their tasks consist fundamentally in the selection, organization and making knowledge explicit, having in this way a limited role in the construction of knowledge itself. The proximity to the knowledge results from the fact that students are the authors of the text that expresses it.

The narratives enable the enforcement of the proximity between students and knowledge. In the first place, the possibility of student intervention is increased, as there is a component of creativity that conjugates the acquisition of knowledge with its application to the characters, the setting and the plot of the story. The student's creative and decision-making space extends to these elements. In second place, the narratives constructed around learning contents leave a place open to subjectivity, the expression of emotional aspects and attitudes, which also take part in the learning process. In fact, the characters, even when they correspond to elements of nature, frequently take on human characteristics, have feelings and emotions, on which the students project themselves. In the case of the learning reports/descriptions, it is the proximity between the subject and knowledge itself that is made explicit. This report/description allows for the emergence of the events of the daily routine together with the discovery and construction of knowledge. The perspective taken on is that of the learners who observe, discover, develop projects, find difficulties, come to conclusions and turn to writing to express the knowledge they constructed through these processes.

We found texts that present descriptions on how students reached knowledge: through research, interviews, visits from different people, observations and achievements throughout the projects with a longer temporal duration. Knowledge is contextualized in terms of the situations that students live and in which they participate. Thus, for example, the rearing of silkworms provides for the recording of not only the observation of the transformations but also how the students experienced them. The same happens when the students build an aquatic environment. The treading of grapes also originates new experiences, together with the visit of the owner of the vineyard and the assembly of a glossary, which results from the students' research. The re-use of garbage to make toys gives origin to texts that talk about the built toys, the parents and relatives' cooperation and their visits to school to talk about the toys. The different possibilities concerning the origin of the town or village's name are expressed together with the report of the interviews made with the elderly of the town or village.

Writing itself can constitute the motive for that "expression". In this way, we found a text that tells of the difficulties encountered to write a text according to a challenge put forward by uARTE (an entity whose role was to give life to the pedagogical facet of the program): the writing of a text with exactly 77 words.

The learning process also lets itself get carried away by the unexpected events of the daily routine, such as a spider that came down its web from the ceiling to the board and then moved around as if it was trying to put the letters together in such a way as to form words.

In the learning reports/ descriptions, although a textual product is obtained, the process acquires relevance. In relation to projects with a longer duration, such as the rearing of silkworms, the written record of events throughout the project are normally contemplated. These records are valued as learning factors and as products that can be published or preserved among the class documents. The school web page enforced the challenge of extending the description of events not only to the major ones but also to the daily activities at school through which knowledge is reconstructed. Once they are posted, they do not wear out just because there has been progress to another topic of the curriculum. Instead, they remain as narratives of the findings for the reader/visitor. On the other hand, contrarily to the means based on the multiplication of copies, their circulation does not originate additional costs when the space of the web page is already available. When publishing on the web page is included from the beginning of the pedagogical project, it enforces the role of this kind of report/description itself in the learning process. Publishing adds intentionality and communicative purpose to the representational means. This enables students to get hold of the benefits writing has to offer, as a representational and communicational resource combined with other modes in the web page [10]. It shows the community students as learners in the process of reconstructing knowledge and values their accomplishments in this process. Publishing on the web page can constitute a means to activate the presence of writing in the pedagogical project, linking these two dimensions: representation and communication of knowledge. In recent years, blogs have come to reinforce these prospects. They call to the participation and interaction with other elements of the community. Commentaries do not constitute the only contributions. Visitors can also send personal texts, chosen so as to participate and interact with the students, as in the case of the blog already mentioned.

Interaction can also take place horizontally, beyond the class. The community of learners can be extended through the interaction with other schools, resorting to e-mails and chats. In some web pages, we can see that type of communication, which can lead not only to the exchange of texts and other products, but also to the execution of joint work, such as the writing of stories [3].

4 Conclusion

The designing of school web pages, in elementary school (grades 1 to 4) constitutes one of the aims of the program Internet@EB1, put into practice in Portugal in the last few years. The analysis of the web pages showed us the activation of some potential of the use of computers in the teaching and learning process and it allows for the opening of doors for the development of that potential. As a means of diffusing developed products, many school web pages have been used to publish student texts, to some extent. Poems and other expressive texts, stories, reports about school trips and festivities found in the school web page a means to be spread to a wider community and to develop students' sense of audience. The texts gain a purpose and function that is not limited to the teacher's marking. However, the fact that there are still many schools that do not take advantage of the possibility of spreading information and the small number of texts that are made present in the web pages show us the urgency in encouraging this potential.

The diffusion of developed products, through this new means, does not represent its only potential, as we can see in Duarte et al. [5]. School web pages can open doors to learning. In this way, it is not only the product in itself but also the path that led to its construction that can be made explicit through writing and published in the school web page, with reflexes on learning. Thus, besides the presence of the textual product, a pedagogical strategy based on the connection between writing and the web page can be put into practice. This strategy reinforces the role of the contextual information that accompanies the texts themselves and the role of the descriptions of the lived experiences during the process of knowledge construction. In these reports/descriptions we can find the explicitation of the initial choices, the alternatives considered, the tasks executed, the problems that appeared, the decisions made and the changes in course throughout the process, the level of satisfaction in the end, the critiques gathered, and so on.

The school web pages constitute windows that allow us to glimpse the learning activity that takes place in school, as we said, and constitute at the same time a mirror, that gives a reflection to both its sides: the student side and the community side. On the students' side, the verbalization of the daily learning experiences makes it possible to show the others what they have learned and, as a mirror, it also allows the students themselves to become conscious of it. On the wider community's side, the publication of texts allows people to discover and accompany learning. But it also allows us to see ourselves as participants, as the interaction with students, the sending of comments and other contributions through e-mail, that make us active elements in their learning community, is made possible. Besides the potential of the computer as a writing tool, which has been focused on the last few decades, the challenge today consists in profiting from the potential of these information and communication technologies, in particular the Internet, to construct a learning community settled on a two-sided participation. On the one hand, we have the participation of the students in the surrounding community, which can be achieved through their texts. On the other hand, we have the participation of the community in the construction of knowledge, as active addressees of those texts, which visit the web page and can find there a possibility of interaction, enriching the students' learning experiences.

Besides the initial impulse, that gave way to the first few steps and made possible the diffusion of texts in many schools, it is necessary a new impulse, which responds to the challenge of integrating the school web page, in all its potential, in the pedagogical project itself on a day-to-day basis.

Acknowledgments

This research is part of the project "Writing – Knowledge Acquisition and Expression", supported by FCT – Fundação para a Ciência e Tecnologia (POCI/CED/69155/2004)

References

1. Barbeiro L (1990) O processo de escrita e o computador. Revista Portuguesa de Educação 3:139–149
2. Barbeiro L (2004) Oficinas de escrita: Trabalhar a linguagem, dizer a linguagem. In: I Encontro Nacional de Oficinas de Escrita. Universidade de Aveiro, Aveiro (in press)
3. Barbeiro L (2005) Writing in a circle of stories. The Reading Teacher 59:380–382
4. Carvalho JAB (2001) O computador e a escrita – algumas reflexões. In: Dias P, Freitas CV (orgs) Desafios 2001 Actas da II Conferência Internacional de Tecnologias de Informação e Comunicação na Educação. Centro de Competência Nónio Séc. XXI, Braga, pp 683–691
5. Duarte JA, Marques T, Tomás A, Pereira MI (2002) As TIC nos primeiros anos de escolaridade. In: Ponte JP (org) A formação para a integração das TIC na educação pré-escolar e no 1.º ciclo do ensino básico. Porto Editora, INAFOP, Porto, INAFOP, pp 40–48
6. Engestrom R (1987) Learning by expanding: An activity theoretical approach to developmental research. Orienta-Konsultit Oy , Helsinki
7. Figueiredo A, Afonso A, Ferreira A (2004) Programa de Acompanhamento da Utilização Educativa da Internet nas Escolas Públicas do 1.º Ciclo do Ensino Básico – Relatório de Avaliação", IPNlis.
8. Flower L, Hayes J (1981) A cognitive process theory of writing. College Composition and Communication 32:365–87
9. Humes A (1983) Research on the composing process. Review of Educational Research 53:201–216
10. Jewitt C (2006) Technology, literacy and learning. Routledge, London
11. Sharples M (1999) How we write: writing as a creative design. Routledge, London

Taking Advantage of the Web in the Portuguese Class: An Experience

Adelina Moura

Escola Profissional de Braga
adelinam@netcabo.pt

1 Introduction

The Internet has transformed our world. The technological marvel of the Internet allows us to communicate, search information, transfer data, learn and share knowledge easier and faster than ever before. Bearing this in mind, the computer network can transform teaching and learning in the classroom.

Despite being difficult to change the actual teaching methods, it is believed that new stages have to be taken into the right direction in order to get a positive feedback both from teachers and students [8].

So that we can face the challenge of the new technologies inside the classroom, we will study their impact on society and on school as well. The students' skills and their learning environment will also be under examination.

We began the project "Portuguese onlinc" during the school year of 2003/2004 at the Professional School of Braga. As mentioned before, our main aim was using the Internet more effectively in the Portuguese subject teaching, always focusing on a new and positive perspective. As a result, we set up a different web site for each class, allowing the students an easy access to the contents of each Module.

We let students work in pairs and showed the greatest respect for their own learning rhythm. The students' positive response greatly encouraged us to continue working in such a recent and innovative experience.

2 ICT – A Useful in the Learning/Teaching Process

The deep transformations that came with the accelerated insertion of ICT in our present society have inevitably changed the way people work, their lifestyles and hobbies, their relations and also their perception of the world around them. In what concerns the socio-educational context, the new trend to take specialization courses is just not enough, since educators are now required to be versatile, self-assured, capable of facing and solving new situations, finding and using relevant information, criticising and assessing results. Moreover, the role of school is repeatedly brought into question; preparing our students for the future is quite a hard task as the prospects concerning the job market loom large. School, more than ever, has to be technologically updated and reorganized, in order to meet the social needs of a fast running world.

Not only will ICT in the classroom require the development of different skills, as interaction and self-interest, but they will also demand the physical, emotional and social development of the participants. Therefore, bearing in mind the utmost importance of ICT attached to their role of informing and being informed, communicating and sharing ideas, they are believed [1] to be fundamental at school worldwide.

On the other hand, the students will be able to bear the acquired knowledge in mind and put it in practice later on. They will behave differently and will be capable of solving new problems. For this reason, the new achievements provided by this learning process are to be underlined.

As far as the collaborative learning is concerned, the student's motivation, self-esteem, responsibility, organization, interaction and communication [5] are promoted by ICT, which, additionally, encourage discussions and activities leading to the actual writing process. The Internet is an effective source of information, communication and publishing means, both for students and teachers. Furthermore, it is a powerful pedagogical tool, as all multimedia applications converge into the Internet and its World Wide Web. The computer-based learning allows participants to learn all they need in the different areas and subjects, either sharing new didactic proposals or innovative projects of regional, national, and international partnerships, allowing teachers to be involved with others globally [2].

However, being the Internet such a powerful technology, how far can it provide a substantial learning and promote a successful schooling? Actually, the growing influence of the Internet on education is the object of study of educators, who continuously reflect on its implications. Some studies [3] have been carried out in order to draw conclusions from this matter. In spite of the positive prospects regarding the use of ICT in the classroom, a long and careful assessment is still to be conducted. Yet, the growing enthusiasm of children and adolescents for the use of ICT on a daily basis develops our increasing awareness of the importance of the Internet in the classroom.

3 Describing the Experience

Being acutely aware that we live in a new era, be it called "global village" or "knowledge society", we were urged to incorporate ICT in the Portuguese subject at school. As a consequence, priority was given to the development of technological competences and multimedia applications so as to achieve the objectives included in the Portuguese language syllabus. We were aimed at finding cognitive and metacognitive strategies that led the student to reflect on one's learning, to pursue one's quest for knowledge through experience and to properly exercise his own judgement.

Therefore, we firstly focused on the organization and presentation of the contents, next on their quality, suitability and graphic design, and lastly on the self and peer evaluation as well as the adequacy of the different communication aids.

Taking into account that information and knowledge are quite distinctive categories, the student's crossing from one to the other is to be carefully contemplated. Information includes facts, observations and sensations, whereas knowledge, in contrast, is the human experience of information. It's often unclear to precisely determine where information crosses into the realm of knowledge. The crossing only occurs when the content conveyed by the information gets involved with our own experience, thus becoming our own knowledge.

Bearing this spectrum in mind, we decided to adopt a new teaching methodology. The cross-disciplinary objectives of each class curriculum, as well as the previously mentioned capacity of transforming information into knowledge were the basic principles of this new methodology aimed at guiding students through their task of "learning to learn".

The Modules were set up according to the elaborated objectives, each class different features and the devised learning/teaching methodology.

Consequently, each Module was structured following the contents of the Module Plan for the Portuguese subject and the peculiarity of the themes to be dealt with. As far as possible the methodologies and pedagogical tools were used differently and according to each learning situation. We made use of a set of interactive pedagogical materials, as diverse and appropriated as possible, creating our own which were to be uploaded and published on the Web. The Web Quest, Web Treasure Hunt and Virtual Tours were some of the selected tools. The Hot potatoes program also provided other activities, such as the multiple choice, short answer, blank filling and matching exercises.

Emphasis must be placed on the module-based development system of the Professional School, allowing a greater respect for the students' rhythm and a significant flexibility towards the structured contents.

In order to work out these ideas, each class was housed in a website learning platform whose addresses are: www.portuguesonline.no.sapo.pt (10th form); www.aulaportuguesonline.no.sapo.pt (11th form); www.aulaportugues.no.sapo.pt (12th form).

3.1 Blog, Forum and Chat Room: Pedagogical Tools

The time lying between the creation of a new technology and its availability and dissemination in society is widely decreasing. That's the reason why all the participants involved in education should take advantage of the new technological opportunities [4].

The blogosphere, the discussion forums and the chat rooms are only three of the web tools gaining considerable ground as a means of gathering information and establishing collaborative knowledge environments.

Early-adopters are beginning to explore the use of the blogs as a teaching/learning tool in educational environments. Actually, this genre seems to be an excellent emerging tool professed by the constructivist learning theory. Both teachers and students may take advantage of this dynamic information tool, create a learning community and promote the development of better communication skills at school. The students may maximize their own insights on the topics, share them, reflect on what they have learned and improve their social and personal attitudes. Thanks to weblogs they are allowed to submerge into a more active and dynamic learning environment. Blogs add another dimension to education because, besides helping students to synthesize what they are learning, as well as articulate and reflect on it, the students' insights are easily published online for free.

Blogging in education is already a very sound didactic and pedagogical tool since the students are given the opportunity to confront the theoretical concepts with the social, moral and political realities of life. This online resource promotes students' writing skills. The class will not necessarily end with the school bell ringing, students and teachers may continue their spirited discussions on the topic beyond the class time. Blogs are expected to greatly motivate students to write and express their feelings on several matters [7].

One of the potentials of weblogs is their ability to promote the high level thinking and the flexibility of the learning/teaching process aside from motivation, interaction, investigation and creativity. On the other hand, it improves the relationship between teacher and student.

For teachers the blogs are one of the most attractive tools for they require little effort to maintain, less than webpages. After having been created, one only has to type a text into a text box, add a selected picture and publish it with just a button click; everything is prepared to facilitate the use of this technology.

Besides blogs, the forum is an ideal means for the students to share and express opinions and feelings, comment on a specific subject and to publish a text.

The chat, on the other hand, allows the virtual meeting with others, through instant communication worldwide. So, to take advantage of this highlighted tool is a school imperative.

It seems the potential of these working tools is unlimited, except on the teacher's mind.

3.2 Implemented Approaches

A blog was set up for each class in order to provide a public space for discussing and publishing the works done in class. Both the 10th Form ttp://trolhasengenheiras.blogspot.com, and the 12th Form http.//somosinformaticos.blogspot.com blogs are run by students; in fact, they are the ones who post their works, leave constructive comments on each other posts, assess their peer's works, suggest possible next steps to the works created by their classmates and report on them.

As blog users in the classroom, teachers think they actually provide a meaningful feedback faster than before, being able to instantly react to the works posting. Pupils can also provide feedback on each other's works, as they are available for others to read and respond to. Aside from this, pupils work a lot harder knowing that their posts are not just for the school but truly public. As witnessed by one of our pupils whose parents live abroad, it is now much easier for them to keep pace with her progress in the Portuguese subject on a continuous basis. That's the reason why pupils try harder to do a fairly good work, asking teachers to edit and provide feedback before posting them [6].

The forum, also put in practice, helps to consolidate both the teacher and the pupil's role in the learning/teaching experience, being the first an optimizer of the process and the second a more interactive participant. Viewing the forum as a meaningful technology, we tried to promote a critical spirit, proposing topics on a week basis, such as the reflection on one's own learning, the successful and unsuccessful educational system, the Internet safety and others.

Thanks to the chat technology, students could meet professor Amélia Pais, an expert in Fernando Pessoa and Luís de Camões, who answered queries about the authors already studied in class.

Despite being early-adopters of the referred teaching tools, we truly acknowledge some of their potentialities and the plethora of advantages they offer.

3.3 The Teacher's Opinion

Trying not to be too exhaustive, we will only present the fundamental advantages of ICT in the educational system, considering our own experience.

It is a fact that information is easily accessed on the web. Wherever they are, students may search the web on their own for resources. As a consequence, they are now actively involved in their learning experience, building up their own knowledge, achieving their autonomy as learners. Students resort to various information sources, select those that are likely to provide the suitable answers and then reorganize them so that they can be disseminated.

Provided that computers are connected to the Internet, a complete and comprehensive set of information is at once supplied to the student. This way, the student's ideas can be enriched by his motivation and enthusiasm when visualizing new and valuable information on the subject topic.

As students can combine the multimedia applications, the pedagogical software and other resources, they are stimulated to work more efficiently, improving competences and technical expertise in multimedia applications and technologies.

When teachers create a site, including all the structured subject contents concerning the module, it is their first purpose to improve the classes quality and, secondly, to monitor the student in his performance, through an organized and directed search, avoiding the hyperlinks complexity and thus saving his time. The technology is used to get and manipulate information, enhancing the student's learning experience. The MS Word, the MS Excel and the databases are the software the students are able to make the best use of.

Students' motivation can increase with the use of interesting activities, like game playing, to introduce and reinforce concepts and contents learned, which otherwise would be tedious and difficult to assimilate.

Students are actively involved in the classroom activities. As their work shows positive results they are encouraged and motivated to learn and remove any constraints. Doing their research in a more flexible environment helps them to develop new literacies and e-learning competences.

3.4 Students' Reactions

Projects will not be viable unless they are assessed. We were particularly curious about the pupils' judgements on this learning/teaching experience. Therefore, the forum was the elected tool to collect the pupils' judgements on the Portuguese subject and other matters, throughout the previous school year and the actual one. Every week a new topic was posed for the pupils so that we might collect their opinions.

From the forty-five answers to the topic "The learning/teaching experience assessment" we report the following (Table 1):

Table 1. The learning/teaching experience assessment

Categories	Percentage
Positive and pleasant feedback	67
New experience and different learning/teaching methodology	29
Motivates and encourages participation	22
Improves final results	11

The experience was reported to have been truly enjoyable and positively assessed by thirty pupils; it was considered a new pedagogical experience by thirteen pupils; ten pupils evaluated it as capable of motivating and encouraging participation; five pupils referred to its capability of improving final results.

One of the students' opinion is believed to be worthy of register as it synthesizes the debated issue: "The Portuguese classes given this way are terrific, because as, nowadays, computers are the new trend, students are quite enthralled by the Portuguese classes and say they aren't as boring as the traditional ones".

On the "Advantages and disadvantages of working in pairs", the presented categories were considered either as favourable or unfavourable, as shown in Table 2:

Table 2. Working in Pairs

Advantages	Percentage	Disadvantages	Percentage
Easier, funny, interesting and less monotonous	63	Difficult to reach agreement	28
Good	38	One's ideas can't be put in practice	18
Sharing of ideas, interactivity	31	One of the members always works more	9
More efficient learning	18	More distractions and noise	6
Allows task division	13	Assessment isn't so objective	3

The answers to this topic involved thirty-two pupils; twenty of them indicated the easiness, enjoyment and interest as favourable factors; twelve mentioned the benefits of working in pairs; the sharing of ideas and interactivity were distinguished by ten pupils; five considered the learning efficiency and four pointed out the importance of the task division and its benefits. As for the disadvantages, nine pupils referred to the conflicts and difficulty to reach agreement; it was stressed by five pupils that personal ideas are in disadvantage; three remarked that the work is uneven; the noisy environment and its effects were emphasized by two and one pupil called the attention to the lack of objectivity in the evaluation.

Table 3 shows, the categories concerning the 20 answers to the topic "Forum and Blog as pedagogical tools".

Table 3. Forum and Blog as Pedagogical Tools

Forum	Percentage	Blog	Percentage
Allows the sharing of opinions and ideas	85	Usefulness	65
Important and useful	65	Easy publishing	50
Dialogue freedom	25	Quick reading and critical spirit	25
Enhances reflection and critical spirit	15	Filing of works and activities	25
		Easy access to all works	15

As far as the forum is concerned, seventeen pupils pointed out that it allows the sharing of opinions and ideas; it was considered important and useful in the learning process by thirteen pupils and to allow dialogue freedom by ten pupils; three pupils gave emphasis to the promotion of critical spirit and reflection. As for the blog, thirteen pupils highlighted its usefulness; ten emphasized the easiness to post works; five mentioned the quickness at reading and criticising the classmates' works; five recognized its value as a filing tool and three remarked on the easiness to access all the works.

A student's comment is thought to be relevant: "In my opinion both the blog and the forum are useful tools in the classroom. Everyone's works, opinions and personal overviews are easily accessed and shared".

In brief, all the students share a positive opinion concerning the use of these tools in the Portuguese subject.

4 Conclusion

The proposed it is our overall goal to emphasise the key role of ICT in the educational process. Actually, the point in question isn't keeping up with the latest fashions or using cutting-edge technology, but the ways in which ICT enhances teaching and learning.

A reflection on the practical applications and implicit challenges of ICT is thought to be of much more importance than discussing their pros and cons. Their educational potentialities go from the simple distribution of information to the sophisticated learning tools.

Bearing in mind that the school is the mirror of the continuously changing society we live in, it was expected that the first would be the pioneer in some areas, namely in the proper use of ICT. However, it seems the gap, between what is happening inside and outside it, is bridging. But there is no doubt that they are the key to innovation and progress.

Their huge impact on education also brings about changes and uncertainties mainly at the beginning. Surely, their role as a means of communication and expression, capable of adding value and achieving successful outcomes is to be stressed. They shouldn't be regarded as a substitute in the teaching/learning practice, but as a fruitful complement. Having these principles in mind and taking into account the teacher's crucial role in the construction of knowledge, not only did we integrate the online communication and collaboration tools in the classroom, but we also encouraged students to reflect on their use. There has been a positive feedback on the methodology.

The buildings with classrooms and school bells are nowadays open and interactive learning avenues. The future does not depend on technical expertise; it rather lies on the repeatedly questioning of what is being done. Only by trying hard, will we evolve to effectively use new technologies, achieving creativity and better practical results.

Network allows data acquisition and sharing, but, we will not be better informed because we have access to so much information. It is our task to do the research, to analyse information, select and organize it. Such valuable and formative experiences will increase our knowledge.

References

1. Duin H, Hansen C (1994) Reading and Writing on Computer Network as Social Construction and Social Interaction. In Literacy and Computers: The Complicatins of Teaching and Learning with Techonoly. New York: The Modern Language Association of America, pp 89–112

2. Eça T (1998) NetAprendizagem: a Internet na Educação. Porto: Porto Editora
3. Gould, D (1980) Experiments on Composing Letters: Some Facts, Some Myths, and Some Observations. In Gregg, L.W. e Steinberg, E.R. Cognitive Processes in Writing. New Jersey: LEA, Hillsdale, pp 97–125
4. Gutierrez S (2003) Projeto Zaptlogs: as tecnologias educacionais informatizadas no trabalho de educadores, Porto Alegre: CINTED-UFRGS, pp 1–19. Available in: http://cinted.ufrgs.br/renote/set2003/artigos/projetoz aptlogs.pdf
5. Hedge T (2000) Writing. Oxford University Press
6. Jarraud F (2004) Enseigner et communiquer avec le Blogue. Available: http://www.cafepedagogique.net/disci/pratiques/54.php
7. Jeffrey S. (2004) In the Classroom, Web Logs Are the New Bulletin Boards. Available in: http://www.nytimes.com/2004/08/19/technology/circuits/ 19blog.html?ex=1250568000&en=33627811ca310596&ei=5090&partner=r ssuserland
8. Morgado C, Carvalho A (2004) Usufruir das mudanças curriculares para uma integração das TIC. Revista de Estudos Curriculares, Associação Portuguesa de Estudos Curriculares, Ano 2, n° 1, pp 85–120

Kitchen Science: Through the Window of the Web

Carla Morais, João Paiva

Faculty of Sciences of the University of Oporto
carlamorais@imediato.pt; jcpaiva@fc.up.pt;

1 (Re) Thinking the School with Information and Communication Technologies

1.1 The School of the 21st Century and the Students of the "Zap Generation"

> "*If you want to see the future of education, don't watch children in the average classroom. Watch children play a video game. You'll see them engaged; excited; interacting, and learning- even if it's only about how to get to the next level of the game*"[1].

School and its teaching-learning methods have undergone enormous alterations over time. From ancient Greek times, in which knowledge was passed on orally, to the appearance of the book, to modern times in which teaching and learning have a wide range of technologies at their service.

Information and communication technologies, supported by an authentic technological revolution, have come to stimulate true change in the educational field. Various metaphors have been used by different authors to explain the configuration of contemporary society using these technologies: "*global village*" (McLuhan), "*post-industrial society*" (Bell), "*post-capitalist society*" (Drucker), "*information society*" (Toffler), "*global web*" (Reich), "*infoera*" (Zuffo). [2] The large quantity of available information and the multiplicity of forms that it assumes characterise contemporary society, so that with effective (quick and flexible) access to vast sources of information, we assume a privileged position in terms of interaction with the world around us.

In this society, it no longer makes sense to memorise information, rather, privilege is given to the capacity to find information from the devices where it is stored and then to manipulate it. In this context, knowledge constitutes something that is under continuous construction, fruit of the multiple interconnections that are established and that are defined in this vast sea of information where we sail like fearless sea farers [3]. At the beginning of the 21st Century, these phenomena lead to some misgivings that pointed particularly to the field of education. The need to correspond to the complex demands stemming from this information era, which were imposed at every moment, was necessarily reflected in education thought and practice towards the definition of a new educational paradigm. Schools need to renew themselves in order to become more attractive to the young people of today, who have needs and interests that originate in the society in which they live.

Sociologists, particularly those linked to company marketing, have been studying and classifying the younger generations, attempting to define markets and evolutionary tendencies. Despite the risk of compartmentalising, it can make some sense to use the marketing perspectives to refer to the school population. Thus, pupils who currently attend primary and secondary schools in the 21st Century are frequently nicknamed the *zap generation*. There are other curious and very suggestive names for these pupils in Anglo-Saxon literature, like *e-generation, generation Z, net generation, homozappiens,* and *Nintendo generation* (as is widely known, Nintendo is a brand of electronic games based on microprocessors of a computer type especially "dedicated" to the task of running games) [1], [4]. The zap generation consists of young adults, born from middle of the 80s on. The main characteristic of the young people of this generation is that they were born grew up in the digital era. For them, the mobile phone, the computer, the Internet, cable TV, and hand-held game devices have been common ever since they were born. They couldn't manage without them and could not even conceive of their inexistence. The *zap generation* is used to "action", that is, they programme their time for a large range of activities, many of which are done simultaneously.

Their lives are a constant *zapping* – they flick though the dozens of cable TV channels with their TV command where the "navigate". They move over to the computer where they open their e-mail, they *surf* the net collecting data for homework projects and communicate with one another in the *chat* rooms. Meanwhile, they exchange SMS messages to confirm Saturday night out and have MTV show their favourite *video-clip* [4]. For these young people the big challenge is to select and organise the enormous quantity of pedagogical and scientific information there is on the

Internet. The quantity of information that reaches these students is enormous, but may not be proportional to the quality. Thus an educational objective is imposed, to induce the students to make a critical analysis of all the information to which they have access. More than teaching, it is necessary to educate towards self learning, thus contributing to the education of individuals who are capable to make a creative contribution to the world today.

1.2 Digital Resources in Teaching and Learning – The Special Case of the Internet

The use of the Internet is something that cuts across important barriers for education, the possibilities and limitations of which are not fully understood, but which profoundly influences the work carried out in schools, promoting cooperative learning that can prepare the individual for a new type of professional activity involving team work.

The spirit of sharing and collaboration are qualities that can result from the use of the Internet, since the Internet favours cooperative and collaborative construction as well as joint work between teachers and students who are close physically or virtually, whether by means of home pages or e-mail, thus constituting a means of divulgation of curricular and extra-curricular activities that take place within the school. The entry of this resource in the classroom facilitates the creation of pedagogical projects, inter-individual exchange and distance communication, thus redefining the relationship established between teacher and student and encouraging critical thought by developing the capacity of the student to analyse other perspectives, other visions of reality or other opinions on a same subject.

From the dawn of the Internet one of its most present values has been solidarity, with countless sites promoting social cohesion. This worldwide network makes it possible to access a series of resources, of which the most important are information gathering resources (World Wide Web, Gopher, Archie, Wais), e-mail, discussion forums (newsgroups), file transfer (FTP), and real time conversation [5]. As a practically boundless source of information, access to it is more efficient when it is well organised and concentrated, for example by means of pointers. This fact translates into a significant reduction in search time comparatively to the time necessary for gathering the same information in libraries or conventional archives. New technologies, new communicational models and mainly the Internet have thus brought about profound changes in the manner in which we learn and teach and the way in which we interact with one another.

The learning environments on the Internet should have in themselves strategies of flexibility in the educative process that are adjustable to the

students, to their cognitive styles, to their motivations and their competences in order to stimulate their development and their ability to "learn to
learn".

1.3 "Getting Down to the Hard Grind", Contradicting the Divorce Between Science and the "Zap generation"

A growing awareness of the apparent divorce between the interests of the
students and the contents and methodologies offered in formal education
appears to cover various social and professional sectors. At the same time,
there is need for this education to be more efficient in terms of individual
and collective comprehension and appropriation (towards improved citizenship behaviour) of the problems that contemporary societies more frequently face, particularly those in which the scientific and technological
aspects are more evident. The importance of scientific education in today's
world is undeniable. Today's society requires scientific education to produce specialists, but also to produce scientifically cultured citizens. It is
useful to consider that in the teaching of sciences, three main aspects are
considered: learning of science – acquisition and development of theoretical and conceptual knowledge; learning about the nature of Science – development of an understanding of nature and scientific methods, thus acquiring awareness of the interaction between science and society; the
practice of science – development to of technical knowledge about scientific research and problem solving. These three dimensions are separate but
related. They are necessary (although not sufficient) and each one contributes to the understanding of the others. Nevertheless, it is scientific research (science in practice) that provides the student with the stimulus
needed to recognise and understand the inter-relation between these dimensions. Adequate practical activities in the teaching of the sciences are
precious resources (vital in many cases) to stimulate significant learning.

So that the teachers can teach sciences, stimulating and dominating specific and didactical knowledge (disciplinary), they acquire competences
and construct multi-disciplinary and interdisciplinary knowledge. [6], [7].

One of the possible motives that bring the *zap generation* to abandon
sciences at an early stage is the lack of motivation that installs itself among
them due to "not feeling the problem", or not "getting down to the hard
grind", since the teaching of the sciences is still very much concentrated on
the transmission of knowledge to be learned off by heart, for evaluation,
for further study, for... By "getting down to the hard grind" we mean
stimulating the natural curiosity of the young person so much that he or
she will approach the problem in as empirical a manner as possible such

that the scientific background emerges later on as a satisfying explanation (and not as a bother or a "pain", or just another equation to learn off by heart...).

In a secondary school classroom the most obvious characteristic of the assembly is its heterogeneousness, not only in terms of tastes and interests, but especially in terms of professional orientations. The only characteristic common to all of these is to be citizens (with future chemists being a minority) and the chemistry that is taught can, and should, constitute a very important general cultural element.

Chemistry is a subject that is labelled as difficult, which study involves concepts that require a certain intellectual maturity as well as a particular vocabulary and discourse. If the approach to Chemistry is made by means of materials that are related to the daily life of the student, based on personal experiences, then greater will be the number of students that pursue the study of sciences. And those who do not will in any case have had a good experience and a greater comprehension of the huge importance of Chemistry in all aspects of life. Thus Chemistry will have greater adherence and longer lasting effects on the lives of the students. [8].

There is a daily activity that, banal as it seems, we forget about when we wish to give practical examples of Science from daily life, especially Chemistry. It has to do with the preparation of food. Food, in its various stages - preparation, conservation, confection – is a process that is akin to the work carried out in a laboratory. In reality, chemists and kitchen chefs have more in common than one can imagine. When we cook food, we follow recipes that are very similar to laboratory procedures. "Beat 6 egg whites into a form, add a few drops of lemon juice or some grains of sea salt until the mixture forms a rigid texture", follows a similar protocol to "Weigh 0.40 g of NaOH, dissolve in 100 mL of water and with this solution titrate a solution of approximately 5% acetic acid". Thus, improvement in the quality of Chemistry teaching could be achieved by defining a teaching method that privileges contextualised experimentation as one of the means to the acquisition o real data, allowing the student to make a critical reflection of the world and to make cognitive development by means of his active, creative and constructive involvement with contents that are classroom topics.

The Internet, computers and technology in general can constitute an important ally in developing the quality of what is taught and the manner in which it is taught, since they are motivating elements and the focus of great interest on the part of the *zap generation*.

2   Digital Interactive Spaces – Kitchen Science (DIS-KS)

2.1   What are they?

The need to motivate students for learning to learn the science syllabi and its importance for day to day life is essential. Therefore it is essential to make science teaching more attractive, more motivating and more up-to-date, which can, in part, be mediated by new information and communication technologies. Informing and motivating young people for science is an evermore pertinent challenge given the growing divorce between these and Science.

Science should appear as it is and not as a caricature of itself. That is to say, science should appear as an interrogation of the world by means of experiment and observation, which to a certain extent are accessible to anybody.

DIS-KS, supported by the *wordcircle* (www.ptdeveloper.net/ead) platform are spaces that seek essentially to disseminate science linked to the preparation of food at home. It is an attempt to combine the two great pleasures of life, eating and learning science, in an agreeable, attractive and meaningful way. Chemistry and Physics are the focus of these, given the background of the authors and taking into account the fact that in the so-called basic sciences, there lie the greatest needs in this country. The creation of these spaces came about within the context of the Open and Distance Learning module of the curriculum of the Masters in Multimedia Education of the Faculty of Sciences of the University of Oporto.

Learning is not the result of development, learning is development. School should create spaces so that students can pose their own questions, manage their hypotheses and models and test their validity. In this way DIS-KS can have an important role in motivating the students for Science, using tools that younger generations are quite attracted to.

2.2   Brief Description of the Digital Interactive Spaces – Kitchen Science

The platform that supports these spaces is organised in three main topics:

Course Overview

This section consists of "welcoming the guests". The users are welcomed, the DIS-KS are presented and their main purpose is explained, that is, the pleasure of eating and the pleasure of science invite the users to explore the other sections.

News

This section consists of an area to disseminate everything that is going on and being created in the DIS-KS. Here the visitors can find all the news related to the updates of the spaces, new publications, forums, links, initiatives, activities and challenges, etc. It is a kind of window upon "Kitchen Science", providing information on everything in terms of publications and initiatives.

Calendar

This section is used to indicate dates of publications as well as to set dates for future challenges and provide information on what will be done and the date on which it will be carried out. This kind of agenda setting can contribute to motivating the users to visit the spaces more regularly to discover activities that trigger their interest and curiosity.

Course Materials

The school should provide challenging enquiries in meaningful contexts, allowing the students to explore and generate various possibilities while explaining, exploring and discussing the contradictions found. According to this conviction, a set of folders can be found in Course Materials, numbered according to date of publication, containing information on the way DIS-KS work, kitchen utensils, kitchen techniques and safety rules. These are examples of what is found in Section 1, which is a kind of introductory session containing the general principles of the space and the structure of the documents that contain the practical activities to be carried out and the challenges to be faced. In the remaining folders, sets of two activities are found structured in the following manner: first the question-problem is presented, which can be solved using simple small experiments that can be carried out in the kitchen and which should be solved and explained. This is followed by a story, a brief introduction to the theme or even an illustration that the users should read or observe carefully; with this the users should "get down to the hard grind", that is, its time to pull up the sleeves and start working on the proposed activity.

Next the users are invited to present their conclusions resulting from the activity and try to respond to the question posed initially, as well as make commentaries, suggestions and form opinions – all of this is done in the forum corresponding to each activity. Finally, the activities that will be published later are announced. Each week two new challenges are published along with the solution to the question-problem from the previous week.

Discussions

In this section there is a set of discussion forums divided into themes related to each one of the activities and challenges proposed in *Course Material*. These are intended as information sharing locations. The discussion forums are centres of debate where any user can participate by expressing opinions or simply reading the publications that are there. In this way, the users interpret and analyse the perspectives of the others, they reflect on their own knowledge and readings, they present their points of view in relation to the challenge or the question proposed for discussion. The forums are an excellent resource for learning, where it is possible to exchange opinions, ideas and experiences.

Chat

The DIS-KS also have a graphic resource that makes it possible for various people to converse without identifying one another – *chat*. It is an essential resource for establishing synchronised communication. It can be used regularly, providing corresponding sessions to classroom situations.

2.3   WebQuest – A Motivating Challenge

The WebQuest concept took root in 1995 in the United States at the hand of Bernie Didge, professor of Educational Technology in San Diego State University. Essentially it seeks to make organised and oriented use of Web resources [9]. A WebQuest therefore, is a research-oriented activity in which a large or whole part of the information that the students interact with are sourced in the Internet, resulting in a product where information transformation exists [10]. The creation of WebQuest – "Science explains the secret of the McChocolate Cake" (www.ptdeveloper.net/ead/webquest or accessible through a had as its main objective the motivation of colleagues of the Masters in Educational Multimedia to explore interactive spaces and to discover in an interesting manner the Science that is hidden in procedures so common in our houses, like baking a chocolate cake.

2.4 Testing the Activity on Colleagues of the Masters of Educational Multimedia

Within the context of a course unit called Open and Distance Teaching in the Masters programme in Educational Multimedia, each student was placed in charge of leading a synchronised class, supported by a WebCT platform and lasting approximately 50 minutes. Some of the students were recommended to use some of the activities described above. It was interesting above all as a way to motivate the users to discover, in an oriented manner (providing clues), the chemistry and physics that are hidden behind the baking of a chocolate cake that after 2 minutes in the microwave oven is ready to delight the sweet toothed.

In this case, the challenge posed to the colleagues assumed the form of the WebQuest. The task that was proposed to them consisted of assuming the role of scientists in the area of chemistry and physics at the service of the most famous restaurant chain, McDonalds. Their mission, in order to make the production of the McChocolate cake profitable, was to explain the function carried out by each ingredient in the cake as well as to understand how a cake can be baked in only 2 minutes in a microwave oven. The receptivity of the colleagues to the challenge was very good and they were quite motivated throughout the process.

3 Development After the Initial Experience

3.1 Some Improvements

Following on from this first pilot experience with students of the Masters programme, and taking into account that the DIS-KS constitute a dynamic project and can be continuously enriched, we plan improve the following aspects: to enrich the practical activities with more scientific questions: to create activities that permit the establishment of a stronger relation with the programme contents of the chemistry and physics syllabi at different levels of teaching, so that they can be used by the teachers of primary and secondary schools to put the themes into context and thus motivate more towards science; to create a section with very intuitive activities in which the challenge is directed at the parents, intending that they carry out the tasks with their children and help them come to an understanding of science; to enrich the DIS-KS with interactive videos, allowing users to visualise the activities in progress and make assessments of what could happen next, or advance ideas, knowledge and explanations that would later be confronted against a scientific explanation (POE-Preview strategy, Observe, Explain); to carry out WebQuests in order to further motivate the participation of the users, involving them in a more genuine and meaningful discovery and understanding of Science.

3.2 Exploration with the Students

The DIS-KS can be explored with the students in different contexts. These spaces can be a good resource in the classroom context for introducing, deepening knowledge or may be more importantly for motivating the students to learn a particular theme of science in general. Its potential can also be used if seen as a complement to the classes, suggesting to the students to explore the spaces, carry out activities that are found there and to participate in forums in accordance with their interests and motivations. At the end of the academic year, the experiences can be shared and conclusions reached in the classroom or the school context. The proposal of project based teaching represents an important form of considering all of the necessary elements in the overall education of the human being. Thus, the harmonious conjugation between the principles of the Project Methodology and the propositions and requirements related to new information and communication technologies makes this of capital importance.

3.3 Evaluation of the Digital Interactive
Spaces – Kitchen Science

One of the essential aspects of any project is its evaluation. Evaluation can include, in a first phase, a small online questionnaire to the users who visit the interactive spaces in order to collect their opinions, ideas and suggestions.

4 Future Projects

We intend that these spaces become better known over time. Thus we intend to develop the following aspects in the near future:

- Dissemination of the resources so that they become better known and provide more a and better benefits;
- Creation of an alternative offline support for those with problems with wide band connections;

- As was mentioned earlier, the current evaluation process is not far reaching and is presented as a pilot scheme that could later become a more systematic evaluation method for these resources;
- To experiment with the tool on primary and secondary school students and assess their impact;
- To amplify the range of proposals, crossing them operationally with the curricula of the primary and secondary curricula in physics and chemistry;
- To include similar participations of teachers who can enrich the spoil of the offer of activities of the site.

References

1. Fino, C (2005) Uma Turma da "Geração Nintendo" Construindo uma Cultura Escolar Nova. Available in http://www.nonio.uminho.pt/actchal01/096-Carlos%20Fino%201027–1048.pdf
2. Quarteiro, E (2005) As Tecnologias da Informação e Comunicação e a Educação. Available in http://www.inf.ufsc.br/sbc-ie/revista/nr4/063RE quartiero.htm
3. Correia, A, Dias, P (2005) A evolução dos paradigmas educacionais à luz das Teorias curriculares. Available in https://repositorium.sdum.uminho.pt/handle/1822/490?mode=full
4. Paiva, JC, Costa, LA, Fiolhais C (2005) " MOCHO": Um Portal de Ciência e Cultura Cientifica. Available in http://www-gist.det.uvigo.es/ie2002/actas/paper-117.pdf
5. Moura, R (2005) Educação e Internet. Available in: http://members.tripod.com/RMoura/ed_internet.htm
6. Santos, M (2002) Trabalho Experimental no Ensino das Ciências. Lisboa: Instituto de Inovação Educacional, 2002.
7. Ministério da Educação (2000) Ensino Experimental das Ciências, 1:37–44, Lisboa, Ministério da Educação, Departamento do Ensino Secundário.
8. Ministério da Educação (2000) Cadernos Didácticos de Ciência, 1:39–53, Lisboa, Ministério da Educação, Departamento do Ensino Secundário.
9. Dodge, B (2005) The WebQuest Page. Available in: http://webquest.sdsu.edu/webquest.html
10. Vieira, M (2005) WebQuest? Aventuras na Net? Available in: http://www.proformar.org/revista/edicao_4/pag_4.htm

Development and Experience in Teaching Biochemistry with a Multimedia Study Environment

Ana Maria Ponzio de Azevedo, Gustavo Brandalise Lazzarotto,
Maria Isabel Timm, Milton Antônio Zaro

Fundação Faculdade Federal de Ciências Médicas de Porto Alegre and
Postgraduate Program of Computer Science applyed to Education,
Universidade Federal do Rio Grande do Sul (PGIE–UFRGS)
Rua Sarmento Leite, 245, Sala 309, CEP 90050-170, Porto Alegre, RS,
Brazil.
anzevedo@fffcmpa.edu.br

1 Introduction: The Needs in the Teaching of Biochemistry

This work reports on a trial performed with medical and biological undergraduates of the Fundação Faculdade Federal de Ciências Médicas de Porto Alegre (FFFCMPA) in using an educational environment which includes, among its activities, the use of a logical sequence game named Ambiente de Estudo Multimedia de Bioquímica (AEMBq), for the teaching of carbohydrates metabolism, one of the topics of Biochemistry. Previous experiences in using the game, both in paper and virtual versions, for teaching biochemistry can be found in [8, 3, 1].

Biochemical contents are particularly difficult for the student to grasp, because they concern abstract concepts (formula expressing the reactions occurring in the cells) and demand previous knowledge on the properties of the substances present in the living organism. In practical classroom activities, it is often necessary to use visual depictions of the reactions that occur within the cell at a microscopic level and, thus, are hardly observable.

Moreover, it is not always possible for an instructor to tailor his teaching to the needs of each student, as each is a unique individual whose characteristics must be respected; flexible methods with multiple forms of representation, access and interactivity degrees are thus welcome.

In this concern, computer science can provide the student with a new approach to the process of knowledge building while also favouring teacher work, as the contents can be presented through interactive, motionless or animated, images that illustrate and facilitate visualization and, thus, the understanding of information and concepts. Hypermedia resources afford a more truthful representation of what does happen during the transformations undergone by the substances in the living organism, allowing as well the planning of activities to explore the variety of skills of each student. In order to facilitate student understanding of the metabolic pathways and provide greater interaction with the contents and thus better learning, a computer-based Environment for the Study of Biochemistry (AEMBq) was developed and is already in use with the students of the FFFCMPA in Porto Alegre (Brazil).

The AEMBq is a computer software which allows the user to learn, study, and review contents concerning carbohydrate metabolism through interactive games with a string of substrates and enzymes of the metabolic pathways, their control, inhibition, role of vitamins in their correct functioning, and their connection with other systems readings on the functions and characteristics of metabolic pathways, as well as historical milestones along their development

The AEMBq allows to store student personal notes in a log file as well as personal statistical data for quantification of performance – time, attempts, multiple versions for essay answers, and hits and misses in multiple choice tests. Privileged access to the system by the instructor enables him/her to collect all student records and comment on their answers. In this case, the software automatically e-mails the comment to the student, who can then reply to it.

2 Structure and Development of the DMVD

The software was divided into a number of functional modules, which served as a basis for structuring the systems: the manager system; the structure of screen and other interface data; the users database; questions, answers and records.

The construction of the graphical interface, as well as the structure of the games, was done using hypertext files (with links between content units). A Tutor Module allows the teacher to follow up the routes taken by the students.

On the game screen the user can interact with the board-like interface, choosing the compounds to assemble (drag-and-drop) the metabolic pathway according to his/her knowledge of the subject. After the student placed the compound at the right place, a text box opens with a question that the student must answer, which leads him/her to make interrelations and new findings. The student himself/herself can correct his/her answer after reading a complementary text, access to which is allowed only after having written an answer. The system also allows the user to proceed in the activity without answering the question, start another activity, or leave. Figure 1 shows a game screen where some of the above-mentioned resources can be seen.

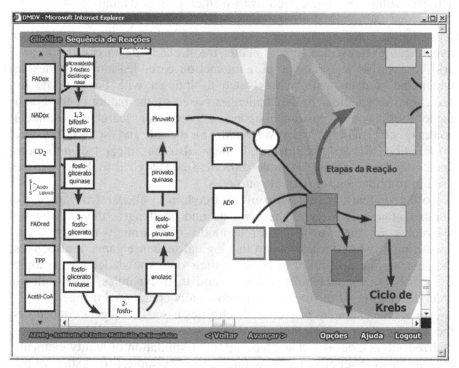

Fig. 1. Game screen with the board-like interface and drag-and-drop pieces

The software can be used by one or more users, providing an individualized teaching that respects the learning style of each student. Each user's interactions are stored in a log file for eventual analysis and each user has access to his/her records in the log link available in the Options menu. These record files can be exported to any relational database, where it is possible to make consultations for statistical purposes.

A preliminary version of the software was developed in C++ language. A more detailed description of the project of a preliminary version of the environment, focused on the content of a single metabolic pathway – the Krebs Cycle – can be found in [2, 3]. The software's current version is being developed in the JAVA platform with complementary data and records stored remotely in a relational databank. The system is made available through an applet interface and can be accessed by any browser at http://dmdv.fffcmpa.edu.br/.

The AEMBq can be used as a teaching tool in regular classes or over distance. The instructor can choose the pedagogical practice he/she prefers as a function of the requirements of the course, the available time for the activity within the course, and even his/her own pedagogical plan. This means that the material can be used as technology and to enrich content presentation only as well as enhance the instructor's own skill to dynamically represent a subject matter traditionally deemed difficult and arid. It may also be used to propose interaction-based learning activities, in which the students will be motivated to interact with the material by searching for solutions to the challenges posed by the nature of the board game itself, whose dynamic engenders needs for searching technical contents and also provides a wealth of visual and sound dynamic information through the media. It may also be integrated into both situations, featuring as a flexible didactical-pedagogical tool that can be used in combination for multiple purposes.

To the students, the AEMBq offers freedom to choose from among a number of access ways to the contents and challenges, thus improving awareness of their own preferred mode of learning: reading texts, answering questions or taking part in a logical sequence game. It also gives the students the possibility of building their own knowledge on the topic by visualizing the metabolic pathways and their dynamics, which allows an understanding of the formulas in didactically operational manner.

Among the examples of proposed activities based on Piaget's concepts is the act of playing, which this author relates to the ludic activity of the socialized subject, besides characterizing the assimilation of reality elements into the existing set of mental structures about the subject (first stage of the cognitive process [7]). Another example: selecting and dragging the piece – matching the function of each element in the metabolic pathway – would be related to motivation, an affective element to stimulate curiosity and improve construction of knowledge structures. Besides this issue, the act of choosing pieces is assumed to inform the student previous knowledge (previous cognitive structures), which, according to Piaget, must be mis-balanced (equilibration of new structures is supposed to be part of the dynamic process of organization of new knowledge). By answering essay questions proposed as a complementary part of the game, the student would be relating his newly-learned knowledge with reverse operations, of negation, of reciprocity and establishing co-relations. In doing so, he/she would likely be developing cognitive processes related to abstraction (formulate answers, analyse existing knowledge, reflect on his/her action), or, in Piaget's terms, will be engaged in reflective abstraction [5].

In assembling the pathway, the student will not only be interacting with the object but also relating his/her own meanings to the actions over the object. Following the same interpretation of Piagetian theories [7], it is suggested that the student will be engaged in a sort of interaction that is characteristic of the logic-mathematical forms, in which he/she will perform activities of seriating and correspondence operation. The next step will imply an application of the result of the previous operation to the object, creating new issues – cause-effects reasoning and classification [6]. It can also be observed the resistance of object against modification, which, in this case, occurs when the system refuses the piece chosen by the student because it does not match with the correct place on the metabolic pathway (i.e., board). The end result of the game would be the characteristic form described in Piaget's process [6], namely, the new form of the object enriched by the action of the subject. Thus, the modifications to the object done by the subject are not lost, while at the same time the newly-built forms are maintained that enrich his/her knowledge. Interactions of this sort would express the simplest form of equilibration, which is established after assimilation of new information into a previous mental scheme, and the respective system accommodation (the basis of the process as proposed by Piaget [7] for the individual construction of knowledge), assuming that the subject may have access to elements compatible with the concrete, operational, formal and hypothetical-inferential levels, all of them present at various moments along the game.

3 Application of the DMDV

After the pilot trials in using the preliminary version of the software, performed in 2003 and reported in [4], a second trial was performed in 2004 with a new version of the software containing contents of other metabolic pathways. The software was evaluated by the students regularly enrolled in the discipline of biochemistry. After a lecture on carbohydrate metabolism, all students could use the software for study during two classes in a computer room. In the following week, before the evaluation of the discipline concerning this topic, the software was made available again through the intranet of the institution. All students were registered on the system, and their access, through use of a personal password, allowed the recording of activities on an individual basis.

All participants were asked to draw a concept map[1] of the Carbohydrate Metabolism before beginning the study in the computer room. A second concept map was performed at the moment of theoretical evaluation but before receiving the questions to be answered, and a third map, two months after the evaluation. It is assumed that the first map expressed the student's previous knowledge on the contents to be worked with; the second should express the influence of the study method itself (using the software); and the third was taken as expressing the consolidation of the knowledge gained.[2] Paper, pencil and pens were the only materials used in drawing the concept maps.

4 Analysis from the Concept Maps

The concept maps presented by the students confirmed the expectation generated by the first experience: the initial maps showed that all students had some previous mental scheme of the proposed concept; new elements were added to all subsequent maps of all students. The students with less previous knowledge (less representations in the first map) showed more expansion of the last concept map.

In the reported trial, some initial concept maps presented a limited number of concepts and relations. The maps drawn after playing the game showed progress concerning the interrelation of concepts, suggesting the effectiveness of the software to facilitate the learning of concepts by the students, not only as fragments but as parts of a whole, whose interconnections are crucial for understanding the content in its more complex sense, which includes generalizations, abstractions and content disposition by order of relevance and meaning. Corroborating the notion that concept maps do express the student's ability of mental representation, it has been found that, as regards the mastery of metabolic pathways, the difficulty seen in the written test was matched by the absence of the topic on the concept maps.

---

[1] As these concept maps were done using pencil and paper, and as a total of 123 maps were turned in, they are not presented here due to space constraints. They are available upon request to the authors.

[2] The fact that these students had previously worked with concept maps and that previous work had already been done on the use of Concept Maps as pedagogic learning and teaching strategy in Biochemistry (Azevedo, SBBQ, 2003), indicated this tool as valid for evaluating student learning.

5 Analysis from Software Records

As the software was available to registered students at the school computers for a week, it was possible to follow up their activities in the environment from the records. Records of 41 users were analysed. Among the 43 enrollees, 41 chose to take part in the activity. The total number of interactions – start and end of the game and answer to questions – was 2568, with a mean 62.63 interactions per user. The lowest number of interactions by a student was 3, and the highest, 211 (space constraints preclude the presentation of the totality of interactions by each student here).

An analysis of the records shows that 44% of the students who started the Krebs Cycle game, under the item of Reactions Sequences, have completed this activity. However, among those that started the game of Energy Balance in the same chapter – considered as a more simple activity, with less pieces to be placed – the completion rate was as high as 73%. The Relations Game, also in the same chapter, presented a completion rate of only 15%, possibly because it is more extensive and requires more previous knowledge from the student.

The structure of interactive activities proposed for the chapter of Glycolysis was different from that for the Krebs Cycle. After completion of the first interactive activity (Substrate Sequence), the system automatically offered the student the option of proceeding to the next activities: Energy Balance in Aerobiosis and Anaerobiosis. This circumstance may explain the greatest completion rate regarding this chapter. Of the 46 students who started the sequence, 30 (65%) proceeded to the next stage, 22 of whom carried it to completion (73%). At the last stage, of the 23 students who began it (one student went directly to the Anaerobiosis item), 18 finished it (78%).

In this chapter, the item Inhibition, considered as the most simple to complete due to the number of pieces to be placed, was finished by virtually all of the students who started it.

The mean grade in the written test about the studied chapter, as required by the institution for student approval, was 7.59, which indicates that most students obtained a grade that was above the minimum required for being approved in the discipline. It is suggested that this result be used as a indicator of the effectiveness of this study method using the DMDV.

The software in its new version is currently being used through the Internet by two groups of students: medical and biological undergraduates, both of the FFFCMPA. The records follow-up has shown good student acceptance and interaction rates with full functionality of the software. Figure 2 shows the new interface of user data storage successfully implemented in the new version, already with the records of a group of students. The answers of the students remain stored on the server, and through these records the instructor can comment on them. The student receives these comments by e-mail and can reformulate his answer in the Options menu, item See comments. After placement of the reformulated answer, the teacher is notified of it by e-mail.

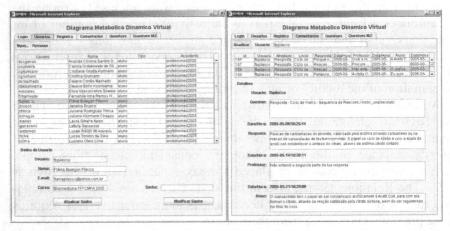

Fig. 2. Records of student activity, stored on the server, allow the instructor to e-mail comments and receive reformulated answers from the student

6 Conclusions

The good results obtained so far indicate that the DMVD not only is operational but also constitutes an activity that stands as a highly effective didactical-pedagogical tool for student learning, as suggested by the average grades obtained in traditional written tests. Furthermore, it is a tool that stimulates student participation and increases their motivation, as indicated by the statistical survey of the accesses and routes taken along the game. The trial also adds value to the methods of application and evaluation of software use, through the use of concept maps which evidence the progress of students, by themselves and by the instructor. As a whole, the present project was also characterized as an opportunity of applying the theoretical concepts concerning Jean Piaget's genetic epistemology to practical situations of didactical-pedagogical nature, pointing to future research on computer science in education and its use in the teaching of science and technology.

References

1. Azevedo A, Fin C, Dutra C, Remião J, Siqueira A (2002) Dynamic metabolic Diagrams for Teaching Biochemistry. In: Anais da XXXI Reunião Anual da Sociedade Brasileira de Bioquímica e Biologia Molecular- SBBq,. Caxambu
2. Azevedo A, Lazzarotto G, Falkembach G, Zaro M (2003) Ambientes Virtuais de Ensino para Bioquímica: Jogo e multimídia como apoio à aprendizagem, In: Anais do SBIE, Rio de Janeiro, pp 728–737
3. Azevedo A, Lazzarotto G (2003) El Software Diagrama Metabolico Dinâmico Virtual In: Actas del Taller Internacional de Software Educativo, Santiago de Chile
4. Azevedo, A, Lazzarotto G, Timm M, Zaro M (2004) Relato de uma experiência com o uso do Diagrama Metabólico Dinâmico Virtual do Ciclo de Krebs. RENOTE – Revista Novas Tecnologias na Educação, 2
5. Becker F (1994) Modelos pedagógicos e modelos epistemológicos. Educação e Realidade 19: 89–96
6. Piaget J (1976) Equilibração das Estruturas Cognitivas: Problema Central do Desenvolvimento. Zahar Editores, Rio de Janeiro
7. Piaget J (1978) O nascimento da inteligência na criança. Zahar Editores, Rio de Janeiro
8. Siqueria A, Remião J, Azevedo A (1992) Dynamic Metabolic Diagrams in Biochemistry. Biochemical Education 20: 97–98

An Educative Application Based on Bloom's Taxonomy for the Learning of Inheritance in Oriented-Object Programming

Isidoro Hernán-Losada, Carlos A. Lázaro-Carrascosa,
J. Ángel Velázquez-Iturbide

Departamento de Lenguajes y Sistemas Informáticos,
Universidad Rey Juan Carlos, Móstoles, Madrid
{isidoro.hernan, carlos.lazaro, angel.velazquez}@urjc.es

1 Introduction

The theoretical concepts in most of sciences or engineering studies are fixed by solving problems. We investigate the systematic development of educative applications within the pedagogical frame provided by Bloom's taxonomy. As the domain of application, we focus on object-oriented programming (OOP).

In this paper we describe an educative application for the learning of the concept of inheritance. In the first section, we summarize Bloom's taxonomy and its application to the learning of programming. Then, we describe our application. Later we show the results of evaluating this application in an OOP course. Finally, we give our conclusions and future work.

2 Bloom's Taxonomy

Bloom's taxonomy [1] is a widely accepted classification to estimate the cognitive level reached for a student in a certain matter. It distinguishes six levels, assuming that a student who reaches a level also dominates the lower ones:

- **Level 1 or knowledge level.** The student is able to recognize or recall information without being necessary any kind of understanding about it.
- **Level 2 or comprehension level.** The student is able to understand and explain the meaning of the information received.
- **Level 3 or application level.** The student is able to select and use data and methods to solve a given task or problem.
- **Level 4 or analysis level.** The student is able to distinguish, classify and relate the information given and decomposing a problem into its parts.
- **Level 5 or synthesis level.** The student is able to generalize ideas and apply them to solve a new problem.
- **Level 6 or evaluation level.** The student is able to compare and evaluate methods or solutions to solve a problem or choose the best one.

The Bloom's taxonomy has been used in programming as a framework for different purposes [2]: to design their courses, to evaluate students, or as a reference to design educative applications.

2.1 Support to Exercises Based on Bloom's Taxonomy

There are a myriad of applications for the learning of programming (e.g. programming environments, correctors, visualizers, etc.), but they are typically designed without clear pedagogical foundations. Therefore, they do not satisfactorily fit any cognitive level of Bloom's taxonomy.

A representative example is the BlueJ environment [5], aimed at teaching OOP in the first course. Another example comes from program animations, whose educative potential is not fully exploited [4].

Our objective consists in designing applications to accomplish exercises at each level of knowledge of Bloom's taxonomy. In experimental sciences, there exists more experience than in computer science in classifying assignments into different levels of difficulty. For example, Herron's proposal [3] distinguishes several inquiry levels (Table 1).

Table 1. Levels of inquiry according to Herron

	Goal	Materials	Method	Answer
Confirmation	Given	Given	Given	Given
Verification	Given	Given	Given	Open
Structured Inquiry	Given	Given part or whole	Open or part given	Open
Guided Inquiry	Given	Open	Open	Open
Open Inquiry	Open	Open	Open	Open

We may think of applications addressed at different levels of Bloom's taxonomy. For example, the interaction facilities of an animation will determine the level of engagement of the student [6] and therefore the cognitive level reached.

Although we are interested in programming in general, we have focused on OOP. In the following section we describe an application we have developed to support the first levels of the taxonomy.

3 Description of the Application

The application provides with theory aimed at the two lowest levels of the taxonomy, as well as assessing the skill reached at the three lowest levels.

The application was developed in Java and implemented as an applet. Its graphical interface is simple and intuitive so that the student does not have to dedicate extra time to learn how to interact with it. The application shows three modules to the user: Theory, Demonstration and Quizzes.

3.1 Theory Component

This module contains an explanation of the concept in study, namely inheritance. The explanation is delivered as Web pages due to its ease of implementation and the educative advantages of the hypermedia. The theory not only is explained with words and code, but also with graphics.

3.2 Demonstration Component

This module permits to experiment with the inheritance concept. It consists of several sample demonstrations of good and bad use of inheritance in Java. At the present time we have two demonstrations, but inserting new ones is straightforward for the instructor. They are implemented in Flash.

The student must interact with each animation, advancing either forward or backward. This forces the student to engage with the animation [6].

Figure 1 shows a demonstration snapshot. It is based on the UML notation. Classes are drawn with rectangles that box up the name in the topside, underneath the attributes and finally the methods. Objects are displayed as ellipses. At the bottom, several sample instructions are shown, highlighting the active one, as well as the forward and backward controls. In the right topside, the object receiving a message is embraced with a thick border; simultaneously, an explanation of the message appears.

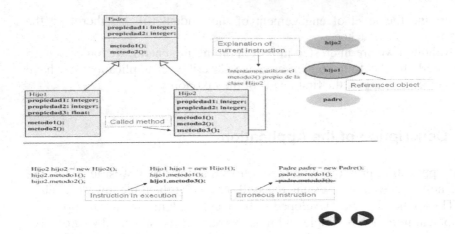

Fig. 1. Demonstration component

3.3 Quizzes Component

This component manages questions and grades answers, as well as stores students' outcomes. There are three sets of questions, corresponding to the three lowest levels of Bloom's taxonomy. Each question consists of a statement, four possible answers and one explanation for each option.

When the application is launched, it asks the student the initial level. Then, questions appear in random order, assuring that they are not repeated during the same session. In order to reinforce motivation, the application increases automatically the level when the student guesses correctly 80% of the questions, provided at least five questions were answered.

Figure 2 shows a lowest level question. Notice that the student may also ask for a longer explanation of the answer.

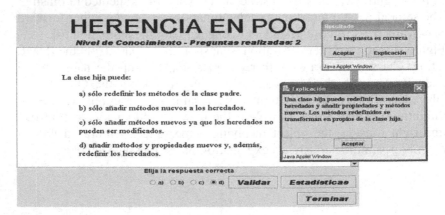

Fig. 2. Quizzes component

4 Test and Evaluation of the Application

4.1 Hypothesis

Two related issues were considered: to determine if the use of the application significantly influences the students' global learning and, to check if it reinforces learning at some level of the Bloom's taxonomy. We adopted an interval of confidence of 95% to reject or to accept the hypothesis.

4.2 Identification of Variables

In order to make the study two variables were selected: the application as the independent variable, and the difference between grades obtained by each group in the accomplishment of the pre-test and post-test as the dependent variable. In order to verify the first hypothesis, the difference in performance is obtained from the final score of the test, whereas for the second hypothesis grade differences are obtained from the score obtained at each level. The objective of the investigation is to determine the influence of the first issue over the second one.

4.3 Population and Sample

The population object of the study were the students of object-oriented programming pertaining to the second course of Computer Science Engineering at the Universidad Rey Juan Carlos in 2004/2005.

The 36 students who regularly attend practical sessions were divided into two groups: experimental and control. Both groups were homogenous. Division was randomly made by their last names and having gender into account, so that two groups of 18 members (13 male and 5 female) were formed. All of the students were given the same theoretical classes by the same professor. Authors of this article did not have previous contact with the students, to avoid slant when generating the test.

4.4 Obtaining the Data

Quizzes consisted in 9 questions, 3 per level of Bloom. They were graded so that right answers counted 1 point and wrong answers, 0 (maximum 9 points). The quiz was carefully designed. The professor collaborated in the questions of the knowledge level, so that their writing was equal to that used by the professor. The remaining questions were independently designed by the authors.

For the assignment, a pre-test on the use of the application was made. When they finalized the pre-test, the control group made the current assignment on the computer. In contrast, the experimental group installed the application and they used it during approximately half an hour. Later, a questionnaire was given to them to evaluate the tool. On the following day, a post-test was given to both groups.

4.5 Results

The test was been responsible for both groups. The results can be observed in Table 2. Notice that three losses in the experimental group and the control group took place, reason why the data of those students have not considered in the results. For the analysis of data statistical application called R was used.

Table 2. General results of the tests

	Pre-test		Post-test	
GROUP	Control	Experimental	Control	Experimental
Mean	5.00	6.28	4.60	5.27
Median	5	7	4	6
Variance	3.14	2.35	2.69	2.64
Standard deviation	1.77	1.53	1.64	1.62
Range	1.8	3.9	2.7	2.8

In order to study the normality of the samples (Table 3) we have used the tests of Shaphiro-Wilk and Kolmogorov-Smirnov that give a value of statistical P. If the value of P obtained in each one of the tests does not surpass 0.05 (due to the criterion of 95% previously chosen), concludes that the sample does not follow a normal distribution. If the samples are normal indicates that the parametric methods for their study can be used.

Table 3. Test of normality of the samples (P)

	Pre-test		Post-test	
GROUP	Control	Experimental	Control	Experimental
Shaphiro-Wilk	0.27	0.49	0.56	0.61
Kolmogorov-Smirnov	0.67	0.56	0.95	0.54

In the first place we verified if the division made in random groups is correct or, however, present some slant (for example, that the most promising students are in he himself group). As the samples have normal distribution, test F of equality of variances was done for the pre-test obtaining a value P = 0.59. As the samples fulfil two requirements (normality and equality of variance) we used the Student's t-test to check if both groups come from the same population (of the same classroom and with knowledge seemed). This test is based on proving that the means of the pre-test do not differ significantly. The following results were obtained.

Table 4. Student's t-test applied to pre-test

T	Degrees of Freedom	P
-1.9828	33	0.056

When obtaining in Table 4 a value of P very near limits (we remembered that if is minor who 0.05 rejects the hypothesis and therefore, it concludes that both groups are not of the same population), was made the calculation of the 95% confidence interval for a mean (95% CI for a mean). See Table 5:

Table 5. Pre-test confidence interval

GROUP	Control	Experimental
95% CI	4.38–6.07	5.54–7.02

As both intervals are partially overlapped, along with the Student's t-test, we did not reject the hypothesis and we affirmed that the differences between both groups are attributable at random and therefore they belong to the same population.

Next we analysed the effect of the application in its learning. In Table 6 are the general results of the dependent variable, which is the difference between both tests (subtraction between pre-test and post-test).

Table 6. Differences between the pre-test and the post-test

GROUP	Mean	Median	Variance	Standard deviation	Range
Control	0.4	1.0	2.69	1.64	–2.3
Experimental	1.0	1.0	3.14	1.77	–2.4

Before making the Student t-test, it is necessary to confirm the normality of the differences and the equality of variances. We are applied tests explained previously. The results are shown in Table 7.

Table 7. Normality test (p)

GROUP	Control	Experimental
Shaphiro-Wilk; Kolmogorov-Smirnov	0.12; 0.56	0.57; 0.80

The variance equality, applying test F gives to a value of P = 0.77, reason why the variances are similar. Student t-test gives the values of T = –0.9625, Degrees of Freedom = 28 and P = 0.34.

In order to study the influence of the application on the levels of Bloom, the same tests have been made. The general results are grouped in Table 8 and the tests on normality in Table 9 and equality of variance and the Student t-test in Table 10.

Table 8. Differences grouped by levels of Bloom

GROUP	Control			Experimental		
LEVELS	N1	N2	N3	N1	N2	N3
Mean	0.93	−0.80	0.27	0.47	−0.13	0.67
Median	1	−1	0	0	0	1
Variance	1.35	0.59	0.77	1.56	0.85	0.51
Standard deviation	1.16	0.77	0.88	1.25	0.92	0.72
Range	−2.3	−2.0	−1.2	−1.3	−1.2	0.2

Table 9. Test of normality (P)

GROUP	Control			Experimental		
	N1	N2	N3	N1	N2	N3
Shap-Wilk	0.07	0.00	0.06	0.13	0.01	0.00
Kolmogorov-Smirnov	0.27	0.31	0.47	0.72	0.34	0.17

Table 10. Tests of equality of variances and Student T

	N1	N2	N3
Test F (P)	0.8	0.54	0.46
T	1.07	−2.15	−1.36
Degrees of Freedom P	28	27	27
	0.29	0.04	0.19

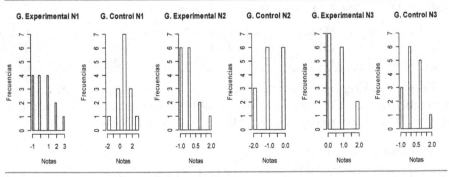

Fig. 3. Differences among both groups for levels of Bloom's hierarchy

Fig. 3 Shows the frequencies of grade differences grouped by levels

An opinion poll was accomplished to the experimental group on his grade of satisfaction with the application. We used Likert's scale, from totally of (5) even agreement totally in conflict (1).

5 Discussion

First we tried to demonstrate that the division made by groups was correct. For it, with notes of the pre-test, we concluded that both samples followed a normal distribution (Table 3) and presented homogenous variances. We applied Student t-test (Table 4) and the test of 95% CI to contrast average notes in the pre-test. The result did not show significant differences between both groups. Thus the differences between pre-test and post-test notes can only be due to the use of the application.

The use of the difference between both test as dependent variable is a habitual practice in this type of studies, because external factors are eliminated the experiment, as different difficulty from the questions between both test (that in fact exists according to show the averages in Table 2). Therefore each pupil makes a comparison himself.

In order to verify the first hypothesis (the application influences significantly in the learning of the inheritance concept), the differences between total notes of the pre-test and post-test were analysed.

As it is possible to be seen in Table 6, the average of the experimental group is greater than the one of the control group, which could erroneously lead to think that the use of the application improves the learning considerably. Nevertheless, the statistical study demonstrates that significant differences between both groups do not exist. This does not indicate that the use of the tool is not effective: it would be necessary to experiment with a greater group to demonstrate or to refute the hypothesis definitively.

The second hypothesis is: The tool reinforces learning in some level of Bloom. The data collected in Table 8 and statistical studies of Table 9 and Table 10 show that except for level 2 (understanding), the differences are not significant. Student t-test for level 2 gives a P-value of 0.04, which is less than the a priori fixed value of 0.05. This means that a significant difference exists, and it is not attributable at random. Exactly our application was designed to support with greater emphasis level 2.

The opinion of the students who used the application was very good. It was not necessary to explain the operation of the tool. As one is in the results, it is intuitive and it obtained a good global valuation.

6 Conclusions and Future Work

We have presented an application to aid the student to learn the inheritance concept. We have briefly described the framework provided by Bloom's taxonomy. Our computer application includes different modules aimed at the three lowest levels. Also, we have shown the results of an evaluation of the application. We conclude that the application reinforces the learning at the understanding level, always considering that the experiment was made on a small number of students (18 in each group).

Our immediate objective is to reach upper levels of Bloom's taxonomy. At the application level, we have thought of an application that generates problems, assists in solving them and automatically corrects them. We also want to enhance the interaction facilities of our demonstrations. These objectives demand a different infrastructure, currently under development.

Acknowledgments

This work has partially supported by project TIN2004-07568 of the MEyC. We also want to appreciate the collaboration of Leandro Martín Molina and Soto Montalvo Herranz in making the evaluation.

References

1. Bloom BS (ed.) (1956) Taxonomy of Educational Objectives: The Classification of Educational Goals: Handbook I, Cognitive Domain. Longmans Green, New York, Toronto
2. Hernán Losada I, Lázaro Carrascosa CA, Velázquez Iturbide JA (2004). On the use of Bloom's taxonomy as a basis to design educational software on programming. In Proc. of World Conf. Engineering and Technology Education (WCETE 2004) pp 351–355
3. Herron M (1971) The nature of scientific enquiry, School Review, 79: 171–212
4. Hundhausen CD, Douglas SA, Stasko JT (2002) A meta-study of algorithm visualization effectiveness, Journal of Visual Languages and Computing, 13(3):259–290
5. Kölling M, Rosenberg J (2001) Guidelines for teaching object orientation with Java, In Proc. 6th Annual Conf. Innovation and Technology in Computer Science Education, ACM Press, pp 33–36
6. Naps T, Roessling G et al. (2003) Exploring the role of visualization and engagement in computer science education, SIGCSE Bulletin, 35(2):131–152

Visualization and Role-play to Teach Object-Oriented Programming

Guillermo Jiménez Díaz, Mercedes Gómez Albarrán,
Marco A. Gómez-Martín, Pedro A. González-Calero

Universidad Complutense de Madrid
C/ Profesor Jose Garcia Santesmases s/n 28040, Madrid (SPAIN)
gjimenez@fdi.ucm.es, albarran@sip.ucm.es,marcoa@fdi.ucm.es,
pedro@sip.ucm.es

1 Introduction

Understanding the interactions among objects in complex object-oriented systems can be a very hard task. On the one hand, reading documentation about the system classes and architecture does not ease this task much. On the other hand, tracing the program execution in a development environment can be even more difficult than following the documentation approach, and the user often gets lost in a mess of message passing and gives the task up. Program visualization is a commonly used technique to enhance the under- standing of software, in general, and object-oriented software, in particular. However, as stated in [12], "visualization technology is of little educational value unless it engages learners in an active learning activity".

Our work addresses the improvement of the object-oriented software understanding for introductory programming courses. We propose the combination of an active learning task with a visualization of both static architecture and dynamic behaviour of a software system. We transfer the role-play approach, commonly used in responsibility-driven development, to a 3D virtual environment, where a user collaborates with a group of virtual participants.

This paper runs as follows: Sections 2 and 3 describe the two main ideas that support our project. Section 4 discusses the way to transfer a role-play session to a 3D virtual environment. Section 5 details an example about a role-play session performed following the approach described in the previous section. The paper concludes with our future work directions.

2 Role-play

Role-play is a kind of active learning where students learn complex concepts –hard to understand by means of abstract explanations– while they simulate a scenario [2]. The role-play supervisor provides information to each participant about the characters involved in the play. During the role-play, participants interact to perform the scenario, learning from themselves, the other participants and the played roles. A beneficial effect of role-play is that students do not only learn about the played roles and the other participants but also they have the possibility to see what they understand. If the student understands the roles in a scenario, then she will know how and with whom to interact [2].

Role-play is typically employed in social skill training but several authors have suggested using it to teach topics from computer science, in particular object-oriented design and development [1, 3]. The work in [2] points out that humans are a good metaphor for objects in the object-oriented paradigm, because "people are autonomous, encapsulated actors, who interact with other similar object". This way, when a student takes part in a role-play that represents the execution of an object-oriented application she is "putting himself/herself into an object's shoes".

Despite the importance of using role-play in teaching computer science topics –it was included in the list of pedagogical patterns [2]– its use in instructional software for object-oriented programming has not been reported. In contrast, there are several collaborative web-based environments, such as TimeScope [15] and Fablusi [9], to teach history using role-playing. In these environments, participants interact among themselves playing a proposed scenario in a forum or chat.

3 Software Visualization

The adage "a picture is worth a thousand words" reflects the enormous communication ability that images provide. Human beings are good at processing visual information. These two facts, together with the rise of modern human-computer interfaces, have led to the massive use of software visualization, both, as a pedagogical tool for teaching programming and as a key piece in software comprehension. Software visualization is the use of typography, graphic design, computer animation, cinematography with graphics technology to facilitate the understanding and effective use of software [14]. Most of software visualization approaches focus on illustrating algorithms, program flow and information. However, we are interested in approaches to visualize static architecture and behaviour of object-oriented systems.

UML models are the most common technique to visualize the architecture and behaviour of an object-oriented system. The class and deployment diagrams provide an architectural view of the system, while collaboration, state charts and activity diagrams are used to represent the dynamic behaviour. Several visualization approaches extend the use of UML diagrams. Grundy et al. [7] propose a complex model that combines UML models with its own visual language for static and dynamic visualization of software architecture.

Other software visualization tools employ metaphors to represent the software architecture. Metaphors provide a way of transmitting software information in a representation that can be easier to understand. A commonly used metaphor is 3D virtual microworlds, where the classes are represented by platforms with incrusted elements –like columns and spheres– to represent the class methods and attributes. The user can navigate through these microworlds in virtual reality [11]. Other applications employ more complex metaphors, as countries, cities and buildings, to represent different software statistics [13]. However, the main disadvantage of most of these tools is that they were not developed for an educational approach but following debugging and software metrics visualization motivations.

Other approaches were developed for pedagogical purposes. Thaden *et al.* [16] proposes the animation of UML diagrams to visualize the execution of arbitrary Java programs. The classes and objects that appear in an UML diagram are translated into animated 3D blocks. Moreover, Alice [5] is a development environment that uses an anthropomorphic metaphor to represent objects. The student designs a world and populates it with characters, whose behaviour is also implemented by the student. When the student runs the developed program, she can visualize the behaviour and the state of the characters in the world. Finally, other pedagogical tools emphasize in both visualization and user interaction. JIVE [6] is a sophisticated debugger to visualizing the execution state of Java programs The user is responsible for controlling the program execution and querying about the objects' state, shown on object and sequence diagrams.

4 Role-play Virtualization

A role-play activity in a classroom requires the collaboration of several participants –one per object that intervenes in the role-play and perhaps a coordinator. Despite its pedagogical benefits, role-play activity is not frequently performed because it is time-consuming. We propose the use of a software tool, an interactive virtual environment where the user learns about the behaviour of a concrete object-oriented system using the role-play approach.

We have selected role-play because it is an active learning approach that can be applied as a program visualization method. In order to translate the role-play to a computer, we need to answer several questions:

- As a visualization tool, we require to answer two questions: What needs to be visualized? and How do we visualize it?
- As an active learning approach, it is necessary to decide the way the user is involved in the simulation.

The next subsections contain the answers to these questions.

4.1 What and How to Visualize

Even a relatively small program can generate too many objects and method calls at runtime. In order to reduce the number of objects in the role-play, the software application is divided into several fragments, simplifying the amount of information visualized. In our approach, we divide the whole application into several role-play scenarios. Each scenario is focused on a concrete application functionality. Thus, the user requires a textual description about the performed scenario.

We have chosen an anthropomorphic metaphor of the object-oriented paradigm. Every object has been represented by an anthropomorphic avatar. The objects are the characters that take part in the role-play. Each character shows the object name and the class that the object belongs to. As in a graphical adventure, every avatar has an inventory, which contains both the state of the object and static information. The inventory contains several items representing the values of the object fields, a reference list with its collaborators and a set with the distinguished local variables in the current scope. Additionally, the inventory includes references to the source code and the signature –methods and fields– of the class the object belongs to.

The message passing is represented by a ball throwing among avatars. The situation of the ball is employed to show the current scope in the interaction because the current active object is represented by the avatar that holds the ball. The ball also contains information about the method currently called, including the parameter values and the returning value, if it exists. According to the message passing, we have considered the following metaphor:

- **Method call.** When an object A calls a method from an object B, the avatar of the object A says *"ObjectName, do MethodName with parameters"* and throws the ball to the avatar of the object B. An object can also call a method from itself, throwing the ball upwards.

- **Method return.** When an object B has concluded the execution of a method called by an object A, then the focus returns to this object. To avoid misunderstandings with the method calls, instead of throwing the ball, avatar B will roll it until it reaches avatar A and says the message *"MessageName is done resulting ReturnObject"* –if the method returns a ReturnObject– or *"MessageName is done"*–otherwise.

- **Object creation.** In order to create a new object we need to represent the class of that object. Instead of using a character, a block with the class name will represent a class. When an avatar creates an object, it says the message *"ObjectName, construct yourself as a ClassName object with parameters"* and it throws the ball to the block. This message will cause the object avatar to appear holding the ball.

Table 1 summarizes the relevant information that will be shown to the user and the way we have chosen to visualize it in our virtual environment.

4.2 How to Involve the Student

Interactive graphical visualizations can present a great amount of information much more effectively than textual representations, allowing the user to control the filtering and abstraction of available information [10]. If our role-play approach presents all the information described previously, the user would be overwhelmed. In order to avoid that, the user can control the displayed information. The objects that participate in the role-play (their run-time class, the active object and the current scope) are always displayed during the simulation. However, the user may request the rest of the information. The user can explore the inventory of any object in the scene to check its current state and its signature. The user can also see both public and private interface of the active object. The ball does not only represent the control flow but also contains information about the last method called. With a zoom-in, the user can "enter" in the ball and explore the method parameters and the returning value or object.

Table 1. A summary about the information visualized in the virtual environment

What	How
Class	Block
Class signature and source code	Inventory
Object	Anthropomorphic avatar
Object name and runtime-class	Visible label
Object state	Inventory
Method call	Throwing the ball among avatars
Method return	Rolling the ball among avatars
Object creation	Throwing the ball to a block
Method signature	Ball
Actual parameters	Ball and dialogue text

The user can act as a passive observer of a performed scenario. However, our virtual environment promotes the student interaction, providing four levels of dynamic interaction during the role-play simulation:

1. Interactive prediction about a specific character. The simulation stops and asks the user for the next step in the simulation. Then, the user should reply in the expected way using actions from graphical adventure games like *Send <Message> to <Object> using <Parameters>*, or *Return Value* when the user considers that her interaction has finished.
2. Performance of a specific character. The user is in charge of a concrete character during the whole role-play simulation, so the user takes part when the object she represents should act.
3. Interactive prediction about several characters.
4. Coordinator. The user decides the steps in the role-play. The user should explore the active object and determine the next method call, selecting –as in the previous interaction modes– the receiver, the method and the parameters.

The user's mistakes motivate for explanations when performing a role in the simulation. If the user makes a mistake during the message passing described above –a wrong message or any wrong parameter– she will be informed with an error message. The user has failed her expectations so she is motivated to revise the information provided by the objects in order to find out the proper message passing in the current simulation step.

5   A Role-play Scenario

To illustrate our work we use the Marine Biology Case Study (MBCS) [4], employed in the Advanced Placement Computer Science curriculum – available at http://apcentral.collegeboard.com– to expose CS1 students to the idea of message passing between objects. This simulator is referred in other works related to role-play exercises [1].

MBCS presents a simulation program designed to help marine biologists study fish movement in bounded or unbounded environments. Every simulation step, the fishes swim in this environment according to a programmed behaviour. The population can change dynamically because the fishes can also breed or die in any given simulation step.

We have created a simplified scenario to understand how the main class creates a fish. Figure 1 shows a sequence diagram that represents our sample scenario. Using the MBCS role-play script [4], we have created the following role-play simulation. The scene contains two avatars –*initial*, which represents a *SimpleMBSDemo1* object and *env*, an instantiation of the *BoundEnv* class– and two blocks –which represent the classes *Location* and *Fish*. The avatar named *initial* is responsible for starting the role-play, so it holds the ball. Then it looks for the *Location* block and throws the ball saying *"location, constructs yourself as a Location object with 2 and 2"*. When the ball reaches the block, an avatar called *<location:Location>* appears. Then this avatar says, *"Constructor is done"* and the ball rolls back to initial. Now, initial looks to the *Fish* block, throws the ball to it and says *"f1, constructs yourself as a Fish object with env and location"*. As a result, the avatar *<f1:Fish>* appears from the block holding the ball.

Let us suppose that the user selects the interaction level number 2 and performs the role of the object *f1*. To obtain help the user can check *f1's* inventory that appears in Figure 2. It contains links to the *Fish* class signature and source code, an item called *myId* (the fish identifier, represented by an integer), and a list with the following references: *theEnv* (the object representing the environment where the fish is located), *myLoc* (representing its position in the environment), *myDir* (the swimming direction), *myColor* (the fish colour) and *this* (itself reference). Besides, the list also contains the references to two local variables named *env*, and *loc*. After consulting the information the user is ready to execute the next message passing in the simulation by means of the send action . Using a visual command interface, the student should select the correct sender –the reference *theEnv*–, the message –*randomDirection*–, and the parameters –this method does not need any parameter. *f1's* avatar says *"env, do randomDirection"* and the ball reach *env*. Then, *env* rolls the ball back to *f1* and says, *"randomDirection is done returning direction"*. According to the user's instructions, the avatar throws the ball upwards and says *"f1, do randomColor"*.

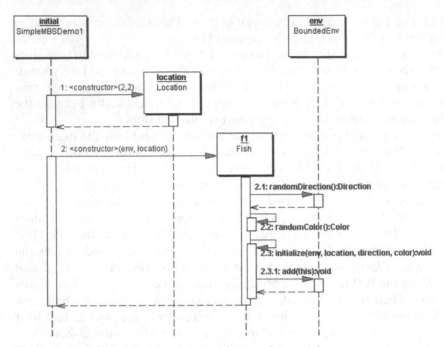

Fig. 1. Sequence diagram representing the sample scenario

Now, let us suppose the user has considered that *f1* can be added to the environment. When she selects the *Send* command and uses the object *env* and the message *add*, *env* tries to execute this method. Unfortunately, *env* displays the error message *"I can not add the fish. It does not have a Location"* because it is not the expected message. After selecting the correct action, *f1* throws the ball upwards and says *"f1, do initialize with env, location, direction and color"*. Now, the user considers the constructor is finished and selects the *Return* action; and, again, *f1* displays an error message *"I have not been added to the environment, yet"*.

After the correct action, *f1* throws again the ball to *env*, but this time it says *"env, do add with myself"* (instead of *"with f1"* or *"with this"*). Avatar *env* catches the ball and returns the ball to *f1*, rolling it and saying *"add is done"*. Now *f1* rolls the ball towards initial and says *"constructor done"*. Finally, when the ball and the focus are on initial, it concludes the role-play. Figure 2 shows the environment during the simulation described above.

6 Conclusions and Future Work

In this paper we have described our approach to teach object-oriented interactions by combining active learning and software visualization techniques. Following this approach, we have developed a prototype called ViRPlay 3D. We have exploited our experience in developing another virtual environment called Javy [8] to design this prototype. Javy is a 3D virtual environment which simulates the Java Virtual Machine (JVM). It is enriched with a pedagogical agent who resides in the environment and teaches the student about the JVM structure and the Java language compilation. Our prototype employs the virtual JVM implemented in that system to execute the source code visualized in the simulation.

Fig. 2. A screenshot from the role-play virtual environment

We are in the process of evaluating the effectiveness of ViRPlay 3D to improve object-oriented software understanding for introductory programming courses. Initial results seem promising and have lead us to consider object-oriented design as new area of application for the same approach combining active learning and software visualization.

Our experience teaching courses on object-oriented design patterns for several years shows that a teaching style based only on lecturing does not fit every type of student. Students lack the experience needed to understand the subtleties and implications of the design ideas given by the patterns In that situation, the student may naively think that the design pattern is the obvious and natural solution to the motivating example used in the lecture. We are running some experiments applying an active learning approach to solve this problem: we make the students collaborate in the elaboration of alternative designs and try to guide them through a trial-and-error process to the solution provided in the design pattern. Designs are obtained through role-play activities where use case scenarios are simulated using CRC cards, a technique usually applied for collaborative object-oriented design. Combining the results from these experiments with the work on ViRPlay 3D, our mid-term goal is to take into a virtual 3D environment what we are now exploring in the real world.

Acknowledgments

Supported by the Spanish Committee of Education & Science (TIN2005-09382-C02-01)

References

1. Andrianoff S K, Levine D B (2002) Role playing in an object-oriented world. In 33rd SIGCSE Technical Symposium on Computer Science Education, ACM Press, Cincinnati, Kentucky, pp. 121–125
2. Bergin J, Eckstein J, Wallingford E, Manns M L (2001) Patterns for gaining different perspectives. In 8th Conference on Pattern Languages of Programs, Monticello, Illinois, USA
3. Biddle R, Noble J, Tempero E (2001) Techniques for active learning of oo development. In 16th ACM SIGPLAN Conference on Object Oriented Programming, Systems, Languages, and Applications (Educators Symposium), Tampa Bay, USA
4. Brady A F (2004) Marine biology simulation case study. Teaching resources. Available online at http://max.cs.kzoo.edu/AP/MBS/index.html.
5. Dann W, Dragon T, Cooper S, Dietzler K, Ryan K, Pausch R (2003) Objects: Visualization of behavior and state. In 8th Annual Conference on Innovation and Technology in Computer Science Education, Thessaloniki, Greece, ACM Press, pp. 84–88
6. Gestwicki P V (2004) Interactive visualization of object-oriented programs. In Vlissides J M, Schmidt D C (eds), 19th Annual ACM SIGPLAN Conference on Object-Oriented Programming Systems, Languages, and Applications, Vancouver, Canada, ACM Press, pp. 48–49
7. Grundy J, Hosking J (2000) High-level static and dynamic visualisation of software architectures. In 2000 IEEE International Symposium on Visual Languages, Seattle, Washington, USA, IEEE Computer Society, pp. 5–12
8. Gómez-Martín P P, Gómez-Martín M A, González-Calero P A (2003) Javy: Virtual environment for case-based teaching of java virtual machine. In 7th

International Conference on Knowledge-Based Intelligent Information & Engineering Systems, volume 2774 of LNCS, Springer Verlag, pp. 906–913

9. Ip A, Linser R, Naidu S (2001) Simulated worlds: Rapid generation of web-based role-play. In 7th Australasian World Wide Web Conference, Coffs Harbour, Australia

10. Jerding D F, Stasko J T, Ball T (1997) Visualizing interactions in program executions. In 19th International Conference on Software Engineering, Boston, Massachusetts, USA, IEEE Computer Society, pp. 360–370

11. Maletic J I, Leigh J, Marcus A, Dunlap G (2001) Visualizing object-oriented software in virtual reality. In 9th International Workshop on Program Comprehension, Toronto, Canada, IEEE Computer Society, pp. 26–38

12. Naps T L, Rößling G, Almstrum V, Dann W, Fleischer R, Hundhausen C, Korhonen A, Malmi L, McNally M, Rodger S, Velázquez-Iturbide J A (2002) Exploring the role of visualization and engagement in computer science education. In Caspersen M E, Joyce D, Goelman D, Utting I (eds), Working group reports from 7th Annual Conference on Innovation and Technology in Computer Science Education, Arhus, Denmark, ACM Press, pp. 131–152

13. Panas T, Berrigan R, Grundy J (2003) A 3D metaphor for software production visualization. In 7th International Conference on Information Visualization, London, England, IEEE Computer Society, pp. 314–319

14. Price B A, Baecker R M, Small I S (1993) A principled taxonomy of software visualization. Journal of Visual Languages and Computing, 4(3):211–266

15. Sharf J, Hsu T, Ryan E (1999) Timescope: An educational 3D multi-user roleplaying environment. In 9th Annual Conference of the Internet Society, San Jose, CA, USA

16. Thaden U, Steimann F (2003) Animated UML as a 3D-illustration for teaching OOP. In 7th Workshop on Pedagogies and Tools for Learning Object-Oriented Concepts in 17th European Conference on Object-Oriented Programming, Darmstadt, Germany, Springer

Making Concept Maps Available on the Web to the Students

Sandra Lopes, Pedro Henriques, Paulo Dias

Universidade do Minho
4700 Braga, Portugal
sandralopes@di.uminho.pt

1 Introduction

Nowadays, the web sites that most of us make available to the students, to support our courses, are mere transposition of the old article material to the computer. This is, our course web sites are just repositories of links and disconnected chunks of descriptions–objectives and course structure, learning outcomes, program (table of contents, or topic index), bibliography and other supporting materials, assessment and marking rules, teaching team, classes and timetables, etc. The interaction of the students with the site and its relevance for the knowledge acquisition process are minimal. This is particularly upsetting when we teach computer science students or we teach computers to other students (engineering, social sciences, etc.)–the best way to convince them of the computer capabilities is to apply it in our own profit. Indeed, teaching how to solve our daily problems with computers, and being unable to take the best of them in our activities, is contradictory.

So, we argue that it is mandatory to transform the web site into a learning object, being an effective aid for students to understand the course subject and acquire new knowledge on that area. Different constituents of the site–like the programme (the index of course units), lesson synopsis and summaries, bibliography, objectives, etc.–should be strongly related in such a manner that students can go through them in a kind of a semantic navigation; In this way, we believe that it can contribute to their learning process. In the article, we suggest the use of Concept Maps to support that transformation.

We advocate that the course planning should be done based on a Concept Map representing the knowledge domain involved. After the planning, this Concept Map should be kept and made available to the students. To be useable, a computer-based tool should support the Concept Maps development and navigation.

In this context and with that motivation in mind, this article aims at introducing a system, NAVMAP, to help teachers create a navigator for Decorated Concept Maps as the result of their course planning activity.

The article is structured as follows. We remember the definition of Concept Map and its role in the course planning process, in Section 2. Then, Section 3 is devoted to NAVMAP; after an overview of the system functionality, we present NAVMAP architecture and detail its two main components: the Decorated Concept Maps Navigator; and the information management sub-system that assists the course planning activity. Section 4 is a short discussion on the benefits of using NAVMAP to build a learning object linkable to a course web site, and Section 5 is the conclusion.

2 Concept Maps and Planning

This section is to introduce the role of Concept Maps in the teaching planning activity (PA).

Concept mapping is a technique for representing knowledge in graphs. Knowledge graphs are networks of concepts. A graph consists of nodes and arcs. Nodes represent concepts and links represent the relations between concepts (see Figure 1 that shows a partial Concept Map taken from our course on *Introduction to Computers*). The Concept Maps may be translated in propositions. Propositions are obtained by going through the graph, reading the substantives (concepts) inscribed in the nodes concatenated to the transitive verbs (relationships) labelling the arcs.

The use of Concept Maps as a teaching strategy was first developed by Novak in the early 1980's [1]. It was derived from Ausubel's learning theory [4] that places central emphasis on the influence of students' prior knowledge on subsequent meaningful learning. According to Ausubel, "the most important single factor influencing learning is what the learner already knows. Thus meaningful learning results when a person consciously and explicitly ties new knowledge to relevant concepts they already possess". Ausubel suggests that when meaningful learning occurs, it produces a series of changes within our entire cognitive structure, modifying existing concepts and forming new linkages between concepts.

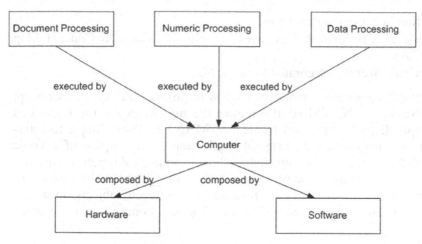

Fig. 1. Concept Map of a course planning

Concept Maps is, also, considered a pedagogical strategy for planning; because it allows organizing the course contents by concepts to be taught. The wide and integrating concepts may constitute the basis of planning while the less embracing concepts are used to select the most specific teaching activities and information resources.

The planning process can be split into four steps: definition of the concepts to be taught; organization the concept network; association of concepts to teaching units and scheduling (distribution of units amongst the course's available time); and choice of resources to use associating them to concepts [8].

However, building and handling Concept Maps is a complex and time consuming task either for the teachers, or for the students to use them as learning object. Therefore, there is a strong need for a computer based system able to process Concept Maps (edit, store, and navigate); for that a rigorous representation system is necessary.

3 NAVMAP

NAVMAP is a web application supported by a database to:
- Define Concepts and Relations;
- Associate Concepts and Relations, creating a true and traditional Concept Map (CM);
- Define course Units, associating them to Lessons;
- Associate Concepts to course Units, producing a Coloured Concept Map (CCM);

- Define Information Resources;
- Associate Concepts to Resources, creating a Decorated Concept Map (DCM);
- Navigate over the Decorated Concept Map.

Figure 2 shows the complete workflow to produce a Decorated Concept Map Navigator. NAVMAP also allows the user to export the Decorated Concept Map to a standard format, XTM (XML Topic Map), to interchange the map data with external applications. The purpose of a Topic Map (TM) is to convey knowledge about resources through a superimposed layer, or map, of the resources. A topic map captures the subjects of which resources speak, and the relationships between subjects, in a way that is implementation-independent [7]. The key concepts in topic maps

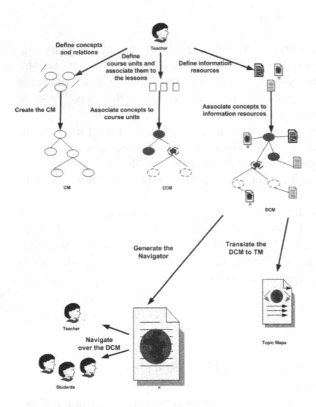

Fig. 2. Workflow supported by NAVMAP

are topics, associations, and occurrences; so Concept Maps can be directly translated to Topic Maps as discussed in [6]. This feature enables the use of other tools that handle that representation (TM) for semantic networks. For instance, we can use the navigator generators Ulisses [3] or Omnigator [5]; or the Concept Maps processor CmapTools [2].

NAVMAP allows exploring course-planning material in three different ways:

- Navigating through the concepts;
- Navigating through the course units;
- Navigating through the information resources.

To accomplish its task, two parts compose NAVMAP: the Back-Office (BO) that supports the teachers' planning, assisting him in the development of the Decorated Concept Map; the Front-Office (FO), available to everyone (teachers and students), to navigate over the Decorated Concept Map.

3.1 NAVMAP Architecture

The two main components of NAVMAP architecture (FO and BO) are supported by a central database, as depicted in Figure 3. The BO is

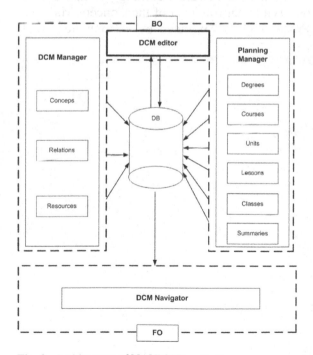

Fig. 3. Architecture of NAVMAP system

responsible for storing and keeping the information in the central data-base, and can be splitted into three parts:

1. A **DCM Manager** that handles concepts, relations and resources;
2. A Concept Maps Editor and Integrator with Course Units and Information Resources (**DCM Editor** in figure 3.);
3. A **Planning Manager** that handles degrees, courses, units, lessons, classes and summaries;

The Front-Office just queries the central database and dynamically generates the HTML pages to visualize and traverse the conceptual network.

3.2 NAVMAP: The Navigator

Figure 4 is a screen of the navigator produced by NAVMAP Front-Office for the Concept Map shown in Figure 1. The page shown is a specific view corresponding to the selection of one particular concept ("Computer"). The selected concept is displayed at the centre of the page; the related concepts are shown around it (in this case there are five concepts). The arrows connecting concepts, three in-coming and two out-coming, are labelled by the name of the relations–observing that fragment of the Concept Map, we can say that "Document Processing" is "executed by" "Computer", and

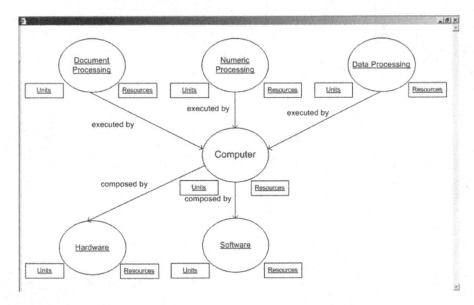

Fig. 4. Screen of DCM Navigator

that "Computer" is "composed by" "Hardware". Units and Resources associated with each Concept are represented, displaying their names inside rectangles locate below the respective node; units on the left and resources on the right.

When we invoke the Navigator, the "Concept Map root" is selected and displayed at the centre of the first page; by default, we assume the root as the concept whose name is the course name.

The student can interact with the page in order to navigate over the Decorated Concept Map; all that he has to do is to follow the link associated with the name of one of the concepts, units or resources, depending on the kind of exploration he intends to do (as previously told, the user can go through concepts, course units where concepts are taught, or information resources proposed to support each concept).

3.3 NAVMAP: The Planning support

The most important characteristic of the NAVMAP Back-Office (BO) is that all the insertion and editing operations are done in textual forms, instead of adopting a visual (or graphical) approach

To illustrate the BO that the teacher uses to build and decorated the Concept Map (creating and updating the database that is searched by the Front-Office to generate the desired navigator), we show some screenshots of the web application.

Figure 5 is the form for adding **course units**. The degree and course names, to which the unit belongs, are initially defined and appear at the top of the page. As can be seen, the units already defined are listed inside a

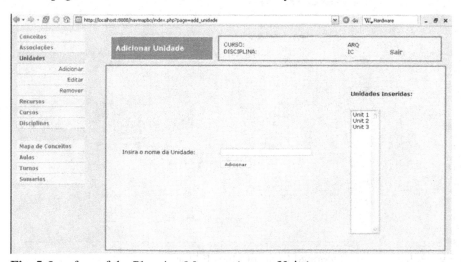

Fig. 5. Interface of the Planning Manager (course Units)

box on the right of the screen; just the unit name must the provided. Another different option should be selected to associate units to lessons, and lessons synopsis and summaries.

Figure 6 is the form to edit **concepts**. The concepts previously inserted are displayed in the list box on the left; the user can select the one he intends to edit, and then update the information shown inside the boxes on the right.

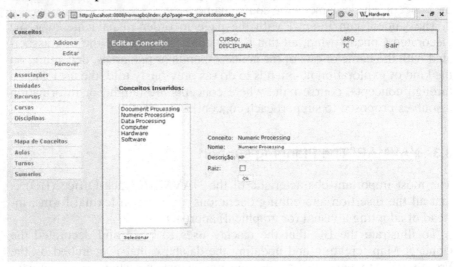

Fig. 6. Interface of DCM Manager (Concepts)

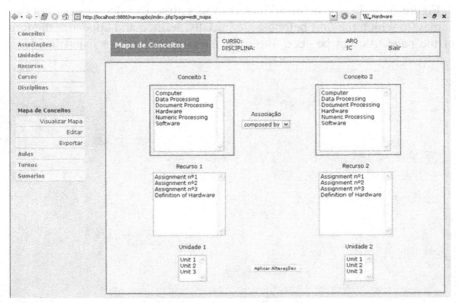

Fig. 7. Interface of Decorated Concept Maps Editor

The form to add/edit resources is quite similar to the previous ones; however, a search facility is included.

After adding the basic components, what should be done is the association of concepts by means of relations, and their connection to units and resources; this task is executed fulfilling the form shown in figure 7.

4 The Outcomes of NAVMAP

In this section we will discuss the pedagogical outcomes we hope to attain with the use of our system in the classroom.

From the teacher's point of view, NAVMAP makes the Planning Activity a simpler and a more systematic process. The edition of the Concept Map and its maintenance becomes much easier, as well as its association with the course units, lessons, and resources.

From the students' point of view, a great advantage of using NAVMAP is that it provides a visual representation of the Concept Map under study in a tangible form that can be remembered very easily. The Concept Map can be readily revisited as many times as necessary. During the navigation the students understands perfectly the concepts' meaning and the relationships established among them.

One general benefit is that course planning becomes useful for both, teachers and students. It is no more just an administrative instrument to exhibit in the first lesson and archive thereafter.

Other general benefit is that the course site is transformed into a learning object and not only a repository of information.

5 Conclusion

To plan a course, the teacher should start by defining the abilities and skills that the students will acquire after following the lessons; in other words, he should specify the learning outcomes. An effective way to proceed, in order to define the course contents and to draw up the course programme is to develop a Concepts Map, in the sense of Ausubel and Novak. However, that task is hard to accomplish and, most of the times, it has not any impact in the teaching/learning process.

We advocate that the Concept Map should be made available to the students, on one hand to improve their understanding about the topics under study, and on the other hand to aid the assessment process (by comparing the student Concept Map against the teacher Concept Map).

In that context, this article discussed the approach and introduced NAVMAP, a web tool to help teachers' planning and to produce a navigator that can be added to the course web site for students' usage. In this way, we believe that a computer science teacher is releasing a much more interactive and up-to-date tool; his course web site is no more just a collection of links, but offers a semantic network of concepts.

The next step is to merge different Concept Maps, allowing an academic manager to get a general overview of a set of courses (belonging to some degree). Such a feature enables the manager to understand where and how some subjects are introduced and discussed, allowing him to balance the institutional teaching offer. This new functionality can be achieved either developing a new module that queries the central database, or using a special tool to merge Concept Maps.

References

1. Ausubel D (2000) The Acquisition and Retention of Knowledge: A Cognitive View. Kluwer Academic Publishers, Boston
2. CmapTools, http://cmap.ihmc.us/
3. Librelotto GR, Ramalho JC, Henriques PR (2003) Ontology driven Websites with Topic Maps. In The International Conference on Web Engineering, Oviedo, Spain.
4. Novak J, Gowin D (1984) Learning How to Learn. Cambridge University Press, New York
5. Ontopia. The Ontopia Knowledge Suite. http://www.ontopia.net/solutions/products.html.-
6. Paz F, Lopes SC, Librelotto GR, Henriques PR (2005) XML Topic Maps e Mapa de Conceitos. XATA' 05 – 3ªConferência Nacional sobre "XML — Aplicações e Tecnologias Associadas", Braga
7. Pepper S (2000) The TAO of Topic Maps. In proceedings of the XML Europe 2000.
8. Ribeiro AC, Ribeiro LC (2003) Planificação e Avaliação do Ensino-Aprendizagem. Universidade Aberta, Lisboa

The Web as a Means of Promoting Reading and Writing Habits: The Netescrit@ Project

Emilia Miranda, Paulo Moreira

Escola E.B. 2/3 Dr. Carlos Pinto Ferreira
Centro de Competência Nónio da Universidade do Minho
emiranda@mail.telepac.pt, paulo.moreira@nonio.uminho.pt

1 The Importance of Children's Literature in the Promotion of Reading Habits

Natércia Rocha [5] states that for children everything is at its beginning, so that thinking about them implies privileging values of the future from the standpoint of the present. She maintains that everything that has an impact on children must be carefully and skilfully tended so as not to imperil their future; and that, among the many things that surround children, books are an active factoring their development, constituting potential modelling agents of future beings, both through their presence and their absence. She adds that a love or hate of reading is not innate; both feelings are generated in the child's early or late acquaintance with this activity. Rocha further states that the function of writers, illustrators and publishers is a causal factor in the affective relationship bound up with the love or hatred of reading.

Reading is a determining factor in the personal and social development of the child, since it enables the access to information, to lifelong learning and, in a school context, to the acquisition and development of the contents of the syllabus.

In the periods of formal learning, students read in order to learn, but it is important to promote reading for pleasure, which contributes to the development of reading habits.

2   The ICT in Literature for Children and Young People

Although they have always tried to keep pace with the transformations that occur in their societies, education and educational systems often lag behind. We are constantly made aware of the yawning gulf between school and society, since society evolves at an increasingly faster pace, while school evolves at a frighteningly slow rhythm.

If we were briefly to sketch the history of education, from the first primitive societies to our days, we would realize that changes in education have always belatedly caught up with the evolution of society.

In the 20th century, we have witnessed a huge and fast technological evolution. This has impacted on all areas of society, obviously encompassing the teaching institutions. These have been through several generations with regard to the use of technology and changes in the role of the teacher.

The first of these generations, corresponding to the 1950s and 60s, witnessed the introduction in schools of several auxiliary teaching tools. These helped the teacher impart knowledge, since they illustrated, through images, what was being imparted through the words of the teacher or of books. These tools, some of which are still in use nowadays, were the epidiascope, the overhead projector, the slide projector, the film projector and also the record player.

It is the second generation, coinciding with the 70s and 80s, that sees the adoption by schools of other technologies, such as the audio and video recorder, the video camera, the photocopier, the television and also the computer.

The third generation, arising in the following decade, sees the introduction of telecommunications and multimedia resources in schools.

In our opinion, we have now a fourth generation. The school, while still resorting to many of the technologies of previous generations, is beginning to realize that it must use the internet as a means that enables the deployment of collaborative processes aimed at creating networks of knowledge of the Information Society.

Information and communication technologies do not in and of themselves install a new pedagogy, but they can be put at the service of varied pedagogies.

There was a time when the need to acquire computing skills was advocated and learning was centred on the computer itself. It was even considered to be 'one other topic of the syllabus and children had to learn its history, the name of each of its components, the professional careers connected to it, etc.' [4]. Later, the computer came to be seen as a tool to teach information technology and as 'a great increment in the teaching of *concepts and programming languages, adding a new area to an already overloaded curriculum.'* [4]

On other current, computer-assisted learning, *'privileges the contents to be imparted, assuming a well-defined curriculum and proposing to help the student progress along it as efficiently as possible.'* [4].

Nowadays, the internet and the World Wide Web attract all those who work in the fields of education and teaching. They make available a huge variety of resources and supports for the use of collaborative strategies in the development of learning processes.

As Dias [2] refers, *'the communication activities supported by the Web promote the appearance of new, more flexible learning practices and the development of interactions geared towards a collaborative learning process.'*

The Netescrit@ project has as its guiding principle to engage children and young people in reading and writing activities. It rests on a collaborative work approach, implemented by means of synchronic and asynchronous communication made available in the platform of the project.

3 The Netescrit@ Project

3.1 Description

The Netescrit@ project started in 1993/94. Its aim is to create a network of schools, students, teachers, authors, and anyone else involved in the development of reading and writing skills in children and young people. It uses the Internet as a versatile tool which enables the creation of varied and challenging learning environments.

Within this project, a learning platform has been developed, sited at XXX. It is geared towards the creation of a work environment conducive to reading and writing. Its objectives are:

- the development of the reading skills of the participating students
- the development of individual and collaborative writing skills of the students
- the development of analysis and synthesis skills
- to implement «Palavras Ilustradas», a meeting of young readers and authors, illustrators and musicians, with the collaboration of the Museum Nogueira da Silva

- to make available bio-bibliographical data on Portuguese language authors who write for children and young people in the project's site
- the constant updating of the site with the collaboration of the Centro de Competência of the Universidade do Minho, both in the information about new authors made available and in interactive proposals
- an analysis of the implications of the inclusion in the curricula of ICT for the development of analytical, interpretative and reading and writing skills.

In this paper, we shall focus on some of the tools we have used, such as the forum, the blog, collaborative writing, interactive challenges and electronic mail.

The forum is open to all and has been developed from the start of the project (under reconstruction at the moment).

The themes under debate are suggested by the participating students or by anyone who logs on.

Whenever we detect any deviation from the theme under discussion, we seek to draw it to the attention of the participants, so that they may get back on track

We also draw attention to spelling inaccuracies or syntactic problems whenever they are spotted.

Furthermore, we try to make the participants adhere to the code of the Portuguese language, rather than to those of text messaging or chat rooms.

The blog is open to the participation of children and young people from various schools and its administration falls to us, which enables us to select the works to be published.

The commentaries section available has proved to be an excellent incentive to writing.

The collaborative writing section is open to all the participants and anyone who logs on through the site.

We currently have nine collaborative writing challenges in progress, initiated by three authors and aimed at the students of the three existing levels of the basic education system.

The interactive challenges are permanently available and the students may, if they so wish, take them up. These are exercises such as filling in the gaps, crosswords, multiple choice questionnaires and scrambled texts, essentially aiming at the self-assessment of their comprehension of the texts of the authors and of the information available on the site.

Electronic mail is used by students whenever they want to send their contributions to the blog or when they need information relating to the themes of reading and writing.

3.2 Implementation Model

The implementation of this project, as far as the exploration of its site by schools and/or students, follows several stages.

Initially, we contacted some schools, explained the aims of the project and invited them to take part.

Whenever a teacher seems willing to collaborate, our work proceeds with his/her collaboration and the strategies for exploring the site are then freely made available.

When no teacher is available to give support to the students interested in taking part, we try to make regular visits to the school in question in order to work with the students.

The meetings with authors, which we have entitled Palavras Ilustradas [Illustrated Words] are developed with the support of the Museu Nogueira da Silva.

This cultural unit of the Universidade do Minho provides the space for the meetings and sends out information to schools.

Up to the present, the meetings shown in Table 1 were realized:

Table 1. Project meetings with authors

Date	Author	Number of Schools	Number of Students
02/02/2004	Vergílio Alberto Vieira	3	132
15/03/2004	Luísa Ducla Soares	3	142
22/03/2004	António Mota	2	160
21/05/2004	Álvaro Magalhães	3	70
22/10/2004	José Vaz	3	65
15/11/2004	Ana Maria Magalhães	2	93
25/01/2005	Alice Vieira	3	125
14/02/2005	João Pedro Mésseder	2	91
08/06/2005	José Fanha	4	139
28/11/2005	Ana Saldanha	2	115
Total:	10	27	1132

The collaborative writing activity takes place when we visit the schools or when the teachers who have agreed to collaborate suggest that activity to their students.

Since this is a free activity, and open to all, when there are unidentified or inappropriate submissions they are eliminated by us.

4 Conclusion

The student population of today's schools is radically different from that of past times and will of necessity be different from that of the future. When they first go to school, children have already learnt quite a few things and *'have developed skills and ways of learning that may be different from the ones typical of a society with little access to information, in which television was not yet a mass phenomenon nor was it, as it is today, the vehicle of communication of a massive amount of information'* [1].

This different mass of children and young people demands of teachers different ways of teaching and assessing. Teachers will have to be able to adapt their pedagogical and assessment practices to new social contexts, to avoid going down a route of collision.

The type of skills that students must possess nowadays is considerably different from the ones required years ago and schools must evolve and seek to keep abreast of the transformations undergone by the societies to which they belong.

If the first objective of a school is limited to imparting knowledge to children and young people through the agency of the teachers and if, for that purpose, it has developed a culture of its own by establishing a series of norms, values and procedures, the use of the Internet in this context will influence the education process and the functions with which it is associated. The information networks enable work and communication, breaking not only space and time barriers, but also social ones. Academic or other titles, social status, race, age, looks, facial expressions, body language are not present. These absences could contribute to a lack of inhibition and therefore, make communication easier. Networks may thus lead to democratizing the participation in the work. Nevertheless, the use of networks such as the internet may have a very important impact in the patterns of communication and the hierarchical status, since it challenges the social and organizational culture of schools, which may well try to defend their authority and their existing norms. Its use may, in a way, call into question the existing school norms.

These challenges must be seen as a great opportunity for all of us and we will then be able to *'reconcile ourselves to the future, bring together the old and the new, the historical archive and the world wide web, welding and CAD-CAM, stucco restoration and graphic computing, if we are capable of overcoming the shame of what is concrete and empirical, the anti-experimental, anti-technical, anti-erudite and slackly conceptualist and rhetorical curse which sustained us while the borders were shut and minds were elsewhere. This is the new frontier of knowledge and know-how. This frontier concerns everyone and nobody can remain indifferent to it.'* [3]

References

1. Azevedo C, Azevedo A (1998) Metodologia Cientifica. Porto: C. Azevedo
2. Dias P (2004) Comunidades de Aprendizagem on-line. Nov@Formação, n° 3: 14–17
3. Gago J M (1996) Os Desafios da Sociedade da Informação: Ameaças e Oportunidades para Portugal. Lisbon
4. Ponte J (1992) O Computador, um instrumento da evolução, 6th Edition. Lisbon. Texto Editora
5. Rocha N (1992) Breve História da Literatura para Crianças em Portugal. 2nd Edition. Lisbon. Instituto da Cultura e Língua Portuguesa, Ministério da Educação

Usage of the AWLA Online Writing Resource for Language Learning

Pedro Sánchez, Manuel Ortega, Angie Phillip, Asunción Sánchez

Universidad de Castilla-La Mancha, Spain
Manuel.Ortega@uclm.es

1 Introduction

The European Union is fostering the development of new learning environments to integrate more interactive techniques in the traditional classroom. The Council of Europe's e-Learning Initiative has established a Common European Framework of Reference for Language Learning (CEF) which regards 'language learning as preparation for the active use of the language for communication and social interaction' [1]. The e-Learning Initiative was adopted by the European Commission in the year 2000 [2], and defined e-Learning "as the use of new multimedia technologies and the Internet to improve the quality of learning by facilitating access to resources and services as well as remote exchanges and collaboration". Following these directives about using the new technologies to develop skills such as the ability to communicate and to work in group, we have designed an online learning appliance to practice the skill of writing in a foreign language by using authentic tools for writing, computers. Computing devices in online learning environments can help us to apply the collaborative learning techniques that are proving so effective in the learning of the oral skills in face-to-face environments (work in pairs, in groups, role play, etc.) to writing activities.

AWLA is an online learning appliance designed to practice the skill of writing in a foreign language. It is based on the new learning theories based on knowledge construction. With AWLA, Web-based ubiquitous technologies enable collaborative work, in situated environments where learners are engaged in a community of learners to produce authentic writing as a means of learning and practising a foreign language as well as for learning any discipline where writing is a necessity. The learners using AWLA can directly practice writing on the Web, with the characteristics of synchronous and asynchronous interaction and ubiquity that the Web offers. This resource facilitates the collaborative edition of text, simultaneously providing access to contents and reference information and offering tools for communication. The text edition can be monitored by the teacher who can control the collaborative edition as well, checking the contributions that each learner individually makes, including plagiarism. With a methodology based on tasks and scenarios, the system has been easily adaptable to diverse educative environments (schools of languages, university centres, researchers and teacher training, in distance and blended learning environments). This is an analysis of the learning-to-write courses and experiences. AWLA is currently being localized to diverse languages and integrated into some online learning systems, such as Moodle and AIOLE, An Interactive Online Learning Environment.

The AWLA System (which stands for *A Writing Learning Appliance*) tries to evolve towards the practice of collaborative writing with computing tools, from the traditional classroom to ubiquitous e-Learning environments accessible from anywhere at any time. The Information and Communications Technologies (ICT) are integrated in the traditional classroom by providing access to the Internet, first with computers connected to the Internet, later evolving to using wireless devices. This will make it possible to apply the e-Learning Action Plan proposed by the European Community in order to acquire new basic skills such as the ones related to information technologies and foreign languages, among others [2]. Thus, learning will be enhanced with a mobile computing system that enables the work in group as well as using the ICT from any classroom, from outside the educational centre, from home or from the workplace. The participants feel really motivated due to the interaction provided and the availability of the learning design, always on display on their writing environment. In the last section, we are presenting here the results of the usage analysis in the first stages of the system deployment.

2 Web-based Mobile Infrastructure

E-Learning in educational centres was first achieved by means of static electronic tools (desktop PCs) in dedicated rooms full of computers (labs). Currently, mobile devices integrated in the traditional classroom are becoming quite common. ICT provide e-Learning with the capacity to be achieved at a distance, in the same place or in ubiquitous environments, simultaneously or asynchronously, and individually or in collaboration.

A technology-enhanced infrastructure has been established to enable writing in ubiquitous and collaborative online environments. For this purpose, a series of computing tools give support to the work in group, taking into account the benefits provided by the new paradigm of human-computer interaction in ubiquitous environments [3]. This has been achieved mainly through Web technologies, implementing the wireless connection in the classrooms in the educational centre, and any Internet-connected computing device outside. The use of ICT should be integrated in everyday life in the traditional class in a similar way as audio-visual media was in the language classroom. Additionally, communications have pervaded in real life in the last years. Adapting the eCLUB architecture, designed by the CHICO Research Group [4], we have taken advantage of the existing infrastructure of Internet-connected desktop PCs installed in the educational centres of Castilla La Mancha, and made it evolve to ubiquitous systems consisting of mobile devices such as laptop PCs, Tablet PCs, and PDAs wirelessly connected to the Internet, used as electronic notebooks in the classroom.

The developed system includes Web based software designed with DHTML hypertext language that makes use of JavaScript and Cascade Style Sheets fully integrated in the user's browser to run on the client side, and of the Perl programming language, on CGI (Common Gateway Interface connection) for the interaction and communication with the Web server. This technique allows the writing of texts, their correction and evaluation saved on the Web server from where they are easily retrieved and accessible at any time from anywhere.

2.1 Pedagogical Aspects

With AWLA the learner easily enters the Web-based writing environment to do the tasks designed by the tutor (Figure 1, right column). The participants do the text-writing tasks (centre), saving them on the server with the action buttons (on the left). They are permanently accessible and modifiable on the Web. Thus, communication of updatable information through technology is offered on the Web, developed simultaneously along the process of learning how to write.

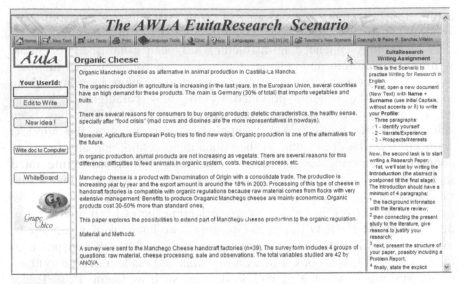

Fig. 1. User Interface of the AWLA System (English)

This system is equipped with Web resources for the learning in group with techniques related to writing text composition from notes in contributions proposed by the learners. These resources are of two types: language reference tools (dictionaries and search engines integrated in the interface), and communication tools, consisting of resources for the synchronous and asynchronous communication with other participants in the same writing task in order to allow the collaborative work between a group of learners and the intercommunication with the tutor, helping the learners to negotiate, coordinate and improve their writing activity. This is done through a Web-based chat, both synchronously and asynchronously, always using the text title as the chat channel. The system allows the integration and adaptation of writing activities from textbooks in tasks addressed to collaborative learning, extending integrated activities in university education and life-long learning, by writing projects, research articles and texts for the development of writing, all this on the Web.

E-Learning has been developed in a ubiquitous environment, which offers the opportunity to access the lesson plan assigned by the tutor (i.e., the learning design: a tasks column for assignments called scenario, which gives name to the activity, possibly with a description of the task, identifying the target learners, their recommended level, instructions, guidelines, and further comments). The system emphasizes the learning design capability that the system offers to the tutor, as recommended by Britain and Liber in [5]. This is updatable and is always on display. It is one of the main pedagogical contributions of the AWLA system. The tutor can easily offer links to internal or external contents such as guides or tutorials, to a similar text for comparison, to multimedia files and to the practice of exercises on the Web, related to the specific writing practice being carried out. As mentioned above, the participants can practice from the classroom, from the computers room or outside the educational centre, at any time. Classroom practice offers more fluid collaboration integrating oral interaction in blended environments to coordinate the texts writing process.

In the initial implementation, a prototype was designed that allowed the work in class guided by the tutor. In the second stage, the interface has been adapted to other languages (Spanish and German; Italian and French are under development), including language tools in these target languages. As to the learning processes, after the initial analysis of the aspects of the class writing activity susceptible of improvement, in the first stage, the system has been completed with models of language learning based on activities, tasks and scenarios.

Currently, the system has evolved after the analysis of aspects such as interaction, learning design and the mechanisms for communication and collaboration. Importance is being given to the possible integration of this tool for writing on the Web in online learning environments, such as AIOLE, originated from AWLA, and MOODLE, the open-source system.

2.2 The Changing Role of Participants

The participants are really motivated by the possibility to publish their texts on the Web, which can be read from anywhere at any time. They are made aware that the facility to find information on the Web about the topics proposed goes along with the facility that offers the system to find plagiarized text. This always takes them to elaborate their own texts, although the information can come from other texts already published on the Web.

The role of the tutor is one of a facilitator and guide (Figure 2, right column), and in the final phase, of an evaluator, which allows to a great extent maintaining technical procedures in traditional education, improving them with the Web technology to adapt to the objectives established in the new education trends proposed by the European Common Framework of Languages [1].

The assessment mechanism of the tutor goes beyond the traditional correction: it includes the control of plagiarism and the tracking of each learner as to the contributions (whether they are proposals or revisions) made in the collaborative writing. The interface adapts when the tutor enters the system to review and evaluate texts, displaying the diverse resources for correcting on the left, and with the possibility at any time of modifying the learning design pathway on the right, as shown in Figure 2:

Fig. 2. Adaptive Columns of the Tutor's Interface

2.3 Usage Analysis

Once the prototype of the system implemented, it was put into operation with real learners in class, developing activities of individual writing first and activities of collaborative writing later. In the first year the AWLA system was put into practice in two courses, (English 2nd year – elementary cycle – and English 4th year – superior cycle in the Official Schools of Languages). After several initial tests, the first writing task was to make a digital newspaper in group, whose results as to level of participation of learners (22), their contributions and corrections can be seen in figure 3:

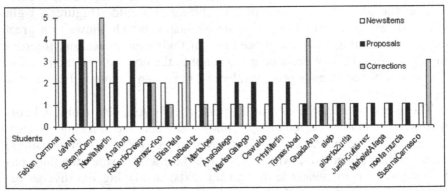

Fig. 3. Analysis of the first environment of collaborative writing; 'NewsPaper'

Later, other types of activities and models of learning were designed and practiced, such as the following ones (referred to in Tables 1 and 2):

1. Activities adapted from textbooks (Textbook),
2. Activities adapted from workbooks (Workbook),
3. Tasks of collaborative writing (Collaborative),
4. Tasks of writing for examinations (Exam),
5. Integrating Tasks in Webquests: information search, reading, design and writing (WebQuest)
6. Other tasks of authentic writing in academic environments (Writing for Specific Purposes such as in ESP, EAP). For example: Course of Writing Research Articles at the University College of Agriculture and another at the Faculty of Chemistry in Ciudad Real in the University of Castilla La Mancha, and
7. Tasks integrated in the Monographic Course of Improving English with the Internet for Life-long Learning (LLL) at the Official School of Languages in Ciudad Real

Table 1. Results in the First Stage: Course 2003–04

Scenario/Task	No. of Texts/ Users	Task Model	Level
NewsPaper	1/22	Collaborative	2°
TravelBrochure	11/20	Collaborative	2°
TreasurePossessions	23	Textbook	4°
FilmReview	10	Textbook	2°
FavouriteFilm	5	Exam	2°
SpendingMoney	8	Exam	2°
FamousPerson	8	Exam	2°
Totals: 7 tasks	72/94 (36 diff)	3 models	2 Levels

In total, 7 different writing tasks were made, which produced 72 texts, with 94 users participating (36 different users, which is an average of 3 texts per user). They can be classified in 3 models of activities in 2 different environments. From the beginning, the collaborative and ubiquitous aspects are of great importance.

Table 2. Results in the Second Stage: Course 2004–05

Scenario or Task	Texts/Users	Task Model	Course-Level
SmartWear	12	Exam 12/04	4° EOI B2 Eng. Students
New Technologies	16	Collaborative	4° EOI B2 Eng. Students
Treasured Possessions	25	From Textbook	4° EOI B2 Eng. Students
BioProfiles	25	From Textbook	4° EOI B2 Eng. Students
Complaint Letters	20	Workbook	4° EOI B2 Eng. Students
Euita Research	10+10 Biodata/10	Teacher Training	EUITA Researchers
TheThirdMan	1	Exam	4° EOI B2 Eng. Students
FamilyLife	9	Exam	4° EOI B2 Eng. Students

Scenario or Task	Texts/Users	Task Model	Course-Level
BadExperience	11	Exam	4° EOI B2 Eng. Students
CrazyHabit	1	Exam	4° EOI B2 Eng. Students
Describing People	13	Workbook	4° & Life-long Learners
CollaborativeTexts	3/6+7+6	Collaborative	4° EOI B2 Eng. Students
Chemistry	9+23 Biodata	Teacher Training	Chemistry Researchers
Technical English	40		University students.
WeekNews	4	WebQuest	Life-long Learners
Freizeit Hobbys	8	From Textbook	5° EOI B2 Ger. Students
(Others: testing texts: external users)	Not counted	Not counted	French Spanish English
Totals: 16 + 2 Biodata	220/ 212 (120 diff)	8 models	7 Levels

In the second year, in the Course 2004–2005, its use extended, not only in the number of participants (120 different ones, which makes a total of 156 in the two years) and in texts (220) but also in the models (8), levels (7) and developed scenarios (7). It has been noticed as a remarkable result how easy it is to apply the system to other educational environments (monographic courses, University courses and training courses for staff development) and the possibility of its integration in online learning systems. The greatest difficulty found as to hardware has been to verify that the use of Digital Assistants (PDA), due to their small size, causes difficulties in the text edition and, due to the operating system used, Microsoft Pocket PC 2003, it does not completely run the functionalities of common forms in JavaScript. However, the system automatically adapts when recognizing the browser interface of the PDA and reorganizes the presentation of the edition areas, the display of the tasks, the menus and the action buttons in the way shown in Figure 4:

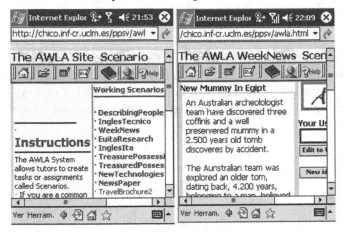

Fig. 4. AWLA Interface for PDAs: homepage with tasks and edition page

The system is being used in its third year integrated in online learning environments such as the CIVIErasmus Courses of Languages for Outgoing Erasmus Students [6], and Moodle Courses.

3 Conclusions

The development of the AWLA system for the learning and practice of writing in a foreign language was initially made in the discipline of English, being later localized into Spanish and German with the corresponding resources to access reference tools, contents and user interfaces, and currently it is being adapted to other languages. Its use will spread to other centres where a foreign language is taught, in non-university centres, such as the Spanish Official Schools of Languages and Secondary Education Schools, as well as in university centres with computers labs or the necessary means for the ubiquitous classroom. It offers technological support for writing collaboratively online, by means of the application of the most recent communication technologies, specially using integrated wireless devices for mobile computing, which has taken to the implementation of the new paradigms of interaction in education and learning design, whose characteristics are deeply related to the new information and communications technologies. The progressive increase of the AWLA usage foresees its extensive deployment with its easy integration in online learning environments, currently focussed on learning design, which AWLA also offers.

Acknowledgments

The AWLA system is being deployed in educational centres in Castilla La Mancha, Spain, thanks to the Project for Cooperation in Research between the University of Castilla La Mancha and educational centres other than the University, funded by the Junta de Comunidades de Castilla La Mancha, Spain.

References

1. Common European Framework of Reference for Languages (2001). Accessible from http://www.coe.int/T/DG4/Portfolio/?L=E&M=/ documents_intro/Manual.html
2. European Commission (2001) The e-Learning Action Plan. Designing tomorrow's education. Accessible from http://www.europa.eu.int/eur-lex/en/ com/cnc/2001/com2001_0172en01.pdf

3. Weiser M (1991) The computer for the twenty-first century. Scientific American, pp. 94–104

4. Ortega M, Paredes M, Redondo, M, Sánchez P, Bravo C, Bravo J (2001) AULA: A Ubiquitous Language Teaching System, Upgrade Vol. II, No. 5, pp.17–22

5. Britain S, Liber O (2004) A Framework for the Pedagogical Evaluation of eLearning Environments. Bolton Institute, Accessible on http://www.cetis.ac.uk/members/pedagogy/files/4thMeet_framework/VLEfullReport

6. Ortega M, Sánchez P (2006) An interactive blended environment for language learning: AIOLE. In García FJ, Lozano J, Lamamie de Clairac F (Eds.) Virtual Campus 2006 Post-proceedings. Selected and Extended Papers, Barcelona, Spain. Accessible on http://sunsite.informatik.rwth-aachen.de/Publications/CEUR-WS//Vol-186/10.pdf

A WebQuest about Tuthankamen

Sónia C. Cruz, Ana A. Carvalho

University of Minho, Portugal
aac@iep.uminho.pt

1 Introduction

It is undeniable fact that we have daily contact with new information and knowledge that comes from the world outside school. If school has progressively lost the monopoly over creating and transmitting knowledge, then education systems must be given a new mission: to guide individual learning paths and contribute towards recognising the set of student skills, including non-academic knowledge.

Today, there are other important arenas for dialogue and research that link youth, the world and the school. For this reason, the school must change its traditional design and must start by establishing bridges with other universes of information and opening up to other learning situations. It has become vital for students to use and learn to use new technologies in the classroom context, providing equal access to the different means of communication. Educational resources such as the use of the World Wide Web and WebQuests must be increasingly present in the educational context as means of research and information selection. This means redefining the teacher's role, the style of teaching, the concepts of learning and a new role for those involved in the learning process.

A WebQuest is a learning strategy, designed and implanted by teachers to be solved by students, which is made available online. The term Web-Quest was created by Bernie Dodge and Tom March, in 1995, to designate the kind of activities that they were developing with teachers, which take advantage of the resource technologies available on the World Wide Web [5]. A WebQuest consists of six parts: the *Introduction* to the theme in question, which must be motivating; the *Task*, which the student will perform and which must be challenging and performable; the *Process* through which the student is guided in order to fulfil the task; the *Resources* available, preferably on the Web, in order to produce knowledge; the *Evaluation*, which explains to the student the qualitative and quantitative indicators that will be taken into consideration in assessing his/her performance; and the *Conclusion*, which recalls the project's final objective and should motivate the student for future research or extend the experience into other domains..

In this way, a WebQuest is an activity of search presented to a group of students by means of a task that aims to be challenging. It enables guided access to multiple information resources, mainly available on the Web, and supports a learning process that promotes the development of critical reflection on the information provided.

The lesson must therefore be seen as a workshop [2] in which the students participate in collaborative work to perform tasks, supported by the teacher whenever they need him/her.

In this way, the teacher fulfils a mission that is required of him/her: to prepare his/her students to seize the socio-cultural opportunities that new technologies offer [4, 6], at the same time as arming the students against the risks that they may entail [7]. In this way, the WebQuest provides a complete piece of work that places the students at the central point.

2 The WebQuest and the Educational Context: Objectives for its Use

It is rather difficult for students to learn and be prepared to learn in learning environments that reserve a passive role for them. Through the appealing resource that the Web provides, active learning is possible because students come into contact with multiple pieces of information and in order to understand them, they will have to deal with the information, which, according to the constructivist model, requires the restructuring of prior knowledge enabling a conceptual change through multiple opportunities and relating processes. In the type of learning enabled by WebQuest, this process is enriched by the negotiation between pairs, making it possible for the group to construct a product. This type of approach enables skills such as searching, analysing, summarising and presenting projects to contribute towards making the students autonomous and responsible for their own learning process. Thus, we have chosen to heighten the potential of this new educational resource so as to understand its pertinence to the learning process.

In the field of historical education, the World Wide Web has already become, for many students, a source of access to historical knowledge. But access to historical sources does not teach students how to exercise historical thinking, a skill that it is important for students to develop [2]. In order to exercise this thinking, it is necessary to understand different points of view of the historical agents, witnesses and secondary sources of various kinds. By associating the constructivist perspective of learning with the introduction of new information technologies, it is believed that the Web-Quest takes on a highly important role since it enables the development of essential skills included on the national curriculum, specifically: the promotion of individual or group historical research, with verbal and iconographic information handling, the use of information technology at the service of History as well as the divulgation and sharing of historical knowledge through direct involvement as the driving force in the class.

Being competent at History implies knowing how to use different sources to understand the human sense of the past and the present in a contextualised way and knowing how to express one's historical thinking effectively through the various means of communication available today.

It is every teacher's wish to have dedicated and motivated students in the class. Having to resolve a challenge on the Web has an immediate element in its favour from the point of view of student acceptance.

WebQuests enable collaborative learning that is characterised by interactivity and negotiation [3]. Working collaboratively implies, per se, cognitive interaction between the pairs, which requires negotiation. What is emerging today is the so-called communal constructivism based on communal learning, where the learners discuss, exteriorise and interpret information. Thus, education must be an interactive dialogue between equals. Online learning favours equality among students who work at different paces. They can reflect upon what they read, decide what to ask or to comment, which requires responsibility in learning. Doing something with someone means using justified discussion to impose one's opinion, not through authority but through argument.

We can no longer deny our students' generalised use of technologies. It is therefore necessary to know how to regard them and deal with them, not as the enemy, but as an ally in the educational process.

With a view to motivating students for the unit Contributions of the Early Civilisations, taught as part of the History syllabus in the 7th year of schooling, we aimed to provide students with more knowledge about aspects of the history of a great civilisation such as the Egyptian, through the discovery of the Pharaoh Tutankhamen, exploring and performing the tasks given in the WebQuest provided at: http://www.iep.uminho.pt/aac/Tutankhamon. The History class would thus be taught as if it were a kind of workshop for developing the profession of historian.

Through this exploration, we aimed to develop the skills necessary in History, namely the use of sources/information handling. In fact, being competent at history means knowing how to use different sources, so that we can understand the past, in order to respond to the challenges of the present and the future. At present, the ordinary citizen is required to have History skills that enable him to read several historical sources, cross-reference information and infer whether sources are true or false in order to understand the view of myself and the others, in different times and in different spaces.

At present, it is accepted that the presence of History in the Basic Teaching curriculum is based on the presupposition that the study of History enables students to form a global and organised view of a complex, plural and constantly changing society [2].

3 The WebQuest About Tutankhamen

On the Home Page of the WebQuest with Tutankhamen site, it explains that it is a WebQuest made for students of the 3rd cycle (7th to 9th grades) for the subject of History. The site also provides Help for the teacher. This Help explains what a WebQuest is and gives the framework of this Web-Quest. The author's name and e-mail are given for any possible contact, as well as the date the site was created and the characteristics for optimal use. The background represents a compilation of elements from the Egyptian culture (Fig. 1).

By activating the Tutankhamen hyperlink, the user accesses the Menu that includes the six components that make up a WebQuest, as well as the student Help (Fig. 2). This Help refers to the components and what they entail, as well as some guidelines for working in groups.

Fig. 1. Home Page of the WebQuest about Tutankhamen

With the menu always available, the user must sequentially access the various components in order to complete the tasks.

Upon activating the Introduction, the student is invited to get to know Tutankhamen and to gather information on this Pharaoh in order to help the director of the sequel to the film "The Mummy" to find a script for his new film, this time related to the Pharaoh Tutankhamen (Fig. 2).

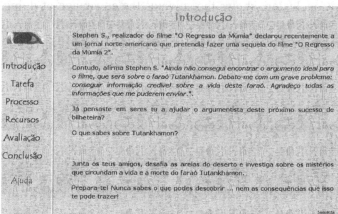

Fig. 2. Fragment of the Introduction of the WebQuest about Tutankhamen

Upon accessing the Task, the user will find information for performing five roles over time so that they can be included in a portfolio, with a view to helping the director to find a script for his new film (Fig. 3).

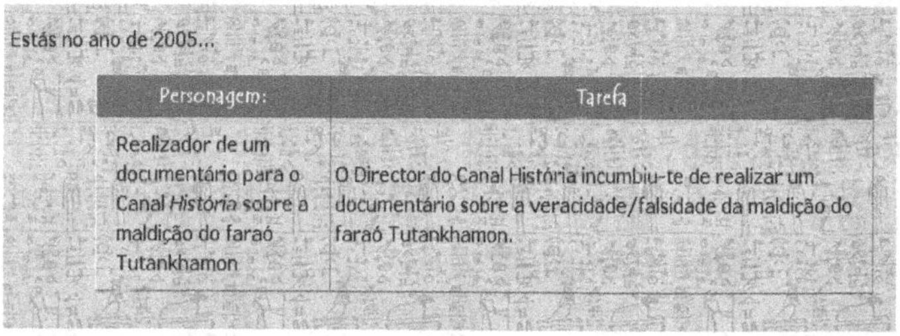

Fig. 3. Fragment of the task of the "Webquest about Tutankhamen", instructing the student to make a documentary on the truth/falsehood of the curse of Tutankhamen

In Process, the students access guidelines on the work to be done, bearing in mind the final production of their work.

In order to gather information for the chosen character, the students must access the *Resources* and consult the sites containing information to research for each character.

In Evaluation, there is a presentation of the qualitative and quantitative criteria of assessment taken into consideration by the teacher for the final assessment of each piece of work. This assessment includes the work done by the students in class as well as the presentation of their collaborative project with colleagues. The information that is gathered constitutes the portfolio aimed at helping the filmmaker find a script for his new film.

A final part, the Conclusion, shows the students the advantage of doing the WebQuest and calls for personal reflection upon Tutankhamen.

4 The Study

This study aims to verify the importance of integrating the WebQuest into the learning process as a means of developing the essential skills included in the national curriculum, specifically: the promotion of individual or group historical research, with verbal and iconographic information handling, the use of information technology at the service of History, as well as the divulgation and sharing of historical knowledge through direct involvement as the driving force in the class [1].

With regard to the WebQuest, the aim is to analyse the students' learning and their reaction to the WebQuest. In this way, we will ask for the students' opinion of the WebQuest about Tutankhamen, the way in which they learnt the content and the performance of the group task. By observing student behaviour, we also aim to analyse: the interested/uninterested way of working; the ease/difficulty with which they work with the Web-Quest; and how they use the information on the sites to produce effective knowledge.

Taking into account the proposed objectives and the conditions available for implementing this study, a case study was carried out.

4.1 Characterisation of the Sample

The sample integrates 27 subjects who attend the subject of history at the Externato Maria Auxiliadora, in the north of Portugal, in the 7th year of schooling of the 3rd cycle of basic education.

Based on the questionnaire used to check the sample's level of computer literacy, it was possible to conclude that the students show some basic knowledge of how to work with the computer as a work tool, with Word and PowerPoint being the most popular programs. Most of the subjects feel comfortable using a computer (69%), while 72% really enjoy working with this tool. The entire sample is familiar with the Internet, including

97% who say they regularly browse the Web. This regularity can be seen through the daily use of the computer by 48% of the students.

The fact that most had used the computer for the first time before starting school, and use it on a daily basis, enabled the teacher to infer that basic knowledge of this technology was guaranteed. Since most of the sample have the habit of visiting sites on the Web, it was concluded that it would not be difficult to work with the WebQuest.

With these skills guaranteed, the path to the correct use of the WebQuest was facilitated.

4.2 Description of the Study

The study ran during the school year 2004/2005 and was done over five classes.

In the first class, the students were told about the activity proposed by the teacher and the objectives of performing the task. Once the challenge was accepted, the students received instructions about how the WebQuest worked and any doubts were cleared up as to the objectives of the work or its assessment. The computer literacy form was then filled in and the WebQuest began.

In the following classes, in order to respond to the challenge, the students performed the respective group tasks.

In these classes, the teacher used an observation grid to record the subjects' behaviour during the WebQuest resolution.

In the fifth and final class, the work done was presented in a large group. It was then collected by the teacher so that the document could be analysed and the knowledge effectively produced could be assessed. The students also filled in a questionnaire to find out their opinion of the WebQuest.

4.3 Techniques and Instruments of Data Collection

The techniques of data collection used in this study were the survey, the observation and the documental analysis. Two questionnaires were drawn up, one entitled the Computer Literacy Form to assess the computer literacy of the sample. The second questionnaire, filled in at the end of the study, asked for the subjects' opinion on the WebQuest, involving three dimensions: site browsing, learning strategy used and group work.

The observation grid allowed the teacher to record the subjects' behaviour in each class during the WebQuest, namely the students' interest as the group work progressed, the difficulties shown by the students and the technical problems that occurred during the exploration of the WebQuest.

4.4 Presentation and Analysis of Results

As already stated, the computer literacy file allowed the sample to be characterised and revealed its skills with the computer as a work instrument.

Based on the data recorded in the observation grid, it is clear that student interest grew as the WebQuest progressed.

However, this interest was not shared in the same way by all the members of the group. The emergence of leaders in each group was also noted.

Concerning the difficulties felt by the students in some activities of the WebQuest, initially, it could be seen that the students did not understand the task that was required of them, which the teacher attributed to poor reading of the tasks.

We now present the data obtained from the opinion survey, by dimension.

Browsing

The questionnaire shows that the fact that the students already had basic knowledge on the use and control of the computer enabled most of the sample (89%) to browse the Web easily, and feel no great difficulty in selecting the information.

Learning Strategy

The majority of the sample (93%) considered the WebQuest challenging, seeing as they appreciated it as a means of research and information gathering. The fact that they performed this experiment enabled most of the subjects (78%) to not only perceive what they knew but also to acquire new knowledge on the theme being taught (93%).

An important piece of data was the fact that the sample was made aware of the need to select information (74%) while doing the work. In fact, in order to perform the tasks, the elements would have to withdraw only the pertinent information in the sense of organising it into ideas and/or main events. In this way, the WebQuest promoted the development of skills, both in the mother tongue and specific to History, namely reading, understanding, research, information selection and written communication.

In addition to bearing fruit in terms of the development of various skills, the implemented strategy also clearly developed a taste for the topic. The sample was unanimous in considering that this strategy, different from those normally used, served as motivation for the contents being studied. In addition, and according to the opinion survey, 96% gained more interest in the subject of History.

Group Work

In performing the activities proposed in the WebQuest, the students had to work in groups. It should be noted that, in general, the group work to some extent benefited the integration of the elements of the group as well as developing other work habits and methods, group spirit and leadership capacity. In fact, 78% of the sample considered that working in a group enabled greater understanding of the contents and 93% of the subjects stated that this strategy allowed discussion of ideas and different perspectives. Thus, the majority (85%) of the elements of the sample considered that it facilitated learning, while 15% of the subjects said that "it neither facilitated nor hindered" learning. We can, perhaps, infer that these elements already have a certain degree of autonomy in performing tasks.

With regard to the documental analysis effectively produced by the groups, we will present a summary of the work done by each group, according to the outlined task.

PowerPoint Presentation on the life of the Pharaoh Tutankhamen

The work presented by this group showed factual accuracy, but it could be seen that the students did not succeed in referring to past times since no cross-referencing was evident. The group stuck too closely to the information given on the Web in the making of the PowerPoint. The presentation showed some weaknesses, since no care was taken to present the information in a simple and motivating way.

Web Page on the Treasures of Tutankhamen

The group completed the topics outlined in the Task, effectively and carefully meeting the criteria outlined in the Evaluation part. It was one of the groups that dealt best with the available information since it handled it well without losing factual accuracy. The page created by the students is simple and functional. In accordance with their knowledge, the students made the page based on the sequential model to provide information on a single page. The page consists of text and images relating to the topic, revealing some creativity.

Diary on Howard Carter's Discoveries

The group completed the topics outlined in the Task, effectively and carefully meeting the criteria outlined in the Evaluation part. It was also one of the groups that knew how to work the available information since it dealt with it correctly without losing factual accuracy. The students identified with the character, managing to narrate the historical events with a time logic. In the diary, they tried to follow the sources presented on the Web faithfully. This group was also noteworthy for the quality of the presentation of the Diary, using visuals to illustrate what was being described.

It is a pleasant piece of work to read, with language that is suitable for the historical moment portrayed.

Report on the Causes of Tutankhamen's Death

The group completed the topics outlined in the Task, revealing some difficulties in the organisation of the information. The students managed to select and present the two views that justify the death of Tutankhamen, but the text is rather confusing. The information was clearly dealt with, but the presentation was somewhat lacking in creativity.

Video on the Possible Curse of Tutankhamen

This group completed the topics outlined in the Task, effectively and carefully meeting the criteria outlined in the Evaluation part. The group researched the information on the Web, gathered what was most important and pertinently organised the script for the film they were going to make.

The film produced by the students showed creativity and dynamism since it managed to explain the problem of the two perspectives in question. Factual accuracy was evident concerning the open discussion of the two perspectives, which were very clear in the film. This presentation was done in an attractive (showing care in the characters' props, social satire) and amusing way.

5 Conclusion of the Study

Once the study was concluded, it was possible to reveal the advantages of the use of this educational resource in a classroom context. It was clear to the teacher that, for the students, the fact that they performed the task from the Web was, per se, motivating.

Through the exploration of the WebQuest, each group was given a specific task to perform, which would have to be presented using a different means (PowerPoint, Web Page, Diary, Scientific Report and Video). In each task, the students had to develop several skills, namely basic skills such as researching, analysing, summarising presenting projects, knowing how to read different historical sources and cross-referencing information to produce a final piece of work. This skills honing was widely achieved, which contributed to the construction of a view of the historical fact in question. The analysis, from sources available on the Web, required them to reflect on the way the information was handled. In fact, most of the students understood what was requested in the tasks, knowing how to put them into practice and aiming to fulfil the topics requested. However, while some of the groups did not manage to free themselves from the information available on the Web in the construction of their final project, others showed creativity in the construction, presentation and transmission of the acquired knowledge. Through observation of the group, the teacher found that, as the group work progressed, the students became aware that cooperative work would have great impact on the quality of the group work. This was clear when elements of the group disagreed and they had to negotiate a solution amongst themselves. This interactivity between pairs required negotiation and, consequently, justified argumentation. This helped each student to feel autonomous and responsible for his/her own learning process.

It should also be noted that most of the groups were faithful to the sources used.

This study not only confirms the importance of taking advantage of Web resources in an educational context, provided that they are challenging and adequate to the students' age range, but also the involvement and effort that can be seen in the students.

References

1. Abrantes P (coord.) (2001) Currículo nacional do Ensino Básico – Competências essenciais. Available: http://www.dgidc.min-edu.pt/public/compeeeenc_pdfs/pt/Historia.pdf
2. Barca I (2002) A aula oficina em História. In: Actas do Colóquio sobre Questões Curriculares. Universidade do Minho, Braga
3. Carvalho A (2003) WebQuest: desafio colaborativo para professores e para alunos. In: Estrela A, Ferreira J (eds), XII Colóquio da AFIRSE/AIPELF: A Formação de Professores à Luz da Investigação. AFIRSE, Lisboa, vol. II, pp 732–740
4. D'Eça T A (1998) NetAprendizagem – A Internet na Educação. Porto Editora, Porto
5. Dodge B (1995) Some thoughts about WebQuests. Available: http://webquest.sdsu.edu/about_webquests.html
6. Harassim L, Hiltz S, Teles L, Turoff, M (1995) Learning Networks: a field guide to teaching and learning online. MIT Press, Cambridge
7. Pouts-Lajus S, Riché-Magnier M (1999) Escola na Era da Internet os desafios do Multimédia na Educação. Instituto Piaget, Lisboa

Blogs: A Teaching Resource and a Pedagogical Strategy

Maria João Gomes

Universidade do Minho, Portugal
mjgomes@iep.uminho.pt

1 Introduction

Weblog or simply "blog" are words that have become part of our daily language, if not of teachers at least of students keen on and more familiar with the use of the Internet. The "blogosphere" already comprises a set of educational tools that embrace a variety of purposes: there are blogs created and moderated by individual teachers and students; blogs with a collective authorship consisting of both students and teachers; blogs concentrating on a particular theme, and those that aim for transdisciplinary reach. Some blogs are digital portfolios of work carried out, and other blogs that act as a web presence of schools, departments or student societies. The type of use and the number of teachers and students involved keeps increasing. The educational blogosphere is increasingly expanding to the different educational stages, from pre-school to higher education.

This paper presents a collection of possible ways of exploring blogs in an educational and teaching context. Specific examples are, in several cases, presented in association with the most common uses of blogs throughout the text. In other cases, proposals for exploitation are proposed that are expected to become part of our teaching techniques.

2 The Explosive Growth of Blogs

Since the appearance of the first blog until 2005, the number of authors and readers of blogs has been increasing at a fast rate. A Marketest.com study [6] (disseminated by email on 9th February 2005) indicates that, in 2004, Portuguese internet users spent 840 thousand hours navigating blog pages from their homes. The same study found that 602,000 Portuguese, aged 4 years old and older, residing on the Portuguese continent, accessed blogs during 2004. This number represents 36.9% of the total number of internet users in that year. During this year, over 57 million blog pages were accessed, averaging 95 pages per user.

There are no blogs directly connected with the Portuguese educational context in the top of most visited blogs, either cited in the study referred to above or in many other sources. However, the interest in using blogs as both educational resource and as part of an educational strategy has been increasing and it is already possible to identify various experiences and practices in this field.

One of the first experiences in Portugal of using blogs in an educational context took place at the University of Minho, Portugal, within a Masters course in Informatics and Journalism, and gave rise to a blog entitled "Journalism and Communication" (http://webjornal.blogspot.com), in 11th April 2002 [2]. Worldwide, the phenomenon of "educational blogs" or "edublogs" is not just an interventional educational tool but also the object of extensive study and research [4].

3 Blogs: Concept, Origin and Main Functionalities

The word "blog" is an abbreviation of the original word "weblog". The expression "blog" was first coined in 1997 by Jorn Bargar [8]. The widely accepted definition of weblog is of an Internet page which is frequently updated by posts, i.e. messages composed by images and/ or texts, normally short, which often include links to sites of interest and/ or comments and personal opinions of the author, which are presented in chronological order, from the most recent to the oldest messages. The natural structure of a blog is reverse chronological order. This last feature is considered as the main characteristic of a blog by Brigitte Eaton, the creator of the main portal of access to blogs – the Eaton portal (http://portal.eatonweb.com/) [8].

The first blogs were created by people with sufficient IT knowledge to generate WWW pages as the current automatic tools for generating, managing and hosting blogs were not available. For some people, Tim Berners-

Lee, the inventor of the World Wide Web [9] and creator of the first web site, is also considered to be the creator of the first weblog.

The concept of a blog has been expanding. The increasing diversity of objectives, contexts and forms, as well as the different backgrounds and nature of their creators, means that the definition of a blog is becoming less universal. From personal blogs, which can be seen as electronic diaries, to blogs aimed at disseminating information for commercial purposes, a wide span is encountered. Authors also range from an individual sharing personal interests and details, to formal institutions, through blogs created and collectively maintained by a group of authors.

Thousands of blogs can be found on the Internet, covering the most diverse subjects, from specific issues to general themes, created with various aims in mind – leisure, informative, political, etc. Blogs can be seen by the author as a private and intimate space, despite their potential worldwide audience, or as a means of maximum reach for the dissemination of the ideas expressed in the blog. A blog can simply be a collection of web links enriched by comments or descriptions by the author. The blog can be a digital record of reflections or emotions felt by the author or it can be a space for exchange of ideas and debate, looking for public scrutiny and inviting the contribution of bloggers who visit the site.

The level of public visibility of a blog can be, to a certain extent, determined by its author(s). Many sites that host blogs allow the users to include, or not, their blog in a database that can be queried by any Internet user. In addition, the author can add the blog to various directories and search engines. A third alternative is to register the blog in portals and directories designed for this specific purpose (e.g. http://portal.eatonweb.com/, http://www.omeudiario.net/ptbloggers, or www.globeofblogs.com, all accessed in 18th April 2005.

Once the blog is available on the Internet, it is difficult for the author to prevent access, should the author wish to keep the blog private and intimate. In many systems, for instance, in blogspot.com, one of the most widely used, although the author can control which users/ readers can intervene by adding or deleting messages and comments, he or she cannot prevent users from reading the messages posted. The possibility of adding "comments" to the blog allows the visitors to express their views making the blog a communication tool on the web, rather than reducing the blog to a simple publication.

More recently, a new system for the creation and hosting of blogs available from http://spaces.msn.com allows the creation of blogs where the author can limit access to authorised users only. This way private blogs can be created for exclusive use of the author and internauts authorised by the author.

A blog can have either an individual or a collective author. In the latter, a group of people is responsible for the creation and management of the blog. On one hand, blogs can be a form of the idiosyncratic web presence of an individual; on the other, they can represent the institutional presence of an institution or organisation.

The success of the blogs is most probably linked to the fact that they provide a space for dissemination on the web, easily used by those without training in the creation of web sites, and that they are often free of charge as there are sites that provide systems for creating, maintaining and hosting for free. One such site, known worldwide, is http://www.blogspot.com; another, with Portuguese scope, is http://blogs.sapo.pt. There are sites providing tools in addition to those mentioned above, such as tools to obtain statistics of access to the blog, identification of the site of origin of the visit, identification of the most read messages, the possibility of updating the blog via email, amongst others, but usually these require payment.

4 Educational Use of Blogs

With the advent of sites for the creation, management and hosting of free and easy to use blogs, the creation of a blog has become possible to all Internet users. As a consequence, the concept of a blog has evolved, being driven by the creativity and imagination of the internauts, and has attracted the attention of researchers, teachers and other professionals with responsibilities in the field of education. The potential use of blogs as a teaching resource and a teaching strategy is vast and we will discuss it below.

Whilst the distinction between "teaching resource" and "teaching strategy" is somewhat blurry and sometimes arbitrary, it will be adopted in this paper as a means of structuring our discussion. As teaching resources, blogs can be:

- A space to access specialist information
- A space for teachers to make information available

As teaching strategies, blogs can be:

- A digital portfolio
- A forum for interchange and collaboration
- A space for debate and role playing
- A space for integration

Before we concentrate on the different ways of using blogs in an educational context, we will identify the reasons why their use in education is both justifiable and desirable. In this paper, we approach some possible ways of using blogs involving students, either as authors or as readers.

Other possibilities such as using blogs as a shared space for different teachers of the same subject or department, or as an interface between school and families will not be discussed here.

As publishing spaces on the web, blogs disseminate the written output of authors "voicing" their ideas, interests and thoughts. Participating in a blog which has an audience can be an invitation to reflect and a stimulus to contribute, as long as there is some moderation and encouragement for this. The school, and the activities carried out there, become more open to public scrutiny but also potentially closer to the communities to which they belong, and new opportunities arise for the members of such communities to participate and collaborate. The medical doctor of the local health centre or the town pharmacist can contribute their knowledge to the development of a blog focusing on health education. The parents of a child from a different country can contribute to a blog on Christmas traditions. The possibilities are immense.

By permitting multiple authorship, thereby allowing the existence of various people responsible for the posting of messages as well as commenting on existing messages, blogs can become spaces for communication in addition to spaces for the dissemination of information.

The creation and animation of a blog with educational purposes can and should be a pretext for the development of multiple competences. The development of competences associated with the search and filtering of information, with the production of written material, and with the mastering of various web services and tools are some of the outcomes associated with the many projects for creating blogs in an education context.

4.1 Blogs as Spaces for Accessing Specialist Information

The use of blogs as a space for accessing specialist information derives from the search and classification of blogs that tackle themes which fit within the curricula or extra-curricula. They should contain scientifically accurate information, appropriate to the age groups with whom the teacher is working and authored by credible and reputable people and/ or organisations. These aspects are particularly important and the teacher must assess the accuracy of the contents and the suitability to the specific age range, before suggesting the students access the blog. This provides the student with an additional source of information with often the possibility of contacting the authors, if they indicate their contact details or if posting of new messages is enabled.

As an example, we refer to the possibility of students accessing blogs related to their personal and social development which they find awkward to approach with parents, teachers and health professionals, such as alcoholism, eating disorders and sex related matters.

4.2 Blogs as Spaces for Teachers Making Information Available

In this approach, the teacher creates and promotes a blog where he/she makes available information of relevance to the students. The teacher keeps the blog up to date by adding new material related to the subjects presented in class. These materials include short texts and personal comments, adding links to sites previously evaluated by the teacher and comments on them, reference to recent news related to the subjects being taught, etc.

The teacher can promote access to the blog by the students by referring to it during classes when appropriate and by providing facilities for the students to access the Internet. One of the positive outcomes of this approach is to encourage continuous access to information and study instead of "cramming" for exams.

Several possibilities exist for using blogs as a virtual space for the teachers to make information accessible, such as the collection construction of a blog on themes common to several disciplines which can foster a multidisciplinary approach of many subjects. This type of blog can be developed with the students' participation as co-authors as long as the teacher ensures the adequacy and accuracy of the information presented.

4.3 Blogs as Digital Portfolios

One of the most frequent uses of blogs in education, particularly in higher education, is its exploration as a tool to develop educational digital portfolios. We can develop a portfolio with different intentions in mind. One of the most common is the "learning portfolio" which can support and stimulate personal and reflexive learning and be a useful tool to register, organize and report learning moments and experiences. Being a kind of "log" of the learning trajectory of each individual student, the learning portfolio can also be an important and significant assessment tool. From the educational point of view, both approaches are valid and, many times, teachers promote students' uses of portfolios with both objectives in mind.

The increasing popularity of alternative assessment forms and tools reflects deep-rooted frustration with traditional approaches to assessment [3]. New assessment tools and approaches and new terminology as "authentic assessment", "competence based assessment", "performance assessment" and "portfolio assessment" occupy an increasing place in the educational "jargon" and practice [3]–[7].

The nature of the portfolio assessment approach implies a longitudinal monitoring of the student learning process by the teacher, for it is an evaluation methodology focused on the "learning process" and not only on the "final product" [10] as is common with more conventional evaluation tools like exams.

The development of a learning portfolio must be a gradual process of reflection and personal maturation more than a simple repository of documents and other artefacts. A portfolio is an intentional and selective collection of student work that should be representative of the student's interests, efforts, reflections, progresses and achievement in a specific area. As is reported in [7] "such purposeful collections include student participation in selecting the contents of the portfolio, increased ownership in the process by helping to develop guidelines for selection, establishment of criteria for judging merit, and evidence of self-reflection".

The educational use of portfolios as a learning and/or assessment tool implies that the teacher follows the student's work by consulting the portfolio and comment on the work done by the student. However, it is not easy to students and teachers to transport and keep portfolios archives. Sometimes, we have the additional difficulty of needing to use different equipment to consult all the materials included in the student portfolio, eg. a video display or a slide projector. It is important to outstrip this kind of difficulty, as one of the advantages of using portfolios to support learning activities is the possibility to integrate documents (artefacts) in different media formats (video, photos, music, animated images and so on).

The kind of practical problems that have been reported can be solved with the adoption of digital supports which support different kinds of media formats like text, video, image animation, simulations, music and other audio files, etc. Digital portfolios can be developed and/or disseminated using support like digital video discs (DVD's) or even being published on the Internet, solving the problem associated with their transport and archive. Although, the existence of specific software to develop electronic portfolios, also in this domain blogs will be able to play a role for its ease of use and, in many cases, for its low cost (usually schools, teachers and students use free blog systems like blogger.com or blogs.sapo.pt).

Some of the available blog systems have the possibility of integrating text, images, video and sound files so that we can create multimedia digital portfolios with the advantage of having it published on the web and so being able to use and refer to websites and other resources on the Internet. These blog-folios have expanded possibilities over some other digital portfolios as many of the blog systems support comments from readers and so it is easy for teachers (or other students) to make suggestions, make a note or writing a comment to the students' portfolios. Digital portfolios on the web, and so blog-folios, can have this new and exciting dimension of collaboration between student and teacher and amongst students. With the appropriate software (which we can find on the Internet as freeware or shareware), we can also save the content of a blog, on a DVD for example, to have a backup copy or to read its content off-line. With weblogs and a simple multimedia computer with Internet access we can create and have access to digital portfolios which incorporate documents using different media languages (text, video, still image, sound, etc.).

Creating a blog as support to the development of a digital portfolio gives students a digital space where they can register, organize, report and reflect continuously on the themes they study and the activities they do on their lessons. A blog-folio can have multiple pedagogical approaches and be developed in different educational contexts and with different kinds of students. We can use blog-folios to register and to divulge in cyberspace the work and reflections from a group of young pupils of primary school or have a blog-folio from a graduate student which is an important assessment element for her/his teachers.

4.4   Blogs as a Space of Interchange and Collaboration Between Schools

The development of exchange programmes between schools is a strategy which has been used for a long time in various contexts with particular incidence in the teaching of foreign languages. The pen-pals which normally comprised students of different schools and different countries using letters and postal mail now interact electronically, using email as the favoured means of communication. This type of interchange, normally cultural and linguistic in nature, can take a more permanent, visible and cooperative form. More permanent, as there is a chronological record of all the messages exchanged; more visible because there is the potential for a world-wide audience; more cooperative as a large number of schools, students and/ or teachers can contribute.

The development of communication, interchange and collaboration projects between schools can take various forms and encompass all sorts of themes. A blog can, for instance, act as a meeting space for a set of small schools with a small number of students, who might be geographically isolated (a common scenario currently in Portugal, particularly in primary schools). This helps to counteract the feeling of isolation and creates opportunities for socializing for teachers and students. A blog can also be used as the support medium for a project of several schools which aims to identify common environmental problems and solutions to them. The possibilities are immense and only dependent on the existence of facilities for basic Internet access, which we believe are available in practically all Portuguese schools, and on the willingness of the teachers and the students.

4.5 Blogs as a Space for Debate and Role Playing

Blogs can also be used as a space to support long debates using role playing techniques. The strategy is to promote a debate on a specific theme among different groups of a class or among classes of one or several schools. Each group participates by arguing its case as if they were the person or entity whose identity they have assumed. This type of approach has wide educational potential, not only because it fosters the development of information search and writing skills, but also because it can contribute to a spirit of tolerance and open mind in the students.

4.6 Blogs as a Space for Integration

Under this classification, we consider two different ways of using blogs, both as means of communication.

In a school with students from different nationalities and cultural backgrounds, the creation of a blog of collective authorship, where all are invited to contribute their own views, experiences and facts, can be a means of promoting understanding and can ease the integration of pupils from ethnic and/ or cultural minorities.

Still under the aegis of "integration", we can think of a student being away from school for an extended period, for instance due to illness, for whom contributing to his/her class blog can help to create and maintain a feeling of belonging.

5 Conclusion

In this paper, different ways of exploiting blogs in an educational context have been presented, all centred on aspects directly related with the process of teaching and learning.

Other possible ways of exploring blogs can be considered such as using them to link the school to the community in which it resides, or as a means of linking the school with parents. A blog can be, for example, a way for a school to present a chronological record of the events it organised throughout the academic year. We believe that blogs are not a passing trend but a new resource that can be used to support various teaching and learning strategies. The availability of free high quality services that ease blog's creation and maintenance, together with the growing dissemination of practical experiences and examples of blog's use by schools of all levels are a good indicator. The widespread use of the Internet, namely with the plan to install broadband in all schools [11] and the increasing number of families with home Internet access is also a positive sign.

References

1. Asyikin N (2003) Blogging Life: An Inquiry into the Role of Weblogs in Online Community Building. Available in: http://www.metablogue.weblog.com.pt/
2. Barbosa E, Granado A (2004) Weblogs – Diário de Bordo, Porto Editora
3. Blood R (2000) Weblogs: A History and Perspective, Rebecca's Pocket. 07 September 2000. 17 February 2005. Available in: http://www.rebeccablood. net/essays/weblog_history.html
4. Georgi D, Crowe J (1998) Digital Portfolios: A Confluence of Portfolio Assessment and Technology. In Teacher Education Quarterly, Winter 1998. Available in: http://www.csubak.edu/~dgeorgi/projects/digital.htm
5. Gomes MJ (2004) Educação a Distância. Braga: Universidade do Minho – Centro de Investigação em Educação
6. MarkTest.com Newsletter by e-mail on 9.02.2005
7. Nisson, S (undated). A Brief Overview of the Linguistic Attributes of the Blogosphere.   Umeå   Universitet.   Available   in: http:// www.metablogue.weblog.com.pt/
8. Reeves T, Okay J (1996) Alternative assessment for constructivist learning environments. In Wilson BG (ed) Constructivist Learning Environments. Case Studies in Instructional Design. Englewood Cliffs, New Jersey: Educational Technology Publications, pp. 191–202
9. UMIC (undated). Iniciativa Nacional para a Banda Larga. Available in: http://www.umic.gov.pt/UMIC/CentrodeRecursos/Publicacoes/banda_larga _pdf
10. UMIC (2004). População Portuguesa – Inquérito à Utilização das Tecnologias da Informação e da Comunicação – resultados 2004 (resultados provisórios). Observatório da Inovação e Conhecimento – Unidade de Missão Inovação e Conhecimento.   Available   in: http://www.umic.gov.pt/UMIC/ CentrodeRecursos/Publicacoes/inquerito_documento.htm
11. W3C® (2004). About W3C Membership. Available in: http://www.w3.org/ Consortium/Prospectus

An Ontology Based Semantic System for Mathematical Problem Solving

Fernando Díez, Rafael Gil

Department of Computer Science,
Universidad Autónoma de Madrid, Spain
fernando.diez@uam.es

1 Introduction

Over the last few years, we have seen the traditional teaching of Mathematics complemented by the appearance of specific learning applications in different contexts. In addition to receiving instruction from the teacher, students also frequently go to the computer science laboratories to make use of specific learning programs. The installation of the new technologies is influencing teaching methodology. There exist initiatives in this area such as, for example, *Calculus Machina* [7], a tutoring system for learning Calculus; *Wiris* [10], a system of numeric and symbolic calculus through the Internet, or *MathEdu* [2], an authoring tool for the design and resolution of symbolic calculus problems. In spite of this, we believe that there continues to be a large gap between authoring tools and the authors themselves [6]. Mathematics is a discipline with a notable difficulty in the definition of contents. This contributes to the impetus for the creation of IES toward applications that encourage purely algorithmic learning, but ignore deductive learning based on concepts. Thus, we believe it is necessary to investigate the creation of applications that allow students to express their knowledge without leaving aside the conceptual supervision of their activity. To carry out the investigation and in collaboration with the Department of Mathematics of the University of Aveiro, we have chosen the field of Affine Geometry as our work context. This context adapts correctly to the representation of concepts like *point*, *line*, *vector*, *coordinate*, *segment*, etc.

2 Student Activity

In order to give us an idea of the difficulty of the type of activities to be analysed, we will outline here an example related to the type of activities that we want to supervise, and that are to be carried out by the user. Let us consider the following statement:

Compute the equation of the line through point P(1,2) and parallel to the

$$line\ s: \begin{cases} x = 2 + t \\ y = -1 - t \end{cases}$$

If we analyse in detail the type of concepts used for the description of possible different solutions, we see that we should use concepts like *vector, point, parametric line, set of straight lines, continuous line form, complete line form* and the *parallel* relationship.

An analysis of exercises related to Applied Geometry as the proposed above, shown us that by means of a small quantity of conceptual objects and relationships we can undertake the solution of numerous exercises. This led us to the idea of that, by means of an ontology representing the type of concepts that are manipulated as well as the relationships among them, we would be able to supervise the student's activity. In short, the problem being outlined is one of representing the necessary semantic information that is contained in the definition of a problem in a particular context, and of being able to generate exercises whose source of information proceeds from the models defined by the teacher as well as from taxonomy of problems. Also, an added value is the guarantee that the exercises generated can only be coincident in the instructional objectives; the data are random and generated in real time in each case. The task of defining ontology that describes geometric objects can be successfully achieved.

The supervision requirements that arise when monitoring the student's activity are of two types. On the one hand, it is necessary to verify the correction, from a semantic point of view, of the objects that the student defines, avoiding the possibility of generating inconsistencies in the knowledge base of the problem. This happens when for example he/she tries to define, in a generic way, a geometric object. For example, suppose that the student declares that P is a point. The system will register it as such, although its definition in terms of its coordinates is still unknown. It is possible that while reasoning the student tries to identify P with another type of object, or tries to use it in a relationship that doesn't admit this object in its reading (for example if he/she affirms that P is perpendicular to r). We will see later on that a component exists in *RAMSys* (Reasoning And Managing System) dedicated specifically to maintaining the consistency of the defined objects at every moment.

A second type of supervision is the one that is required when the student writes mathematical expressions. In this case, it is generally necessary to check the equivalence between two expressions, or if a certain relationship is completed. Such a case is presented when the student has defined a line like eq. 1.

$$r : x + y - 3 = 0 \qquad\qquad (1)$$

and he/she affirms, in another part of his construction, that this line is parallel to the line of the eq. 2.

$$s : \begin{cases} x = 2 + t \\ y = -1 - t \end{cases} \qquad\qquad (2)$$

In this situation he/she should carry out a semantic verification of the activity, checking that the relationship is applicable to the two geometric objects. Given that both are line objects the semantic confirmation is correct. A second part remains and that is the mathematical confirmation that, indeed, r and s are parallel. In *RAMSys* we have incorporated another component, which makes use of the symbolic calculus program *Mathematica* [9], which is charged with these types of confirmations.

In addition, *RAMSys* incorporates another form of supervision that allows us to evaluate when the student has achieved the defined instructional objectives for the exercise type that he/she is solving. The significance of these is equivalent to that of a group of predicates. When the teacher defines an exercise type it should specify, among other elements, what the objectives of that exercise are. For each task that the student carries out the system checks if it is completed or not and until this is done the system doesn't register the solution. In the case of the exercise in the previous example the defined objective is

And [Parallel [Line [$l1$], Line [$l2$]], Incident [Point [$p1$], Line [$l2$]]]

The defined objective requires that the two conditions demanded in the proposition exercise be simultaneously verified. On the one hand, that the line that the student defines (labelled as $l2$) is parallel to the given ($l1$), and on the other hand, that the line that the student obtains should be incidental with the point that is provided in the proposition (labelled as $p1$). As we have already indicated above, until this objective is completed, the exercise cannot be considered concluded.

In summary, we have analysed the supervision requirements necessary when developing a system capable of controlling the activity that a student carries out for the solution of a mathematical exercise. It is quite probable that other forms of supervision can be defined that impact more in certain aspects that we have not yet covered, such as the reasoning process in itself. However, in order to approach this type of supervision there are undoubtedly greater difficulties.

3 Description of the System

3.1 Architecture

The distributed architecture of the system is composed of a series of modules that work in different virtual machines. The system is structured in two main subsystems:

- A web server that controls communication with the users (teachers or students) by means of corresponding editors that work on a standard browser.
- A system of knowledge, *RAMSys* that serves as a database of problems, support for symbolic calculation and a module of representation of knowledge.

Communication between both modules uses the RIACA OM Library[1] (ROML) [8]. This library is oriented to communication among applications by means of OpenMath. On the other hand, the module that houses the part of representation of knowledge (the classes of mathematical objects and their relationships), and the logical verification of the student's actions, is based on the language OWL[2] [1, 4]. As a consequence, beyond the semantic possibilities of representation that OpenMath offers us, by means of the use of ontology we can verify, from a logical point of view, the objects and the relationships among them that the student defines. These objects can be defined in an incorrect or incomplete way, but the system must be able to process this information in order to let the student know that he/she has made an error. In such situations OpenMath is not able to carry out the semantic confirmations of the type that we will analyse in the following example of the next section.

---

[1] http://www.riaca.win.tue.nl/products/openmath/guide/omguide.pdf
[2] http://www.w3.org/TR/owl-features/

Definition of the Ontology: Their Added Value

In order to define the classes of the ontology, we have used the *Protégé* [3] ontology editor. We suggest that the reader refer to the excellent information available on the Protégé webpage or the text [1]. In order to have an idea of the kind of information that we manipulate, we are going to give some details with respect to the implementation of the ontology. For example, Fig. 1 shows the definition presented by the properties of the defined class *RAMSysProblem*, which is one of those used for the representation of problems.

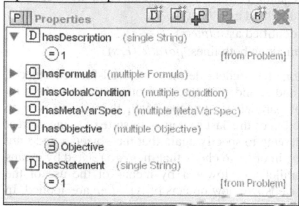

Fig. 1. Properties of a problem in *RAMSys*

These properties means that all problems in *RAMSys* should have a description and a statement, represented by the numerical value inherited from the class problem. Furthermore, an objective should also exist for the problem (represented by the existential quantifier of the property). It can also be appreciated that the property *hasObjective* is defined as a multiple, giving the idea that it can have different objectives in a problem.

For a detailed description of the type of data used in the definition of problems, consult [2], where we have used in the ontology the description of the problems that is used in the declaration of problems in *MathEdu*.

Given the above-mentioned, beyond the semantic possibilities of representation that OpenMath offers us, by means of the use of an ontology we can verify, from a logical point of view, the objects and the relationships among them that the student defines. It is possible that during his/her activity using the system, the student manipulates objects in an incorrect or incomplete way. The system should be able to process this information to call the student's attention to its incorrectness. In such situations Open-

---

[3] http://protege.stanford.edu/

Math is not able to carry out the semantic confirmations of the type that we will analyse in the following example. Let us consider the following problem, - a small variation of the previous case:

Compute the family of lines through $P = (x_0, y_0)$ and parallel to the line of the direction vector $\vec{u} = (u_0, u_1)$

Let us suppose that a student carries out the following tasks of definition of objects starting from the data contained in the statement. To carry out these tasks he/she has an equations editor accessible through the Web:

- Define the *line* object identified as *r*: *line(r)*
- Define the *line* object identified as *s*: *line(s)*
- Establish the parallelism along both lines: *parallel(r, s)*

With the first two actions the student defines two well-formed objects: two lines identified as *r* and *s*, and with the third one he relates them by means of the property of parallelism. In OpenMath there is no way to verify the semantic correction of this last sentence, in spite of being correct mathematically, without having to specify again that the objects *r* and *s* are lines, including their types, in order to check that they are related by means of the relationship of parallelism. However by means of the use of the ontology, in the first two steps two new objects of type *line* are applied. In this way the system knows what properties and what relationships can be applied on the objects defined by the student and it is not necessary to specify the types again. For example, if the third action had been $r \in s$ (represented by *in(r, s)*), an inconsistency would have been detected in the *is-an-element-of* relationship between the objects *r* and *s* in the ontology. The system would have detected the error since two lines cannot be related by means of the *is-an-element-of* relationship.

As we have just seen in the example of the ontology, the instances and relationships associated with the actions that the student carries out are incorporated dynamically. To maintain the consistency of the knowledge base it is necessary to analyse the coherence of the new actions with regard to the previous ones by means of the use of a system reasoner. For example, if the student has defined *A* as a *point* but then later on tries to use it or to redefine it as a *line*; or the case where he might use an object not yet defined in a relationship. In these circumstances the system must take into account the inconsistencies generated and should advice the user.

Returning to the architecture of the system, Fig. 2 shows an outline of it. As it can be appreciated, we have divided it into two large modules: on the left the part corresponding to the Web server that establishes the system communication with the teacher and with the student, and, on the right, the part of the reasoning module that stores the definitions of problems and the encoding elements and verification, etc.

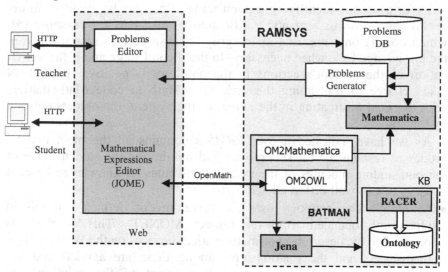

Fig. 2. System architecture design

The communication between *RAMSys* and the users is carried out through an editor of mathematical expressions housed in a web server, whose role is to disseminate the system through Internet. For the edition that we need, we use the JOME (Java OpenMath Editor [3]) that provides an interface for the edition and communication of mathematical expressions by means of standard OpenMath. The interface that JOME provides has been efficient for the purposes of the developed prototype, although if we consider a more continuous use of the tool, it would be necessary to improve this interface.

With respect to the teacher, he/she has access to an editor of problems in order to define the statements and their characteristics, which are stored in a database of problems.

At the moment of solution, a problem-generating module accesses the solution and obtains a model of the problem. If it is needed, the generator obtains the necessary data for the generation of problems for the student to solve from the system of symbolic calculation Mathematica. In the case of the student, each one of his/her solution actions is coded in OpenMath. The resulting code is processed through the module BATMAN (Bivalent AnnoTation MANager) in a process that involves two stages. In the first one they are translated into OWL code in order to make the annotations and corresponding verifications in the knowledge base. All the annotations are made dynamically by means of the *API*

Jena Semantic Web Framework[4]. Each annotation requires that the integrity of the knowledge base be checked, so that all possible inconsistencies (for example, identifying a point with a line) can be avoided. In order to carry out this semantic verification we use RACER reasoner [5], which doesn't only preserve its integrity but also derives new facts from the knowledge base when necessary. In the second stage and if the verification of the student's actions in the ontology is positive, BATMAN takes charge of translating the code OpenMath to code Mathematica, with the goal of creating in the kernel of the system, the objects defined by the student.

As we have indicated above, *RAMSys* contains all the mathematical processes responsible for supervising and monitoring the student. One of the outstanding modules of the system constitutes its knowledge base. It consists of two well-differentiated parts:

- Ontology: The ontology uses the taxonomy of defined symbols in OpenMath obtained from the project MONET[5]. This ontology is oriented to the description of mathematical services on the Web and in it the objects and the relationships among these are applied that the student defines. Therefore, at each moment of the solution, the knowledge base has all the elements (objects and relationships) implied in it. It also uses another taxonomy defined clasess which represents the concepts needed to modelize a problem.

- Reasoner: RACER assures the coherence of the defined concepts and their relationships as well as deriving new facts from the information contributed by the student.

Finally, we must refer to the system of symbolic calculation: *Mathematica*. We have already indicated the use that is made of it in the generation of the random parts of the exercises offered to the student. Additional use can also be made of it in the execution of the possible calculations that the student requires, as well as in the verification of the syntactic correction of the formulas that he/she may introduce. For example, to define the equation of a line that goes through point $P = (2, 3)$ and in the direction $\vec{v} = (1, -1)$. The student should make the opportune calculations and introduce (making use of JOME) the equation of the resulting line

$$x + y - 5 = 0 \qquad (3)$$

The system, with the same data, verifies that this equation is correct, or informs the student of his/her error. Thanks to its pattern matching system,

---

[4] http://jena.sourceforge.net
[5] http://monet.nag.co.uk/

Mathematica is qualified to accept as correct both the previous statement and any other equivalent one, for example:

$$x + y = 5 \text{ or } y = -x + 5 \tag{4}$$

Given the questions relative to the benefits that are provided by the use of semantic information integrated in an ontology and the diverse tools that accompany it, we will describe in detail, in the following epigraph, some considerations related to the communication scenario among the different components that are integrated in the system.

3.2 Communication Among Components

The solution of any problem, which has already been modelled by the teacher, is preceded by a phase of random generation, delivered in an automatic and transparent way for the student. Additionally there is a phase of interaction between the student and the system, which initiate the resolution process.

In the first phase, the internal structure of the problem contribute in a decisive way, which is coded as another class in the ontology and for whose representation the taxonomy developed for the MathEdu system has been used [2], with a new class Objective incorporated. To generate a concrete statement the problem should be processed. In order to do this a link is established with Mathematica, calling on the function that generates the formulas present in the statement. This function manipulates three lists of objects. The first list contains the formulas. The second contains the meta-variables and the third contains the conditions so that the generated statement is valid. Until the conditions of the statement are not met, this is not revealed to the student. Once the formulas have been generated the problem is constructed in HTML + MathML exporting the formulas of Mathematica into the format MathML. At this point the problem is ready to be presented to the student by means of the Web server.

In the second phase, which is the solution of the exercise, the system waits for the student to introduce a mathematical expression by means of the JOME editor. The introduced expression is translated to OpenMath so that it can be interpreted in the module BATMAN. In order for it to be interpreted, BATMAN has to communicate with RACER through the API Jena. At this stage, it is necessary to transcribe from OpenMath to OWL statements in order to incorporate the new information into the ontology. The translation of OpenMath to OWL is based on ROML, which offers classes to easily manage OpenMath objects. The OWL code is based on lists with the format (*subject, relation, predicate*), the object *subject* relates by means of the *relation* relationship with the object *predicate*. It is here that the new information is integrated. In the case where there are inconsistencies the error is pointed out by means of an exception. To detect inconsistencies Jena incorporates a mechanism by which, once the new statements have been introduced, the resulting ontology is validated and a validity report is generated. This report contains all the detected inconsistencies as the previous ones pointed out in the example addressed in the epigraph above. If the report is empty this means that no inconsistencies have been detected and the system continues with the mathematical verifications. To carry them out a new translation is done in BATMAN. In this case the object OpenMath is translated to the Mathematica code and its content is evaluated. If it is necessary to carry out a calculation it will be done at that moment.

Finally, once the stages of logical verification (consistency in the ontology) and mathematical one (confirmation that the mathematical objectives of the problem are verified), have been carried out, the system responds to the student through a Log space in the interface of the system. This process continues until all the objectives in the model are satisfied.

4 Conclusions

We have presented the architecture of *RAMSys*, a problem solving system based on ontologies. *RAMSys* makes use, among other technologies, of a knowledge base of mathematical concepts defined by means of ontologies. The definition of mathematical concepts constitutes one of the key questions when developing systems that are able to deal with interactive solution of problems. Due to this difficulty up until the present time, the tendency has been one of guiding the creation of IES towards applications that encourage purely algorithmic learning but which do not attend to deductive learning based on concepts. We believe therefore, that it is necessary to investigate the creation of applications that allow students to express their knowledge without ignoring the conceptual supervision of their activity. The architecture described illustrates two questions that in our opinion are fundamental:

- The complexity intrinsic to a system with the characteristics of *RAMSys* having the capacity to interpret sequences of non-predetermined actions.
- The necessary trend towards the use of standards that allow communication between processes and which facilitate the re-usability of the software components used [6].

In our case we are making an intensive use of components developed in centres like Stanford, RIACA, or the consortium MONET. Their use guarantees us the reliability of the components used as they have been previously tested. In spite of this, we have found that it is necessary to increase the number of classes and relationships described by the ontology with other new ones that adapt to the requirements of the context in which we are working. Moreover, we have checked that it would be necessary to make a partial load of the ontology that describe mathematical objects, since at the moment we load them in their entirety, which over-loads the reasoner and slows down the process of confirmation of the integrity of the base. Therefore it would be necessary to establish some filter mechanism. However this supposes a difficulty not only for the filter and the selective load of parts of the ontology, but also because when the student is acting, he/she could try to make use of concepts or relationships as yet unseen, for the resolution of a certain exercise. Thus, it may be necessary to look to a dynamic loading model of the definitions of classes in the ontology.

Finally, in this respect, we would also like to say something about the purely didactic aspects of the tool. At the moment, except for the system's verification of the attainment of objectives by the student, we have not thought about the introduction of any type of didactic help. The student's activity within the system is entirely free and is not guided. The student cannot be given any type of needed help or direction if he/she doesn't know how to act. However we think that, for the type of information of the problems and of the domain that we have represented, it is possible to extract a very basic information with respect to, for example, the type of objects that should be used to construct a demonstration. This could be the first level of help. At the moment we have not contemplated the possibility of other didactic characteristics of the tool. Both with respect to these questions and others that may arise, we are very open to the possibility of any type of collaboration.

Acknowledgments

This work has been supported by the Inter-ministerial Commission of Science and Technology (CICYT), project number TIC2002-01948; as well as by the program of Collaboration Scholarships of the Ministry of Education and Science from Spain.

References

1. Baader F (2003) The description logic handbook. Theory, implementation and applications. Cambridge University Press, Cambridge

2. Díez F (2002) Diseño y resolución interactiva de ejercicios que involucren cálculo simbólico. Ph.D. Thesis, Universidad Autónoma de Madrid

3. Dirat L, Buffa M, Fedou, JM, Sander, P (1999) JOME: OpenMath on the Web. IV International Conference on Technology in Mathematics Teaching, Plymouth

4. Gómez-Pérez A, Fernández-López M, Cork O (2004) Ontological Engineering. Springer, London

5. Haarslev V, Möller R (2001) RACER System Description. International Joint Conference on Automated Reasoning, Siena

6. Mizoguchi R, Ikeda M, Sinitsa K (!997) Roles of Shared Ontology in AI-ED Research: Intelligence, conceptualisation, standardization and reusability. In: Boulay B, Mizoguchi R (eds) IOS Press, pp. 537–544

7. Quinney, D (2002) Calculus Machina: An intelligent tutor providing computer based support for teaching undergraduate calculus, II International Conference on the Teaching of Mathematics, Crete

8. Riem MN (2004) The OpenMath Guide. A practical guide on using OpenMath (Report from the Research Institute for Applications of Computer Algebra RIACA)

9. Wolfram S (1999) The Mathematica Book, Cambridge University Press, Cambridge

10. Xambó S, Eixarch R, Marquès D (2002) WIRIS: An internet platform for the teaching and learning of mathematics in large educational communities Contributions to Science vol. 2:2 pp. 269–276

LOMEditor: Composition and Classification of Learning Objects

Antonio Sarasa, Javier Piquer, Raúl Arriola, Susana de la Iglesia

Facultad de Informática. Universidad Complutense de Madrid.
asarasa@sip.ucm.es

1 Introduction

The new technologies revolution has led to the emergence of proposals in the field of education to shift to the computer work environment the elements of attendance teaching (computer-based teaching systems). Among these proposals, one notably suggests creating educational resources from minimal reusable units of information called learning objects. This approach responds to the need to reduce development and implementation time of a computer-based teaching system, and to the maintenance/ adaptability problem of educational applications (knowledge is created and transmitted progressively, and must be lasting. Therefore it is necessary for the applications to be transferable to another computer system when the system they run on becomes obsolete). In this sense one of the objectives is to simplify the creation of resources down to a simple assembly of existing resources which may be situated locally (in the system itself) or remotely (in other systems interconnected by means of a telecommunications network) [7–8], and constructed for heterogeneous platforms. In this article a learning objects authoring tool, which is being developed as a final degree project, is described. It provides the basic editing and creation of learning objects functions, in addition to two particular functions, namely the composition of objects, and the automatic evaluation and classification of objects. In the following sections a learning object is defined, the principal characteristics of the LOMEditor tool are described, some sections are devoted to dealing with the special functions in greater detail (composition, and automatic evaluation and classification), and, finally, conclusions are drawn and future work is touched upon.

2 Reusable Learning Objects

On a conceptual level, a learning object is the combination of three elements: contents, behavioural descriptions of the object, and a set of metadata which refer to the objects [1]. The aim of the learning objects proposal is to provide an answer to four questions which previous alternatives have either not answered properly or have not tackled at all [2]: a) Accessibility. It is the possibility of accessing and using educational resources from any place, b) Durability. This is the ability to support technological changes without the need to redesign, reconfigure or recodify everything from scratch, c) Interoperability. This is the possibility of using resources developed anywhere and implemented using any kinds of tools and for any kind of platform, with different tools and platforms from those which served to develop the aforementioned resources, c) Re-use. This is the flexibility to incorporate resources in multiple applications and contexts.

3 Lomeditor: A Learning Objects Authoring Tool

In the recommendations the learning objects are considered as units called bundles. The purpose of bundling is to group together interrelated contents so that they are treated as one unit and to make it possible to: 1) Structure the structures that make up the bundle. 2) Associate descriptions with it. 3) Facilitate their re-use and make it possible to locate them in content repositories. 4) Facilitate the attachment of different bundles so as to make bigger bundles. Although the implementations of a bundle may be very varied and have special features, what they all have in common is that they implement objects as units composed of a document which describes the contents and how they relate, and the contents described by the document.

To develop LOMEditor the recommendations of the IMS consortium have been used as a basis, specifically the specification "IMS Learning Resource Meta-Data Information Model Version 1.2 Final specification" and the specification "IMS Content Packaging Information Model" [4]. So LOMEditor is a visual tool capable of managing learning objects implemented in the way outlined in these recommendations (see Figure 1). It is made up of a main window where 2 main panels may be identified and a toolbar in the top part where the different functions of the tool are displayed in drop-down menus. The panel on the right is reserved for showing a tree-shaped display of the learning object's metadata. The panel on the left is divided into 3 panels, a top panel to provide a user-friendly display of the manifest document and two bottom panels which respectively serve for the user to input values for the object's metadata, and to display information to help the user to create the learning object.

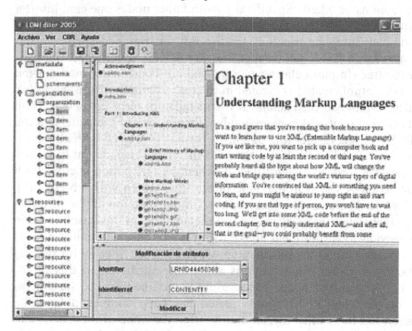

Fig. 1. Lomeditor screenshot

The basic functions that the tool provides are: 1) Open learning object previously validated against its schema and display of object in browseable tree. The objects must be zip files and be chosen from a browser window. They are then checked against the schema included in the bundle. If they pass the test, they are displayed in a browser tree which is displayed in the left panel of the tool (otherwise display is not permitted). The tree represents in its ramifications and nodes the metadata hierarchy which defines the learning object, which is extracted from the imsmanifest.xml document. 2) Editing a learning object. In editing a different treatment is carried out according to the type of metainformation: a) LOM Metadata [3], and b) Other Metadata. For type b) metainformation, editing operations are performed directly on the browser tree; however, for type a) metainformation an independent screen is used with an exclusive browser tree for this type of metadata. In either case, two types of metadata may be distinguished: those that can have offspring (composed of other metadata, and considered as Father nodes) and those that cannot have offspring (not composed of other metadata; what they have is a particular value. They are considered children or leaf nodes). So regardless of the kind of node, each one has related dropdown menus which can be displayed by pressing the right mouse button after situating the cursor over the node. These menus, depending on the type of node being dealt with, enable the user to carry out some actions or others. Specifically, with father nodes one can: insert a node, eliminate a node, add attributes and modify attributes; and with child nodes one can: insert information, modify information, add attributes and modify attributes. Every action that the user selects is reflected immediately in the tree. In particular when a metadatum is created, a node of the type of metadatum created is created in the tree, stemming from the father of the aforementioned metadatum. If the metadatum to be created is a son metadatum, that is, it will contain a value, then in one of the panels on the right (the lower one further to the right), a form is displayed with all the information details which the user must fill in for the metadatum to be defined. Once the form has been filled in, when the OK button is clicked on the information is stored in the node of the tree, which will subsequently serve to create the manifesto document. A similar function to that of creating a son metadatum is modifying a son metadatum. In this case the same panel is used as to fill it in, but unlike the previous case where it is empty, it now appears with all the information which the user filled in for the latter to modify it. Other similar actions are adding attributes, modifying attributes or eliminating a node. Once adding to the tree the necessary metadata of the learning object being created has been completed (and the information has been filled in), an option offered by one of the menus can be used which enables an ims bundle to be created from the information stored in the tree. 3) Save an open learning object in compressed form. The bundle created is stored in the directory which the user indicates through a browser window. Note that the bundle created is a zip file in accordance with the specifications outlined above. 4) Creation of a learning object from scratch. A single node is created called manifest, which represents the whole manifest, and which will act as the root of all the metadata associated with the object. This node will determine if the succeeding are metadata that a manifest can have. This first node has the editing functions of a father node, so that from these functions the learning object is constructed. 5) Evaluation of the quality of open learning objects (it is a manual evaluation which is saved with the object in a document) and persistent storage in a database. 6) Queries to a database containing information on learning objects. 7) Automatic classification of learning objects in accordance with the same attributes used in their evaluation. 8) Composition of learning objects.

4 Application Model

One of the most important features of the tool is its independence from the schema followed to construct a learning object. In this sense for each object opened in the tool an internal model is created dynamically from the schema this object contains. In this model any of the successive changes brought about by the action of any of the upgrading functions that the tool has are reflected. In the same way, this model is used to create the manifest when it is decided to save an open object in the tool. The model is composed of the following elements: a) Validation or reference model: This is obtained from the grammar of the learning object, (manifest and metadata xsd files). All the metainformation of the learning object being dealt with is saved in a data structure. Its main uses are for the extraction of data to be used in editing the object and to validate the manifest of the learning object, b) Document: Represents the manifest of the learning object. The manifest is parsed with JDom, and a Document type object is recovered. This object will be the reference to the real model, from which the object data will be taken, and where the modifications will be saved. Its structure consists of a set of Element objects distributed in the shape of a tree, which represent the labels of the XML document and their distribution in this document, c) Temporary tree which will represent the model: This is the main object of the application model. It is a Java Tree (DefaultTreeModel). Its construction implies the union of the real data of the Document with the metadata obtained from the validation model. In this way, for each Element of the Document we shall generate an XML Node, which we shall enrich with the information which the validation model gives about the latter, d) Metadata Node: It belongs to the tree previously generated, but given that Metadata receives special treatment, as regards editing and display, there will be a reference to it so as to work on it, e) Composition tree: It represents the model of the tree used in the composition of learning objects. It is the main object in the learning objects composition model. It is a DefaultTreeModel. Its construction implies the union of the data saved previously in the Java Tree with the metadata obtained from the validation model. So, for each learning object shown for its possible composition with another object, an Organizations node will be generated, which will only show the information of the Organizations node of the object in question, though enriched with the information which the validation model gives on it.

The construction steps for the internal model of the application are: a) The Validation Model, and the Document object are constructed, b) A Tree type object is constructed which covers the Document resourcefully in depth, and for each Element found a class XMLNode is created. (It is a class which will extend from DefaultMutableTreeNode, so that it enables a

DefaultTreeModel to be constructed directly (the tree of the Tree class) and avail of the work methods on nodes and trees (insertion, elimination, path, etc)). For the construction of this XMLNode the information on the Element it will represent is needed, and the meta-information on the aforementioned Element which the Validation Model offers. Subsequently the XMLNodes are joined up so that their structure imitates that of the Document's tree. An XMLNode will hold relevant information: 1) Name of element. 2) Reference to Element, in order to modify the Document in real time. 3) List of node's possible sons: Each one indicating if it is obligatory and its maximum appearances. 4) List of Node's possible Attributes: Indicating whether they are obligatory and their default values. 5) Flag indicating whether node is Simple or Complex. 6) Only for Element Metadata: The XMLNode which will represent the Metadata label (Element Metadata) holds a reference to its "tree", but do not figure as sons for the Java interface. In this way we can hide this information without losing it, or diminish the model's efficiency by having to look for it elsewhere, c) Organisation of tree (DefaultTreeModel) of Tree class: 1) In the resourceful generation of the tree, the XMLNodes are inserted in the same order in which they appear as labels in the imsmanifest (in the Document), so as to be properly displayed to the user. 2) This organisation also enables each XMLNode to contain a very important piece of information: Its current offspring. Since it is a Java tree and the XMLNodes are enriched Default-MutableTreeNode, we have all the data that a tree structure can offer, so we do not need the XMLNode to manage a list of current offspring. Efficiency is gained as the same solution is valid for two problems (display and editing), d) The compound tree model is created, for which composition-type objects are generated which extend to the DefaultMutable-TreeNode class; with this all work methods on nodes and trees can be availed of. We store the Organizations nodes of the current learning object in these objects, e) Final construction of JTree. The final advantage of this design is the Model-View independence that the Swing slim model offers. That is, its graphic objects, JTree in this case, may be constructed from an internal model (our DefaultTreeNode), so that any modification of it may be viewed without having to carry out an operation whatsoever on the JTree. Moreover, JTree may provide interesting methods for capturing events which will permit work on the internal model.

5 Lomeditor Composition Function

This function enables two learning objects to be composed, that is, to obtain a single object from two initials objects [5]. To access this function one of the toolbar menus containing a compose option is used. On selecting this option, the learning objects to be composed may be chosen (each click on this option allows a single object to be opened; the same one cannot be opened more than once). The objects opened are shown in the left panel, only the metadata referring to organizations being shown (their contents may also be viewed by means of a user-friendly presentation in the right panel). When at least 2 objects have been opened the composition options are enabled both in the menu and in some buttons which appear in the toolbar. There are two composition possibilities: a) Parallel (if the object that acts as content will be a direct son of the root of an organisation). b) In depth (if the object that acts as content will be a son of some internal son of the root of an organisation). In either case, the procedure it follows is common. One of the composition options is compose. On clicking on this option a form is opened showing the names of all the learning objects previously opened together with boxes that can be marked (which will be the organisations in the case of parallel composition, and the items in the case of in depth composition) and an "OK" button. A single object must be chosen, which will be the containing object. Once the form is accepted the same form is opened which shows again the names of all the objects except the one chosen as containing object in the previous form (this time only the organisations for both types of composition are shown). Another object must be selected, which will act as contained object. On clicking on OK in this form the composition is carried out: a) The newly composed learning object is validated, b) The tree is updated showing the new object and concealing the contained object, c) If more than 2 objects remain open in the browser tree the composition options remain enabled; if not, they are disabled. As regards the other composition options, we have: Display (allows the content of the object selected to be viewed by means of a user-friendly presentation in the right panel) and Exit Composition (leaves the application screen blank).

6 Lomeditor Automatic Evaluation and Classification Function

This function enables a quality assessment of a learning object open in the tool to be performed [6], according to the contents of its metadata. (Currently the assessment is only performed depending on the contents of the LOM general metadata (General Label)). Learning objects may be assessed in two different ways: manual assessment and automatic assessment. Using the manual assessment option, the user is empowered to assess the learning object's different labels. For this purpose a form is displayed in which each label appears in rows, the content of the label and a drop-down list with different scores or ratings: (Very Good, Good, Fair, Mediocre, Bad and Very Bad) for the user to choose one with which to assess the content of the label. Finally there is an "OK" button. Internally with this information the general assessment given to the learning object is conducted. In this first version of the tool, assessment simply consists of working out the average of each of the values entered by the user, with the following correspondence: Very good (4), Good (3), Mediocre (2), Bad (1) and Very Bad (0). Next, the learning object and its associated score are saved in a database. This second way of assessment enables a learning object to be assessed without user involvement by means of a case based reasoning strategy (CBR) on the system database. To this end, an assessment button by means of CBR is offered among the assessment options. Internally objects are extracted one by one from the database (which will serve as test cases). For each test case a similarity estimation regarding the object being assessed is conducted; this provides a similarity value between the test case and aforementioned object. Having assessed all the test cases, we will know which object is most similar to the one we are attempting to assess and we shall assign the assessment of the object most similar to the current one. A form is then displayed with the score achieved, and the user has the option of choosing "OK" and saving both the object and its assessment in the database, or of manually changing the assessment automatically generated. The database can also offer the user the possibility of formulating queries on the objects it contains. Specifically, it allows objects to be recovered by means of queries involving fields which represent general metadata of the objects of the base. The result shows all the objects that verify the query, and the route where they are stored. In order to perform the queries there is a button among the assessment options which gives access to a form where the names of the fields appear beside blank spaces. The user fills in this form which represents the query.

7 Conclusions and Future Work

As regards future work four areas will be developed:
- Editing. Specifically, LOM metadata labelling or modification can be improved, so that this is not performed through the visual tree but through a form in which all the labels and their contents can be seen at a glance and be edited directly.
- Interconnection of functions. Currently functions are independent and one cannot be used while another is being used. In this regard an improvement would be the possibility of using them at any time, linking actions from one to another. So, it would be interesting, for example, to

compose two objects and subsequently be able to edit the result of the composition.

- Assessment. As regards manual and automatic assessment, they must be completed so as to take all metadata into account, not only the general kind. Also, more sophisticated assessment functions than the arithmetic average must be used.

The conclusions of this project are:

- With regard to learning objects design, composition enables greater granularity in objects (we can create an object based on the composition of other objects, and the latter based on yet others, and so on). Apart from this way re-use of learning objects already created is facilitated.
- The assessment function is not complete and has a demonstrative value of how quality assessment of an object might be conducted, and how this information facilitates the implementation of other functions such as automatic assessment or recovery of objects with similar characteristics.
- As regards editing, the advantage this tool offers is that it enables basic editing of an object but regardless of the schema used to create it, as a particular model is created for each object that is opened.

References

1. Cm Multimedia Systems (2001) Learning Objects Does Size Matter?. Cm316 Multimedia Systems Coursework
2. Friesen N (2003) Three Objections to Learning Objects. In McGreal R (ed) Learning Objects and Metadata. London: Kogan Page
3. IEEE Learning Technology Standards Committee (IEEE LTSC) Learning Object Metadata (LOM)
4. IMS Global Learning Consortium
5. Knolmayer GF (2003) Decision support models for composing and navigating through e-learning objects. In Proceedings of the 36th Annual Hawaii International Conference on System Sciences, Hawai
6. Rovinskiy D, Synytsya K, Podgornov A (2003) Quality assessment for collections of learning resources. In Proceedings of IEEE International Conference on Advanced Learning Technologies, Athens, Greece
7. SantaCruz-Valencia L, Aedo I, Breuer T, Delgado Kloos C (2002) A Framework for Creation, Integration and Reuse of Learning Objects. Learning Technology newsletter. Vol 5. Issue 1
8. Shih TK et al. (2003) An Intelligent E-Learning System with Authoring and Assessment Mechanism. In Proceedings of the 17th International Conference on Advanced Information Networking and Applications, Xian, China

Arguing On-line in Order to Learn How to Argue

Maria José Loureiro, Anabela Pinho, Luísa Pereira, António Moreira

Dept° Didáctica e Tecnologia Educativa; Universidade de Aveiro
{zeloureiro, apinho, lpereira, moreira}@dte.ua.pt

1 Collaborative Skills, Argumentative Skills and the SCALE Platform

It is commonly perceived that students who work in environments involving Information and Communication Technologies (ICTs) invest differently in solving learning tasks, since these environments promote relevant progress in the conceptual changes of learning and of educational innovation [1].

One of the skills the school currently aims at developing concerns using ICTs collaboratively, exploring their full potential in an effective way, in order to stimulate innovative educational activities.

In distance learning and in web-based environments, on-line identities are created through text and its authorship, and most interactions happen in written form. People only exist on-screen when they 'act' or 'speak'. They can only be defined through written language. They create and recreate themselves in collaborating, interacting and negotiating with their peers [2, 3], namely in argumentation related to controversial or 'hot' issues. Students question, justify their opinions and come to conclusions. Following this, they reach new conclusions; add reasons and counter-arguments and are thus driven towards new premises. This way, according to [4], they develop their ability to coherently express their points of view, enrich their persuasive intelligence and refine their knowledge. Such abilities will be extremely important for their daily life and for their on-line collaboration: when using them, they will have greater possibilities of negotiating conflicts and of reaching consensus, which will result in more effective sharing and greater and better involvement in the learning community, aiming at a true network of ideas and learning communities. This was one of the objectives of the SCALE project (Support Collaborative Argumentation-based LEarning in secondary schools).

The SCALE Project, developed by a team of European research centres, consists of an on-line platform for teachers and students, offering scenarios and pedagogical guidelines on how to learn to argue and how to argue to learn, as well as communication tools and analysis of results,. Therefore, it is an Internet-based tool to guide and support collaborative learning of argumentative discourse, whose use alone results in benefit for the teaching and learning process, as well as for teachers and learners.

On the SCALE platform, specifically focused on acquiring argumentative language, learners experience the cognitive and social conflict of being confronted with ideas contrary to their own. Hence the creation of the term social-cognitive conflict [5]. Students' power of argumentation and the development of such skill leads them to defend their points of view in a more convincing way – or not – in the dialogic synchronous interactions among the participants.

The SCALE tools comprise, in addition to a free CHAT, a structured CHAT – ALEX – where the dialogic interaction is previously defined by models of statements which students must choose and emerges structurally organised. JigaDREW is another Internet tool used in the visual representation of the debate, since it automatically creates argumentation graphs of the chat sessions, though students may also create them manually. Furthermore, the platform offers additional tools of support to the process of learning and its analysis. The Pedagogical Website (PWS) contains the necessary software and help for the creation and use of learning sequences [5].

2 Argumentative Skills

Activities aimed at working on argumentative text, suggested in several textbooks, often show a simplistic, linear and reductive conception of such texts, with consequences for teaching and learning. What's more, they are introduced and trained too late in the schooling process.

Argumentative text and discourse are widely mentioned in the subject Philosophy, in relation to classical Rhetoric and Logic, as well as in the syllabus of Portuguese A (11th grade) – both seeking the acquisition of argumentative text and discourse in oral and written form. However, they are difficult to find in other school years and subjects, where discourse activity is limited mostly to understanding and producing narrative or descriptive texts, since argumentative texts are considered too complex for students.

It is thus neglected that, besides narrating and describing, all of us argue in our daily life from early childhood, in the most varied circumstances and contexts, as state several authors dedicated to this topic [6, 7, 8, 9]. Some authors even defend that before entering primary school, one spontaneously uses argumentation, though in an unconscious way. Hence the claim that such skills should be consolidated through formal learning, in order to be used adequately in diverse situations, some of which may be more complex [10].

We must also highlight the fact that the teaching and learning of argumentative text is not yet practised systematically. As [9] states,

> "the difficulties in managing oral and written production of such texts are clear and, according to some scholars, its 'spontaneous' acquisition is tardy. However, other researchers [6] suggest that the slow acquisition of this type of text results, above all from the lack of explicit teaching of the argumentative text from early on[1]" [9:478].

In fact, several authors unanimously claim that argumentative text is poorly trained [6]. The importance of argumentation in knowledge construction and conceptual changes has been frequently referred to largely referenced, namely in relation to Science and alternative conception, that is, changing students' conceptions based on common sense and previous knowledge [11]. Still, the problem of lack of argumentative skills is felt throughout all levels of schooling, since they are either not taught or poorly and tardily taught [12].

In Portuguese Higher Education, our analysis of the course syllabuses shows some references to the formal teaching of argumentation and/or Rhetoric in degree courses of Philosophy, Law or even Business Management and, to a more advanced level, in post-graduation courses in similar areas. In Humanities courses, our search on the Internet showed us that the references to argumentation in the syllabuses are rare or inexistent, at least at degree level.

Two University teachers of Humanities [12] mentioned the existing weaknesses in academic work of argumentative text, and the skills (clearly insufficient) at it showed by secondary students or even Higher Education students, a situation which may result in lack of success. In a 1996 study, published by the Institute of Educational Innovation, about the academic preparation of secondary school students, Higher Education teachers emphasize the poor writing of first year degree students. Foreign researchers confirm this opinion, concluding that secondary school students usually

---

[1] Translated by the authors.

write reports or essays, text types far from those demanded in Higher Education. An article called «La escritura en los universitários», [14] outlines some of the difficulties most commonly felt by students at this level:

"Nevertheless, one of the most important problems of those arriving [at university] is the difficulty in understanding academic texts – in terms of categorical and conceptual content – and in writing argumentative essays and articles, as well as inferential or final texts. Students have serious problems in understanding scientific texts and in organizing information in written form; and find it difficult to identify main ideas and hidden ones among the information given[2]" [13, 14].

The same problem is mentioned in different contexts. In the business world [15], the difficulty rises from the fact that, in Portugal, argumentation is perceived as amateurship, and thus not suitable to be taught at university level. Moreover, according to the author, one teaches formally neither argumentation nor in more vast conceptions critical thinking, which consists as "examining ideas, detecting arguments, and analyzing arguments such as sub-skills of analysis" [16:4] –, among other abilities like interpreting, analysing, evaluating and inferring, as well as taking into consideration evidence concepts, methods or contexts on which judgement/thought is based upon [16:13].

Actually, academic writing – in general, of argumentative core – requires the subject's critical thinking, due to the fact that it is a text of ideas which teaches to think and to learn.

Argumentation has, in fact, specific structures and characteristics that differ from other types of discourse. It is based on a mechanism of persuasion which aims at convincing someone or changing one's opinion to reach consensus. One of the fundamental questions of this type of discourse is giving the speakers the useful tools (abilities) for solving conflict between contradictory statements.

Both research projects approached the argumentative skill from its social dimension, as a constitutive element of interaction among speakers (face to face or at a distance), and from the linguistic dimension of discursive organization, as this type of discourse is made of micro-structures (connectors), which, when articulated and integrated in the arguments, will generate the macro-structure of the argumentative text [8, 10, 17, 18, 19]. The speaker must then be provided with the necessary argumentative techniques for producing a persuasive, convincing and consistent discourse. What is most important is, thus, the aimed linguistic skills, such as the necessary distance from one's own discourse and the anticipation of opposing arguments to be debated and contested effectively. Such skills are

---

[2] Translated by the authors.

acquired by analysing texts in their macro e micro-structures, breaking them into conceptual pieces and examining the difficulties felt, so that one finds the necessary strategies for solving them [18, 19].

The dialogic dimension of argumentative discourse is more easily understood if one sees argumentation as defending personal points of view, as mutually understanding, refuting, changing, extending and improving a group of arguments and counter-arguments, among two or more subjects, aiming at resolving tension or a conflict resulting from a problem-situation, considering a particular context and target reader.

Choosing a pedagogy based on negotiation and collaboration, according to Vygotsky and his followers [6, 7, 9, 20, 21], is undoubtedly important for teaching in general and even more – due to argumentation's dialectic character – for optimizing students' argumentative skills. As [22] states,

> "it is apparent, therefore, that peer perception and all useful cognitive activity that it generates for the purpose of learning, cannot easily be fostered by conventional classroom conditions. The transcripts provide evidence that the process occurred when participants interacted and were on a par with one another." And he adds that, in such situations, "the use of computers is strongly recommended" [22:350].

In the context above presented, both our studies gave particular importance to the development of computer-mediated collaboration, as well as to the improvement of argumentative competence in mother tongue.

3 Describing the Aims of the Projects

We underline, once more, that the same corpus was analysed in both pieces of research: one more focused on proceedings analysis at the level of selecting and organizing information from written argumentative text (Project 1) and another more focused on production analysis (Project 2).

3.1 Project 1: «Processes of Organizing Information from Written Argumentative Text in an E-Learning Environment – A Study with Students from the University of Aveiro»

Objectives/Aims:
- To describe the procedures used by students when they de-construct and graphically represent argumentative texts.
- To analyse in what way note-taking and graphical representation procedures influence the development of the argumentative skill at the level of text planning.

- To determine how the SCALE/Blackboard tools contribute to the development of the argumentative skill at the level of selecting and dialogically negotiating information.
- To outline strategies for academic writing in Higher Education at the level of planning and organizing the argumentative text.

3.2 Project 2: «Constructing the Argumentative Discourse in an E-Learning Environment – A Study in Higher Education»

Objectives/Aims:
- To analyse the mechanisms of dialogic collaboration used by students in activities of planning and producing written argumentative texts.
- To identify the mechanisms of dialogic collaboration used by students in activities of planning and producing written argumentative texts.
- To understand how these mechanisms show in argumentative textuality
- To determine the contribution of SCALE and Blackboard tools to the development of the argumentative skill in written text production.
- To outline didactic proposals on the construction of academic writing.

4 Methodology

The studies developed are fundamentally based on a qualitative/descriptive approach, since we intended to clarify the procedures and causes of the research object and also since this research area is still an emerging one.

The pilot study and the research were developed with a second year class from the degree course in Primary School Teaching of the University of Aveiro. The pilot study involved 4 students and the experiment involved 16.

The research work was organized, in general, according to the stages below described.

4.1 Work Developed by the Researchers and/or Team

- Building the data gathering tools:
- Questionnaire for characterizing the sample in terms of attitudes towards ICTs, reading and writing skills and argumentative skill;
- Test on knowledge of note-taking and production of argumentative text.
- Grids for categorizing the analysis of dialogic interactions;

- Grid with criteria for observing intermediate production (contributing to the forum) and for observing and evaluating the final products[3].
- Selecting argumentative texts and organizing didactic sequences in SCALE and Blackboard.

4.2 Tasks Performed by Students

- Answering initial questionnaires.
- Individual reading of opinion texts.
- Note-taking.
- Initial diagnosis – Entry Test – based on note-taking, producing an argumentative text on Genetically-Modified Organisms (GMOs)
- Chat discussion in argumentative pairs on the note-taking performed
- Creating argumentative graphs based on the texts read
- Discussing the set theme in ALEX.
- Participating in a forum on the topics to be discussed, with contributions corresponding to the type of text under study (Blackboard).
- Completing the final test and answering the questionnaires for subsequent data triangulation

5 Results

The results presented here reflect primarily the analysis of the pilot study, given that the analysis of the products resulting from the research project are only now in its beginning. Our analysis intends to put forward the benefits resulting from pair negotiation, work strategies used for gaining argumentative skills and the participants opinions on this form of interaction and training.

In relation to skills in Technology, all students had ICT for one year in secondary school. Students stated that they prefer working alone on the internet, in order to be free to navigate it according to their own will and criteria. They also prefer studying alone for better concentration. If they mentioned they preferred to work in pairs at the computer, it was due to their low self-confidence in relation to the technology, or to the difficulties in the task to be developed.

---

[3] Besides these, other tools for content analysis will be used: Rainbow methodology and QDS ("Quality of the Debating Space"), the former for the analysis of computer-aided debates and the latter for the analysis of argumentative graphs produced in the SCALE environment.

Regarding argumentative text, students generally believe they are skilled at writing argumentative texts and their answers show some degree of awareness of the characteristics of these particular texts. On the subject of note taking, all students (except one) enjoy performing it and do it on a regular basis. They consider themselves able to take notes because they easily cope with separating important information from unnecessary one and they study from their notes and have good results. Nevertheless they all admit they need to learn more on the technique.

However, their answers and their online discussion about this skill are contradictory, as well as their production in which they reflect a lower control of this type of textuality. In fact, their texts evidence that students don't differentiate their opinions from the text's perspectives, having difficulty in distancing themselves from the ideas and thoughts of authors they read. In addition, they misunderstand the rhetorical characteristics of expository and argumentative formats and lack critical and synthesis skills. They also show difficulties in selecting and organising relevant information, in note taking (since they often cannot understand, summarize and organize the information they read), in sequencing and expressing their own ideas and reflections.

Regarding the SCALE platform, students agree that it helps them to develop more solid opinions, to structure their own points of view and to deconstruct arguments which facilitate understanding. However, they think they must be more familiar with the platform tools, in order to benefit as much as possible from SCALE.

Concerning the interactions' logs, there were a lot of off-task messages containing social elements, due to the familiarity existing between students. One might speculate this is due to the fact that students knew it was a pilot study, so they felt less constrained to offer serious discussion. Nevertheless, for the same reasons – their familiarity – they did not hesitate in requesting clarification of points not clearly understood or of ambiguous opinions.

Students preferred to work with regular chat instead of the *Grapher* or the *structured chat – Alex*, because they were more familiar with it. Learners entered the chat clearly predisposed towards learning from and with the peers with whom they feel comfortable. It was common to witness short dialogues like "I'm not very sure of this topic" – "Don't worry. I will help you".

When compared to the *Chat, Alex* was perceived in a different way. Students found it confusing and consequently contributions were in more limited numbers and of inferior quality. Furthermore, the existence of templates in ALEX led to a lack of spontaneous exchanges and to poorer or non-existing explanations and clarifications, as well as to a shallower reflection. Consequently, and the analysis of *Replay* interactions confirms this, the most important difference lies in the lack of challenge and explanation cycles that characterize positive interchanges in chat, guiding students towards the strategies of learning from peers.

6 Projects' Relevance and Impact

In such studies one does not intend to attain results which contribute with indisputable truths to the scientific knowledge in the focused area.

We intend to describe the difficulties a significant part of Higher Education students show in selecting and organizing information and in producing written argumentative texts, seeking, at the same time, to contribute to the validation of strategies for on-line training and to precede other research paths to be followed in such a neglected area of study.

Acknowledgments

We would like to thank Patrícia Alves and Tim Wallis for their precious participation in this work.

References

1. Dias P (2001) Comunidades de Conhecimento e Aprendizagem Colaborativa. In: Seminário Redes de Aprendizagem, Redes de Conhecimento. Lisboa, Conselho Nacional de Educação, pp 85–94
2. McAteer E, Tolmie A, Harris R, Chappel H, Marsden S, Lally V (2002) Characterising On-line Learning Environments. In: Proceedings of the Networked Learning Conference, Sheffield, UK
3. Tickner S (2002) Charting Change in Networked Learners: What can we learn about what they learn? In Proceedings of the Networked Learning Conference, Sheffield, UK
4. Wen L, Duh C (2002) The influential Factors in Argumentation-based Teamwork Problem Solving. In: Proceedings of Internet Society Conference 2002, Taiwan
5. SCALE (2003) Test instruments for assessing the quality of students' argumentation, and results on school experiments for teaching collaborative argumentation in secondary schools, Deliverable 8, Project funded by the European Community under the Information Societies Technology (IST), Programme (1998–2002), Document prepared in collaboration by University of Jyväskylä, and University of Utrecht
6. Dolz J, Ronveaux CH (1994) L'objet construit à travers l'interaction didactique: le texte d'opinion et la subordonnée relative. In: Actes du Symposium

S 1, la discipline comme on l'enseigne entre curricula et modèles. Université de Genève

7. Perelman F (1999) La production de textos argumentativos en el aula. In: Revista En el aula, 11, Argentina: Ministerio de Educación de la Nación, Febrero, http://www.cerlalc.org/Escuela/datos/textos.doc

8. Adam J-M (1992) Les textes: Types et prototypes – récit, description, argumentation, explication et dialogue, Éditions Nathan, Paris

9. Pereira MLA (2000) Texto argumentativo. In: Dicionário de metalinguagens da Didáctica, Porto Editora, Porto

10. Masseron C (1997) Pour une didactique de l'argumentation (écrite): problèmes, objets, propositions, II. In: Pratiques: enseigner l'argumentation, décembre, 96:35–64

11. Ravenscroft A (2000) Designing argumentation for conceptual development. Computers and Education, 34:241–255

12. Veiga MJ, Baptista MM (2004) Argumentar, Ver o Verso Edições Lda., Maia

13. Bono A, Barreira S (1998) Los estudiantes universitarios como productores de textos. Lectura y Vida, Año 19 (4):13–20

14. Romero F (2000) La escritura en los universitários. In: Revista de Ciencias Humanas, 21, Universidad Tecnológica de Pereira, Colombia

15. Germano V (2004) A argumentação na comunicação empresarial - Entrevista a Desidério Murcho. In: Crítica, Revista de Filosofia e Ensino, http://www.criticanarede.com/filos_entrevista.html

16. Facione P (1998) Critical Thinking: What It is and Why it Counts, Santa Clara University, California Academic Press, http://www.insightassessment.com/pdf_files/what&why2007.pdf

17. Jespersen J, Reichler-Béguelin MJ (1997) Argumentation et discours rapporté: présentation d'une séquence didactique. In: Pratiques, enseigner l'argumentation, décembre, 96:101–124

18. Garcia-Debanc C (1996/97) Pour une didactique de l'argumentation orale avec des élèves de 10 ans. In: Enjeux, décembre/mars, 39/40:50–79.

19. Erard S (2000) Le point de vue, séquence didactique, rubrique, argumenter. Corome

20. Amor E (2003) Didáctica do Português. Fundamentos e Metodologia, Educação Hoje, Texto Editora Lda, Lisboa

21. Järvelä S (1995) The cognitive apprenticeship model in a technologically rich learning environment: interpreting the learning interaction. In: Learning and Instruction (3), 5:237–259

22. Gélat M (2003) Taking Others' Perspectives in a Peer Interaccional Setting while Preparing for a Written Argument. In: Language and Education, (17) 5:332–353

Use of ICT and Project Work in Teacher Training at the Public School System

Danielle Santos, Elisa Schlunzen

Paulista State University – Technology and Sciences College
Rua Roberto Simonsen, 305, CEP 19060-900, Presid. Prudente, SP, Brasil
dani_asn@yahoo.com.br

1 Introduction

We intend to discourse over a research that arouse from the wish of approaching the theme "Formation of Teachers in work", having in mind the assertive that they have to be in a continuous process of formation and transformation of their practice, re-elaborating the knowledge they utilize, with the purpose of building up in the school a space not only of work, but also of research, action and formation [1].

The investigation started in the year of 2003, beginning from the holding of the "I Symposium about Inclusive Education", which took place at the FCT/UNESP campus. One of the pedagogical training and teacher in work in a school of the State Public System of Presidente Prudente/SP/Brazil, who participated in the event, worried with the students' high illiteracy and consequently, their undisciplined behavior, gathered together with her other colleagues and looked for the person who orientates this research, who also works with the subjects: Formation of Teachers, Informatics in Education and Inclusion. Thus, they asked her to help them in the work with projects and to apply them in the Informatics Operating Room (IOR), which had never been used before. These changes could make the pedagogical practice more attractive and interesting, and could also provide a diminution of the high indiscipline rate of the school and an improvement of the teaching and learning process.

As the work started in 2003 was basically useful to help to carry out a diagnosis of the school reality and to form the teachers concerning the Constructionist approach[1], the teachers, still worried and anxious about a change in their practice, thought about the importance of continuing the work throughout 2004, in order to achieve a real change in the classroom pedagogical action. It appeared then the possibility of finding answers to the following anxiety: How to form the teachers to work with projects using the computer and technological resources in order to promote a significant knowledge in their students?

In this way, to carry out this research for the Master degree, we agreed to go along with teachers of the 3rd and 4th grades of the Fundamental Teaching System (which corresponds to the 7th and 8th grades), who taught classes during the day period and who were open to a change in their behavior regarding their practice. This, we began to dialogue with those teachers in order to apprehend, in a better way, the universe of the research. We discovered that the teaching staff, in a diagnosis (Bimestrial Exam) accomplished in the first (1st) Bimester of 2004, detected that 90% (ninety per cent) of the school students, including all of them who attended the day and night periods, were functional illiterates, that is, despite the recognition of some letters, they couldn't link phrases or interpret texts with either objective or subjective language.

In the presence of this sad reality, considering the problems of indiscipline and of functional illiteracy among other ones, we selected some strategies of acting to make the teachers aware of the importance of the work with projects (including space of practical living, considering the students' daily life to, afterwards, work the curricula concepts, in order to favour the construction if knowledge.

So, the teachers, themselves, indicated the classes with the greatest problems referring to the illiteracy and indiscipline rates and, after a distribution of schedules, we decided for working directly with the students of the 7th grade "D" of the morning period, with students who came from the resource classrooms and regarded as "the worst of the school", "the most undisciplined".

In this context, after being defined: universe, subjects and objects of the research, the investigation really started to be accomplished in April 2004. The objective was to investigate the process of formation of the teachers in

---

[1] The Constructionist approach [2] based on the construction of knowledge using the computer as a potential tool arises the student's interest and motivates him to explore, research, describe, think over, and clarify his ideas. Such approach provides the resolution of problems that appear in the classroom and the students, with their teacher, decide to develop, with the help of the computer, a project that makes part of their lives and context.

work so they would incorporate to their methodological practice "Projects of Work" and the use of the ICTs, guaranteeing that their students were the actors of their own learning process, to modify their functional illiteracy rates and to promote dynamics of cooperation and spirit of group.

The formation of the teacher must be seen as a continuous process, considering the importance of a new pedagogical doing and, in it, the ICTs and the projects of work allow the search of equilibrium and of flexibility, that is, then makes possible the adaptation to differences in the learning rhythm and in the life experiences [3].

It is very important to emphasize that the teachers' biggest fear was not related to applying the ICTs, but how to behave in a way of diminishing the indiscipline, the inattention and the disinterest of the students. This, understanding that the formation of the teachers must search the development of a teaching own style individually thought about [4], which will produce in the students a significant learning, we noticed the importance of this fact to be understood by the teachers themselves inside the context of their work.

Still under this perspective [5] the formation of the teachers considering the incorporation of the ICTs to their pedagogical practice must start from the same presupposition of the formation to the change, combined with the appropriation and the pedagogical usage of the formation, must be stimulated to have the conditions to develop a critical thought over a style of his/her own to act towards technology.

From the premise that the pedagogical practice mediated by the work with projects stimulates the teachers for a critical glance over their role, which is decisive to the development of this new methodological practice [1], the idea was that the teachers and the students would become themselves the actors and the co-actors in the teaching and learning process, in a constant act/do [6, 7].

This is the condition that sets the teacher up into a cyclical and continuous movement between doing and understanding [8] through the thought over the action [9], in which the teacher's mediation is essential in order to promote the considering and the depuration of the process under development by the student and to promote learning. Therefore, the teacher being formed understands and interprets facts and ideas from the world he/she lives in, becoming the co-creator and the co-author of this/her formation [10].

When the teachers have chances to discover degrees of freedom to think over the teaching process during and after its practice, they try to catch the sense of their own work and they put to test their own work and they put to test their own understanding of the process in which they are involved. In the process of formation in work, the thought over acquaintanceship provided, in fact, concerns which induce them, in a way, more conscious and aware of their role [9].

Regarding these perspectives, the purpose was to persuade the teachers to place the students' apprenticeship as the core of their practice, providing spaces to cooperation, dialogue, creativity and the practice of the critical spirit [11] willing to accept a change in their behavior referring to their role as the stimulating and learning process, causing, therefore, the equalization of the students' opportunities and rights, suppressing every other aggressive behavior and favouring not only the cognitive but also the social and emotional students' development.

Considering the fact that we live in a society of knowledge, where the computer and the other ICTs are getting more and more present in the daily life of children, youngsters an grown-ups, another question arose referring to the use of the school IOR (Informatics Operating Room), with available machines that could provide the knowledge construction and help the activities development.

The use of the ICTs must be connected to other materials: paper, ink, other resources as clay and plaster or logical blocks, blackboard, etc, because the computer operates as an extra tool and not as the only one [12]. However, we observed that nowadays it is one of the pedagogical devices that con offer the greatest possibility of combining several sources and resources.

Therefore, the use of the ICTs, together with the work with Projects, helps teachers and students to apply the technology in the development of activities and/or the solution of real problems. This makes the students able to produce something of their own interest, learning with the experience and with the concepts included in the development of a proposal.

2 The Research

In accordance with all the above-mentioned perspectives, the methodological approach followed in the research development, with a qualitative mark [10] close the natural environment (a public school) as a direct source of data, combining the action with the solution of collective problems, being the researcher and the subjects of the research (three teachers and 30 students) involved in a cooperative and/or participative way. Thus, it was accomplished an exam of the "real" situation of the teachers' pedagogical practice, of the daily school living and of the classroom existing relationship.

The qualitative research works with the universe of meanings, motives, aspirations, beliefs, values and attitudes, transforming itself in a space of deep relationship of the processes and phenomena which cannot be reduced to the variable performance [13].

In the course of the investigation, aiming at the formation in work, it was necessary to go along with the teachers and to help them. Thus, the data collecting was done throughout intensive direct observation, using open dialogues and semi-structured interviews in which the researcher had a real participation in the group under analysis [14].

In the direct and intensive observation (participative observation) there were accomplished:

- Weekly meetings to elaborate and develop the activities which were held in the classroom and in the IOR (when the utilization of technological resources was necessary)

- Development of activities in the IOR, in which the computer and all the available technological resources were used as maximization tools of the students' abilities, in the development process of emerging activities of the work with projects arisen from the themes: "Hunger" and "Environment". It is worth emphasizing that the theme "Hunger" was chosen from a consideration over the reality of some students in the classroom. Related to their family low income, fact that results many times in expense restriction with food (many of them used to go to school without breakfast and could count only on the meals offered in the school context)

- Use of software: Word text editor, Excel electronic Plane and Internet web, to build up activities related to the research about food with the objective of analysing their nourishing value, their classification in types among others. These activities included: text production (Portuguese Language), chart and graphic construction (Mathematics), a script elaboration for a theatre play (Arts).

- Analysis, of the change process in the teaching practice, besides the attendance of the teachers' work together with their students in the classroom. We also held meetings, making good use of the Collective Pedagogical Work Hours (CPWH) (Figure 1), to study and think over the proposed methodology as well as to plan the activities which should be carried out in classroom, to analysis and thought over with the purpose of planning the actions for next activities.

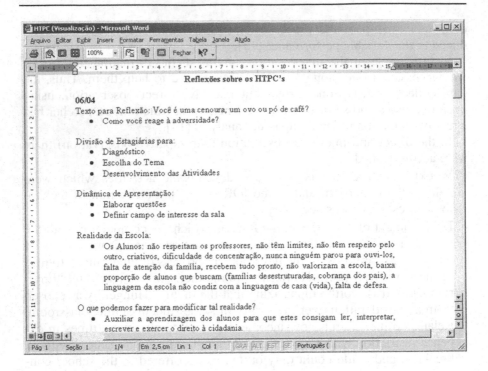

Fig. 1 Considerations about the Digital CPWHs in Word

In the interviews (the semi and the non structured ones) we maintained a constant dialogue, organizing only a scheme so that the answers could fulfil the research purposes and could be offered both in formal and informal situations, trying to guarantee the non-directed answers of the interviewers (the teachers), with the aim of being really acquainted with their personal, professional and emotional universe, searching for the analysis and interpretation of their living experiences.

Following the teachers' work, planning with them the activities that were developed in the classroom and participating in their execution, there was a constant thought over the teachers' and the interviewers' action, to define changes and alterations when necessary. All the thought over arose from a constant dialogue and partnership relation, together with the theoretical reading and analysis, in the sense of guaranteeing the validity of the collected data in the investigative process.

From the diagnosed reality, which faced a high illiteracy rate and serious problems concerning the students' indiscipline, the teachers were attentive to the purpose of helping the students' learning, so that they could read, write and interpret, as well as tie bonds to create group works.

In accordance with the above mentioned, the proposed activities included reading and writing dissertative texts related to the suggested subjects, researches in sources as magazines, newspapers, Internet, interviews with parents, construction of charts using Microsoft Excel (Figure 2), preparation and performance of theatre play.

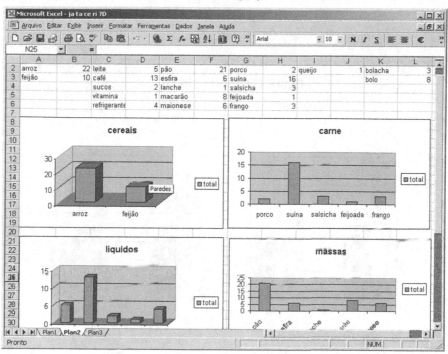

Fig. 2 Chart built up by one of the classroom group regarding a research made with the parents

It was possible to follow up the students' progresses observing the work accomplished and the relationship established between themselves and their teachers, in which they got more capable to dialogue and to cooperate.

Formerly undisciplined students, they started to have a more effective participation in the classroom activities, to research at home, and to collaborate with their classmates and teachers. The figure above is a work from a group of students that had never participated in any of the classroom activities, but became so motivated that succeeded in doing the best charts and graphics. After some months of this work, at the end of the process, the São Paulo State Education Bureau carried out the examination of the Evaluation System of the Municipal School Efficiency (SAREM).

All the students of the school took this examination. The result was surprising, because the classroom under study (7th D), got the second better general mark among the 7th grades comprised between the interval of 20–25 points, in a scale of 0–30 points (Figure 3). The mark detected at the beginning of the year was 11 (unsatisfactory), based on the some scale.

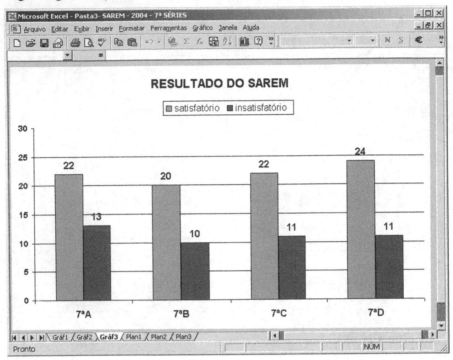

Fig. 3 Graphic build up by the School Administrative staff based on the performance of the 7th grades in the SAREM Examination

The data obtained from the teachers' testimony and from the students' performance permitted that the research looked upon an external validity, referring to the process, since it was proved that the adopted methodology generated a significant change [10]. In the same way, it was possible for all the research subjects: actors and co-actors, to express their perspectives and to change the reality by means of a constant dialogue.

This could be achieved through a work strategy with projects and also with the use of the ICTs as potential tools. In this process, the teachers also became learners and realized that they were not the only "knowledge owners" anymore. And to face this courageous perception, which passed by their formation principles, (considering the fact that they were formed to transmit the systematical knowledge), it was more than evident that they should adopt this apprentice behavior, being able to take out from the other, in the case the students, teachers and researchers, aspects as important as the contents they "mastered".

3 Final Considerations and Future Perspectives

We finished this article considering the affirmation made by [9]: when teachers find degrees of freedom to think during and after their practice, they try to give a meaning to their own work and so they put to test their own understanding of the process in which they are. Such critical living together was, in fact, of great value, and also to our formation.

Starting from the positive perspectives regarding the accomplishment of a in work formation process, trying above all to use the ICTs as potential tools to develop the students' abilities of transforming their practice and, consequently, the classroom reality.

And, even more strongly, the living in the schools context shows that we need to form teachers who accomplish not only their daily "task" of mere information transmission, but also fell that their function brings them the possibility of believing and, why not saying, of dreaming with a more humanized, fair, truthful and joyous society, with the participation of all citizens aiming at the development of some basic values as self-respect, respect towards the other and to the environment in which they are inserted.

Which these perspectives, the intention is that the teachers consider the students' apprenticeship as the core of their work, opening spaces to creativity and the practice of the critical spirit [11], making themselves opened to a change in posture concerning their role of stimulating and facilitating elements in the teaching and learning process, promoting in this way the equalization of theirs students' opportunities and rights.

On analysing the whole process of formation in work, and on considering all the experiences already lived, in which anguish, criticism, questionings and solutions arose naturally, and where the change in the pedagogical practice brought extremely significant improvements to the students' cognitive and social performance, we learned that, on developing work projects applying the ICTs, there is a possibility of including all of the mentioned students' dimensions, allowing them to learn through their already living fixed contents, releasing their ideas and bringing to the apprenticeship environment a motivation that could build new knowledge in a dynamical, spontaneous and creative way.

Acknowledgment

We would like to thank the São Paulo State Research Support Foundation (FAPESP) for the financial resources supplied to the research carrying out.

References

1. Hernandez F (1998) Transgressão e mudança na educação: Projetos de Trabalho. Artes Médicas, Porto Alegre
2. Schlünzen E (2000) Mudanças nas práticas pedagógicas do professor: criando um ambiente construcionista contextualizado e significativo para crianças com necessidades especiais físicas. PhD Thesys, Pontifícia Universidade Católica
3. Nardi R (2001) Perspectivas de Mudanças na Abordagem Educacional da AACD a partir da Proposta de Informática na Educação. In: Valente JA, Freire FMP (orgs) Aprendendo para a vida: Computadores na sala de aula. Cortez, São Paulo
4. García C (1999) Formación de Profesores: Para un cambio educativo. Porto Editora, Porto
5. Almeida M (2003) Educação, Projetos, Tecnologia e Conhecimento. Proem, São Paulo
6. Thurler M (2001) Inovar no Interior da Escola. Artmed, Porto Alegre
7. Almeida M (1999) Informática e formação de professores. Ministério da Educação/MEC, Brasília/DF
8. Piaget J (1974) Aprendizagem e Conhecimento. Trad: Equipe Livraria Freitas Barros. Livraria Freitas Barros, Rio de Janeiro
9. Schön D (2000) Educando O Profissional Reflexivo: Um novo design para o ensino e a aprendizagem. In: Nóvoa A (ed) Os professores e sua formação. Dom Quixote, Lisboa
10. Lüdke M, André M (1986) Pesquisa em Educação: Abordagens qualitativas. EPU, São Paulo
11. Moraes MC (2000) Descobrindo fluxo e aprendendo a desfrutar da aprendizagem e da vida. Versão Preliminar para Estudo, São Paulo
12. Valente JA (1993) Por que o computador na educação? In: Valente JA (org) Computadores e Conhecimento: Repensando a Educação. Gráfica da Unicamp, Campinas
13. Deslandes S et al (1994) Pesquisa Social: Teoria, Método e Criatividade. Vozes, Petrópolis
14. Lakatos EM, Marconi M (1991) Metodologia do Trabalho Científico. Atlas, São Paulo

The Production of Internet Pages by Visual Impaired PSENs through a Computer Mediated Distance Learning Program

Lizandra Estabel, Eliane Moro, Lucila Santarosa

Computer Center in Special Education (NIEE)
Federal University of Rio Grande do Sul (UFRGS)
Porto Alegre – Rio Grande do Sul – Brazil
estabel@cpovo.net, lucila.santarosa@ufrgs.br

1 Introduction

The use of computer by People with Special Education Needs (PSENs) has provided their social and digital inclusion in society. On reference to the visual impaired PSENs, partial sight or blind ones, the use of Communication and Information Technologies (TICs in Brazil) is presented as a way to include them digitally, communicating and interacting to each other so that neither they realize their own limitation. Assisting and Adapting Technologies provide this communication and interaction process where the focus is on the capacity for sharing, learning, interacting and building collectively into a society where many times they are excluded.

According to data from The World Health Organization (WHO) exist, approximately, 40 millions of people with Special Needs and Visual Impairment in the world, of which 75% are originated from the social-economic low income regions. In Brazil, the incidence of PSENs with visual impairment is at the rate 1.0 to 1.5% of the whole population, being one in each 3,000 sight impaired children and one in each 500 partial sight ones as well. The proportion is 80% of partial sight people and 20% of absolutely blind ones.

The 2002 scholar census, data from The National Study and Educational Research Institute Anísio Teixeira (INEP/MEC in Brazil) enlists 20,257 students with visual impairment in basic education of the Brazilian educational system. The analysis of these data reveals that many children, youths and adults with visual impairment are off school.

Data from 2000 Census from Geographic and Statistic Brazilian Institute (IBGE in Brazil), points out that 14.5% among Brazilian population is formed by PSENs and of these 48% are considered visual impaired PSENs. It is considered that, according to the presented data, the half of PSENs population has visual impairment, becoming necessary and urgent an implementation of governmental politics for social, digital and educational inclusion with an access to TICs.

Based on that, it is necessary lecturing the instructors and conduct them to attend these visual impaired PSENs students on their needs, propitiate to them an environment where they can be agents for their own knowledge building process interacting with each other. Through this Distance Learning Program Mediated on a Computer, it is been administered the National Computer Program in Special Education (PROINESP in Brazil), where instructors, some of them PSENs, who work directly with special needs students, consider themselves able to instruct their students on this cooperative and collaborative construction process on which it is built on a collective shape starting from communicating and interacting with the whole group.

In this article, it intends to pronounce the construction process of a personal internet page by a visual impaired instructor/student from PROINESP, overcoming her own limitation, accepting a task through a collaborative construction mediated on a computer that, initially, it was impossible for her.

2 Visual Impaired PSENs and Collaboration

The interaction among visual disabled people and healthy ones should be characterized as a process structured on dialogs and communication. Vygotski [3] points out that the font for compensating blindness it is not in the development of touching or better harness for hearing, otherwise it is the language and utilization of social experience in communicating with normal vision people. And he says "the word conquers blindness".

A writing communication process among normal vision people and blind ones, for many times it is not established when there is not domain over the Braille system. For a normal vision person, who has ever been in touch with that system, it turns impossible reading a Braille text. For a vision impaired one, when accessing an ink printed paper sheet it is the same as taking an empty page. This verification serves to emphasize the importance of language as an instrument for mediating the process of communication among visual impairment PSENs and normal vision ones. Only in the 90's, with uprising of screen readers and voice software that situation has changed, when a writing text is accomplished at the moment the visual impaired access the computer. Computer is a facilitator method to access TICs. The PSENs with visual impairment will consider themselves digitally included, minimizing differences and propitiating iteration with others.

As Ferreyra emphasizes [1] the five senses: hearing, touching, smelling, tasting and seeing connect the human to the world. The author states that the culture of technological methods has provided an expanding that intensified the human senses to promote a new reality, a point that "some scientists of human communication has considered that as stretching all our senses". A lack of one of senses, in case, the vision, could be overcome in the measure in which assisting and adapting technologies enable the introduction of a PNEE with visual impairment to a digital environment.

Yet to Vygotski [4] "the new theories do not valorize blindness in itself neither to its deficiency, but the capacity enclosed in itself and the fonts to overcome and stimulating the individual development".

Rego [2] affirms that the whole development of an individual depends on accomplishment which is assembled in a sort of cultural group, starting by interaction with other individuals of his own specie.

Interaction among PSENs with visual impairment and people with same limitations or not, enables to overcome obstacles since the moment they interchange to each other. The individual is responsible for its own learning feedback and to the others as well. To engender a learning method it is necessary a sharing process in collaborating and cooperative construction mediated by instruments which enable the access this people into the digital environment and the use of information and communication technologies. Vygotski remarks that the most appropriated meaning to mediation is the use of mediators to strengthen human possibilities on a search for reaching an edge, a target, supplying such needs in a chain of social relations.

Collaborative learning based on computer should be a educational strategy where one or more individuals shape their own accomplishment on debating, reflection and decision-making, having the computer as a mediator instrument. To this process happens, instructors and students should be disposed to collaborate and building it together.

As Vygotski denotes, there are two levels of development: The real and the potential one. The real development (Real Development Zone – RDZ) represents the conquering that it is already consolidated by a person, what he has learned and dominated by himself; The potential development (Potential Development Zone – PDZ) constitutes on actions that a person has made with help of others (colleagues, instructor, specialist). "The development zone today, will be the development level for tomorrow, or better, the children who make with assistance today, it could be able to make it by itself for tomorrow" [3].

It is necessary that the visual impairment individual overcome his obstacles and becomes more self-sustained. However, only with collaboration of others he will reach more independence. It will be an opportunity to new relationships, to know better each other and discovering in others theirs abilities and offering collaboration to the group in a process of learning and building acquaintance.

To strengthening the group, working for cooperation and collaboration it is necessary the presence of dialog, participation and collective construction. The crew members should have common objectives where all of them have to contribute to the others. Each member of the group should be responsible for his own learning and as well for the others, doing an evaluation of the process so that they can retake the dots that should be improved propitiating a reflection upon a process of collaborative construction. Nevertheless, that process only occurs whether all tools which propitiate collaboration are used.

3 Computer Mediated Learning Environments and Collaborative Learning

Using Learning Environment Mediated on a Computer (LEMCs) is the key to include people into the digital atmosphere. To manage distance curses, it is necessary a meticulous choosing of an environment which enable the students interaction, but in a way that they can be agents for their own learning process, staying the instructor just as a mediator, allowing the exercise of cooperation and collaboration in the execution of the activities.

The TelEduc, a learning environment mediated on a computer, is an atmosphere of easy utilization and presents tools of communication as: e-mail, dairy board, conference forum, screen board, chat and others. These tools enable the student getting autonomy to make the activities proposed and it can establish a communication among others members of the group, with no intervention by the instructor.

That environment is been used in the National Computer Program in Special Education (PROINESP in Brazil), from the Special Education Secretary of the Ministry of Education (SEEsp/MEC in Brazil) administered by members from the Computer in Special Education Center (NIEE in Brazil), of the Federal University of Rio Grande do Sul (UFRGS in Brazil), coordinated by Prof. Dr. Lucila Costi Santarosa. The course began on March 7th, 2005 scheduling 120h. PROINESP event had approximately

310 instructors from 155 public schools and non-governmental institutions with computer laboratories. The objective is to capacitate instructors from these institutions to work on a computer in a way of including their students with special educational needs in the digital environment, enabling them to exercise citizenship and inclusion.

Those instructors were divided in fifteen groups of approximately 22 participants in each one, deriving from institutions located in different regions of the country. In one of the groups, among the participants, exists 4 visual impaired instructors with special needs.

Within the proposed activities, weekly, in the module of Pedagogic Uses of the Internet, there was a construction of a page in html, individually or collectively. That proposal was an utilization of a Front Page software to built the page and utilize components from that software aggregating text, image, sound and another sources. The page built should be published in a TelEduc environment, with allowed access just for the participants of that course and making it available on the internet for free access afterward.

In the case of visual impairment individuals, there should be a care in relation to accessing pages. The sites might show sparse problems of accessibility when built in html. There should be a special care in utilizing Flash and Apple Java by a reason of those sites could become inaccessible; avoid using frames and diagrams that turns hard to navigate; the figures should include an "alternate name", the attribute "alt" in html, with its description, so that they know what it is and in case the figure being a link, it should be accompanied by the function which symbolize it. At the conclusion of the page it is interesting verify whether it attends the criteria of accessibility submitting it to a checker program as Bobby (http://www.cast.org/bobby); the W3C (http://validador.w3.org); the TAW (http://www.tawdis.net) or the Da Silva (http://www.acessobrasil.org.br), the first accessibility checker in Portuguese language.

One of the participants with visual impairment denominated M.S. (to preserve her identity), felt herself defied to execute the activity in building a personal page on the internet, by the reason of all tools available do not facilitate the visual impaired PSENs adaptability and accessibility on that task.

Upon that challenge, the wish for overcoming the situation was more powerful than the discouragement to compose the proposed activity in that course.

4   The Challenge of Building His/Her Personal Page

When requesting to the instructors/students a construction of a page in html, immediately, M.S. sent an e-mail as following:

Date: 04/23 – 03h10pm
"I (do not) know html language (...) this Front Page is (not) accessible for blind. I'll try to copy here an index.html of a friend and create some attempted page on Intervox, where I've already had an account of ftp. (...)I'll see whether I can get it".

In this way, maybe the reaction of the instructor, nomenclature utilized to determine the responsible tutor for the class, could be to decide an execution of another activity or considering the fact that she is a visual impaired instructor/student and discharging her from that activity, excusing itself by the lack of accessibility on available tools. However, believing that, besides all limitations in relation of accessibility, it is possible to seek other alternatives, the instructor has stimulated M.S.:

Answer – Date: 04/23 – 03h17m pm.
"Take it easy darling. Let's take it in parts....You have one more week to do that. The text must be written normally as it does on Word. The most problem is links and figures. Would you like to try? We can do it together on distance. You write the text and I conduct you in relation of images and etc...I'll wait you".

The answer was immediate:

Date: 04/23 – 04h01m pm
(...) I accept your help; let me try it seeing the index.html page of a friend".

The answer was the decision to accept the challenge, then a relationship of complexity has been established and a faith in the possibility of a collective construction. It is necessary to establish a relationship where what is ZDP today will be ZDR tomorrow, because through interchanging, one who has a specific knowledge will share it with others in a collective, collaborative and cooperative construction.

Vygotsky express that a good teaching is the one which advances beyond the development, or better, that leads to the psychological functions which is still in a way of accomplishment. This prospective dimension of the psychological development it is of a great worth for education, because permits an understanding of the process of development that, despite the fact that it is present in the individuals, do not need intervention or collaboration of the more experienced partners on the culture to consolidate it and, consequently, it helps to define the field and the possibilities for pedagogic actions [2].

At the same day, when being defied to construct the page, M.S. wrote:

Date: 04/23 – 06h55min pm
"(...)I'm already in the third chapter of a book I have about html. I'm always used to say that for us, blinds, the ways are more tortuous and crammed with shortcuts. It's like we always have to do things in a natural

way, noticing all scheme, anything that a quick click can solve. I could send you the text to you setting me off from this but I wouldn't never know how the process could be".

The relationship of construction and collaboration has been established. It can be observed that M.S. assumed an active role for building her own acquaintance when she let her posture of just accomplishment a task, sending a text and standing her "free" from that activity otherwise she proffered her collaboration being opened to be helped too. And she continues:

> "I'm in a phase of tests. I'm alone at home and there's not anyone who can say whether my picture is on the link. I'll give you the address where you'll see my first test with no embellishment. That's just a little text and a link displaying my picture. Please, Access it up and tell me whether or not it is already there to check if I am at a right way".

In this situation, yet it is not possible to use an assistive and adaptive technology that attends that demand, as well as it is not a barrier to execute the activities when it is believed being possible to construct with one other a connection to cooperation. Whereas technology is a human hand extension, interpersonal relationships are the encouragement for humans overcoming its own limitations. In this case, the tutor bestows her perception to that requirement, being conscious that the instructor/student is able and just intervening more directly in that matter when the apprentice can not execute it by herself. There is a relationship of cooperation, but in any moment the tutor has mediated for her apprentice. That is a collective construction leading to autonomy of one whom in any moment has experienced limitation. The tutor has a mediator role in that process.

> (...) You are the mouse and I am the keyboard and commands! I am making a list of commands in html, I'll print it and it gets easier to use it. To tell me the result, access Intervox...

During the activity, M.S. mentions one of the obstacles that it is the use of a mouse by sight impaired people; it is an instrument that it is not utilized due to the difficulty of spatial organization and its localization on the computer screen. Blinds utilize the keyboard and it is not necessary being in Braille because the letters "f" and "j" are marked, so they place their hands on it and making use of shortcuts they can utilize most resources available on the computer.

When accessing for the first attempt to create html pages, M.S. used an initial title which was: "My first paths". There was a recorded greeting for one who has accessed her page leading to a link including her picture. That link was working perfectly. Furthermore it introduced to a link containing her e-mail and a voice message welcoming the visitors, but it was take too long to initiate.

After some observations about her page, on following day, M.S. sent this answer:

Date: 04/24 – 09h25 am
(…) Yes, I want it! Send to me the way how accessing the page with an automatic sound on it. Tell me where I use that command, on account of being a page to blinds; I like better dealing with sounds. I'll also set up on it the size of the fonts; I was reading much about html yesterday. It's a shame that I'll never know how it could be aesthetically, but what can I do? Send to me everything you have about html, these commands are the hassle (hard) but we go copying".

In this message, M.S. points out one of the characteristics presented on most sites built by/for visual impaired people: using an archive of sound. Generally, the pages have sound attachments. In the case of that student, besides her page presents a welcoming message when accessing it, it also introduces to links with music by her own interpretation because she is a singer too, having programs by her own authorship transmitted on a virtual radio. Another question mentioned in that e-mail is in relation of the page aesthetic. Due her visual limitation, M.S. reveals that she'll never know how the aesthetic results could be but she trusts in the opinion from others who help her. Furthermore, she wonders about the shape on which the page is being executed, so that when people with normal vision access it, they'll have a suitable page layout due the fonts size and colours used on it.

At the first contact, there was a complaining about the use of the Front Page. In a next moment, M.S. was questioned about the kind of software it would be utilized to build her pages:

(…) I am executing the html archives on edivox indeed; but I could use the note book because, anyway, I'm already on the f t p vox , so I'll be there reading the html and trying to use its commands.

The edivox is one of the operational programs DOSVOX, which is a sound program, with a voice synthesizer that has more than 70 programs as: lettervox (e-mail), chatvox (chat), webvox (to search on web), intervox (homepages creation), calcuvox (calculator) and others. That software helps to edit texts to visual impairment PSENs.

M.S. proceeded exploring her page and asked for help to expand new commands. In such moment, she requested support to put a link which it sends to the top page or initial page.

The different rhythms, behavior, experiences, trajectories, family issues, values and accomplishment levels of each individual engrave to school routine a possibility of sharing repertoires, points of view, confrontation, reciprocal help and consequently to strength their individual abilities [2].

Despite she has never built a page on html, M.S. employed the use of technologies and the internet for a long period of time. That experience enables her to make her own evaluation about her site, comparing it to some resources utilized in other pages. It can do this statement upon the following requesting and other ones which it was made before:

Date: 04/24 – 5h23 pm
"(…) perhaps I should know some commands, as how setting my name on the top…I'll brainstorm a title! I was doing everything by enthusiasm! (…) Now I am thrilled! I'll keep it going and always looking for your tips.

When getting this message, it can be compared to the first one. At a first moment, it couldn't believe that it was possible for the student to execute the page. However, she was defied to try it and she accepted it and the activity could be concluded.

To exist appropriation it is necessary internalization, which implies the transformation of external process (being solidified in the activities among people), in an intra psychological process (where activity is rebuilt internally). The long path of human development follows, however, the direction from social to individual [2].

Along the process it won't lack incentive terms and conviction that she could get it if being supported and encouraged to continue. "Now I'm thrilled! I'll keep it going and always looking for your tips!" (M.S.).

In this message, we can observe an internal motivation and a trustful relationship of mutual interaction between the tutor and the student. The tutor makes the process mediation, conducting her and supporting her on learning process. The student shows enthusiasm when inviting other people and colleagues to access her page:

(…) a friend told me to insert subtitles about me on the side of the photo, but I think it is not necessary.

In this message, M.S. points out one of the difficulties in relation to the accessibility. When the images do not show any description, they lost importance while accessed by a visual impaired person. When searching pages using a screen reader, one will just hear graphic words. It is necessary to use the attribute "alt" describing what appears on the screen.

Answer: Date 05/25, 10h34 am
"(…) about the picture, it can be made a description. Therefore, your page will follow the accessibility rules. The description serves to describe what appears on the screen when the reader goes to the image. Otherwise, the reader will say: photo and kb. Now, let's enhance it…the main is already done".

The image M.S. inserted on her page is a personal one, where she is sat on a garden bench. This description was input on her page. One of the descriptions she made was in relation to the materials published on her site. She preferred to put texts and programs from the virtual radio and music interpreted by her own authorship. The page created by M.S. has her own authority and authorship, built through interaction and overcoming her limitation over technological tools.

At the end of this first construction, as any page is always being built and never finished, M.S. choose the title: Special in Education, because according to her own words, special is to believe that it is possible to overcome limitations starting from building with others and knowing that you can defeat restrictions when you believe it is possible.

Her last message along these three days of much interaction was:

> Date: 04/26 – 0h16m am
> (…) I've already made the alterations. I called my son to see it! He loved it! He's requested one for him! Imagine that! What a work! They know that they have spent all weekend not using the computer! Kisses and Thank You!

After some days, M.S. sent an e-mail informing she is working in elaborating pages with her visual impaired students.

In her auto-evaluation about the execution of the page, M.S. commented on this:

> I've learned to build collectively, conjugating the collective, because without the tutor support it would be impossible this construction. I've learned to valorize the unconditional availability of someone who is ready to help us; it seems a 24h SOS! (…)I've had an internal disposition, a motivation because I learned what I wanted to learn, it was a psychophysical action; it is exhaustion and much commitment as says GRAMSCI. That was the more accelerated execution by the exigencies to the course activities, the ones which did not make me anything bad. I'll improve that page, registering it, turning it more and more accessible. Learning is a verb conjugated "ad infinitum"! (M.S.).

Learning is really a verb conjugated infinitely, because it propitiates a changing in its initial setting to everyone involved in a growing process. At such moment, there was no more instructor/student and apprentice. Both of them shared the desire of building and learning. It was a new situation, where it was necessary to seek a lot of alternatives, communication ways, suitable technologies and, above all, being itself in a posture for sharing where each member has much to cooperate, donating itself in a search for a collective construction and overcoming its limitations, whether physical or technological.

5 Final considerations

Since the first moment, when it was proposed the activity of building a page in html, it was clear how difficult that task could be due the obstacles in using some technologies, the physical distance and all limitations presented in the lack of vision, because that construction were being mediated on a computer.

However, all that difficulties and obstacles could be overcome if there was, above all, a desire for building, overcoming and accepting challenges. Vygotski [5], in his studies about PSENs was more interested on his own capacity than deficiencies". It is believed that through sharing, interchanging and cooperation it is possible to overcome limitations. Interchanging roles between the tutor and the student, in many cases, where each one supporting, suggesting, interacting and informing simultaneously, it has turned possible that activity. It would be easier if another activity were proposed upon the difficulties and the first reaction of M.S., when the student could just copy another page and altered some items; it could be a lot of justifications to avoid the execution of that activity, but there was a challenge and the certainty that the obstacles and limitations can be overcome when people interchange with each other. It is necessary unbalancing to balance it again, abandoning a passive position and assume the role of an agent for its own acquaintance.

Today, M.S. is able to build her own pages, updating them in a permanent building process and teaching her students, visual impaired PSENs, to execute this construction.

This report could be just at the first message, but it didn't happen because yet there are people who believe that it is possible go beyond that; that it is possible to overcome barriers because limitation is inside people and it is necessary much courage and support from others to do that.

In Brazil, there are 20,257 students with visual impairment in its basic education. It is necessary to capacitate instructors so their students can be better attended, but with a collaborative construction proposal, propitiating to these students autonomy through interchanging with each other. The difficulties to be defeated are much: accessing of information, the qualified special materials to attend their needs; using assistive and adaptive technologies and, mostly, a posture of the tutor in mediating this process, propitiating an active role to the student building his acquaintance. Overcoming limitations is inside of each human, it is necessary to believe in it and executing it.

There are many examples for overcoming a process as it was presented in this article, but it is necessary other way to look at it, believing that deficient is the society which exclude PSENs or do not let them to be included into a society of a lot of differences.

References

1. Ferreyra ER (1998) A Linguagem Oral na Educação de Adultos. Porto Alegre: Artes Médicas, 1998
2. Rego TC (1995) Vygotsky: Uma perspectiva histórico cultural na educação. Petrópolis: Vozes
3. Vygotsky LS (1984) A Formação Social da Mente. São Paulo: Martins Fontes
4. Vygotsky LS (1997) Obras Escogidas: Fundamentos de defectologia. v.5 Madrid: Visor
5. Vygotsky LS, Luria AR, Leontiev AN (1988) Linguagem, Deselvolvimento e Aprendizagem. 2ed. São Paulo: Ícone

Index